D0349878

BODY AND SOUL
Sexuality on the Brink of Change

BODY AND SOUL
Sexuality on the Brink of Change

ANNE STIRLING HASTINGS, PH.D.

 INSIGHT BOOKS

PLENUM PRESS • NEW YORK AND LONDON

Library of Congress Cataloging-in-Publication Data

On file

If you would like to be on a mailing list for workshops given by
Anne Stirling Hastings, please write to:

Anne Stirling Hastings, Ph. D.
P.O. Box 40083
Bellevue, WA 98015

ISBN 0-306-45400-9

Insight Books is a Division of Plenum Publishing Corporation
233 Spring Street, New York, N.Y. 10013-1578

An Insight Book

10 9 8 7 6 5 4 3 2 1

Printed in the United States of America

To Rex,
without whom I could not have learned
about bodies and souls

PREFACE

§

I decided to study sexuality after becoming a psychologist because sex was confusing to me. I couldn't think about it clearly. I knew that most of what went on around me wasn't very healthy, but I couldn't see any alternatives. Over the years since I completed my Ph.D., I have created experiences for myself that have yielded new understandings, but to get there, I had to stumble around in the dark time after time. I am still in the dark in some ways, but I have managed to interact with enough recovering people to grasp a much healthier view of sexuality.

When I began my search, I had little information about my childhood sexual experiences. It emerged as I let myself think about that time and as I questioned my mother and siblings over a period of years. I learned that I had been sexual with my father, and that I was a sexualized child (see *Sexualized Children*[1] for more information on this surprisingly common phenomenon). When I was three, I was sexual with my sister, who was eighteen months younger than me, and when she objected to it, I stopped and turned instead to sexual play with my dolls for years. When that seemed too likely to reveal my interest in sex, I left the outer world and moved into my mind, where I played everything out in fantasies. I wrote whole romance books in my head.

After childhood, I was surprised to discover that I had no reaction to direct breast or genital stimulation, including intercourse, when I became sexually active at age seventeen. My sex life had been limited to fantasies for many years, and that was the only way arousal occurred for the first year of sexual activity.

I fantasized about the sex I had just had or the sex I was about to have. But soon after that, I learned about feeling "horny," and my addiction to sexual feelings graduated from those created in my mind to real interaction with men.

I had no understanding of monogamy, except as a rule that must be followed so my partner wouldn't have an excuse to be sexual with anyone else. It seemed odd that after growing up in a morally strict family I was perfectly able to have sex with a married man. I didn't mind taking men away from other women and actually enjoyed doing so. I seemed to have few sexual morals, in spite of what I had been taught. I didn't question it then. It seemed right that the "bad" person in the family—me— would be immoral, whereas the rest seemed to follow the rules.

After I left my first husband, I launched into serious study of my sexuality and began to learn the lessons that have led to writing this book. I had an affair with a married man, and as he prepared to leave her for me, his previously lukewarm wife passionately decided she wanted him. When he ended our relationship, I grieved for my role in interrupting their bond. He had a role too, of course, but that didn't change the fact that I did. I began to understand monogamy—real inside-out, natural, effortless monogamy—and went on to examine all the rules that our culture superimposes onto sex. As each one fell away, I could glimpse the truth that lies under the cultural artifacts. My second marriage, in which we tell the truth as soon as we know what it is, became a laboratory for these new discoveries.

Well into my learning, as I was already beginning to write, I found out the truth about my "moral" family. My father was a sex addict, having sex with men into his seventies. He contracted AIDS. I was shocked and affirmed at the same time. Surprised and not at all surprised, I began to realize why this moral-looking family produced a child who had few sexual morals. Of course, I was unconsciously perceiving the truth that lay behind the lies. The benefit of taking the position of the immoral one is that I had motivation to recover from damage to my sexuality once I could learn what it was. It also made sense of my almost lifelong desire to hear the truth, even when it is painful, and to tell it. I wanted a world that made sense instead of one in which I acted out the family secrets.

I began writing as a way to learn more about healthy sexuality and to offer my own and my clients' emerging understanding. My first book, *Reclaiming Healthy Sexual Energy*,[2] focuses on sexual addiction and how to recover from it. It includes specifics on sexual addiction and exercises for reducing shame. My second book, *Discovering Sexuality that Will Satisfy You Both*,[3] and the audiotape *Healthy Sex*[4] show examples of what healthy sex is like. *From Generation to Generation: Understanding Sexual Attraction to Children*[5] is a compassionate look at the need for sexual healing from attraction to children and sexual boundary confusion, told through the stories of many who are healing.

This book has emerged out of my growing understanding of how cultures inhibit healthy, unfolding, inside-out sexuality. The picture I paint of the new sexuality is based on my own experiences of recovery and on those of my clients, colleagues, and friends.

The stories that follow are all personal. I have experienced each discovery I present, either as the adult or the child with the adult. I invite you to join me in taking a look at how we have been trapped in the beliefs of our families and communities, unconsciously passed down through the generations. We can change the culture now. As each one of us refuses to be involved in the old ways and seeks to find our inherent, effortless, sexual health, the culture will change too. Then our children and grandchildren need not go through what we have.

§ MISUNDERSTOOD SEXUALITY §

The basic sexual paradigm of our culture has resulted in a misunderstanding of sexuality throughout history. As a result, we have all been encouraged to treat this vast and vital energy as if it were something to be ashamed of, and at the same time, something to be skilled at. In decades past, sex was viewed as entirely private, something that men enjoyed and "good" women didn't. Now it is presented by the media as recreational "fun."

Traditional views contain glaring contradictions. Among them are the belief that intimacy (defined as knowing another and being known to him or her) and sexual fantasy can occur at the same time. Traditional sex therapists state that intimacy in sex is ideal and, at the same time, encourage the use of fantasy while having sex—an activity that takes us away from our partner. Experts also encourage us to tell the truth yet recommend withholding certain truths about sexual feelings and activities. Sex is called an important, vital part of being human and then described as if it were an exciting game of tennis. Men are taught that monogamy and commitment are necessary to adulthood and are also pressured to respond sexually to "sexy" women to whom they are not married.

The combination of cultural beliefs, family silence, shaming, and the absence of models of sexually healthy adults makes it virtually impossible for any of us to make it into adult life with a healthy sexuality. When those of us who have actively begun sexual healing are able to see and feel the real nature of sexual energy, the inconsistencies and abuses of culture become glaringly evident. In coming out from under the influences of our past and our culture, we are able to recognize that *practically everything in our society having to do with sex is not healthy.*

Now it is changing. And as it changes, it provokes a crisis—a useful crisis, one that will rip apart our staid beliefs and allow us to discover the truth. In this book, I will explore how culture represses sexuality, and how we have become sexually reactive in order to continue the species. I will offer an idea of how it might have started, review how we are now changing, describe the crux of the crisis, and relate all of this to the social ills with which we live. Each of the chapters that follow provides information about aspects of this crisis: how sexuality is shamed, and how to remove that shame; how practices designed to remove shame (such as the circumcision of African women or the desire of American men to maintain an erection) become

acculturated and how these practices take on a life of their own;
how jealousy can be healthy; what it would be like to grow up in
a sexually healthy culture; how sexual harassment is a function
of culture's sexual distortions; the function of sexual services for
those who want to reduce feelings of shame; and how traditional
sex therapy is often not a solution to sexual difficulties but
instead can make things worse. Throughout, I show how readers
can join the millions who are now healing their sexuality.

§I Know My Own Culture Best §

Our world and most of the cultures within it do not know how
to use sexuality in a healthy manner. The United States and
other Western cultures have created a crisis by beginning the
healing of sexuality. Because I live in the United States and have
been part of both the unhealthy culture and the healing movement, I know this culture's distortions the best. Ideally this book
would reflect all cultures' uses of sexuality and the impact of
healing, but to do so would require traveling to every country
and producing many volumes of text! Consequently, I have
mostly concentrated on the sexual culture of the United States
and Canada, which reflects the events going on in many Western
cultures. I have also selected Africa and India to describe more
fully because of glaring practices affecting many millions of
people. Even though cultures may appear different, they all have
in common the shaming of sexuality and the need to remove
shame in order to discover the real nature of sexuality. The
principles described here apply to all cultures.

§If You Have Feelings while Reading §

You may find yourself having a variety of feelings while reading
this book. Among them might be sexual arousal, disgust, anger,
shame, sadness, and pleasure. Or relief, excitement, and joy. I would

like to invite you to have these feelings and know that shame inhibits healing unless it can be felt in a way that allows it to flow out of the body. Breathing deeply can help make this possible.

§ THE PURPOSE OF THIS BOOK §

The chapters ahead provide information about the many ways we are living with the results of deeply embedded sexual shame. By naming them as symptoms of a culturewide disease instead of normal human sexuality, I hope to provide a mirror for those who are deeply involved in retrieving sexual health and who may not have found words for what they know. This vital movement is about far more than sex. It is about retrieving our bodies and souls, our families and community, and our world.

ACKNOWLEDGMENTS

§

Laurie Harper, a tenacious agent, encouraged me to put my ideas down on paper and, after reading rough chapters, offered criticism that really was constructive.

Mathew Grace and Jamie Comption gave thoughtful time and attention to ideas and contributed their thinking and experience.

Louisa Turner, Jill Seipel, and Cindy Rushin Galliger gave monthly support by reading, reacting, and sharing their own work with clients with sexual issues.

Clients and others told their stories and faced their shame.

Those who have come up to me after talks and workshops, with open faces and words of gratitude, have provided mirrors for the accuracy of my writing.

CONTENTS

§

CULTURE IN CONFLICT

§

Sexuality is changing. Sexual abuse is increasingly under-stood, and millions of people are in therapy to examine the damage done to their sexuality. The growing numbers of people in sexual addiction recovery are making clear that much of what is called normal male and female sexual behavior is actually harmful to the person involved, serving functions other than loving oneself or a partner. We are moving toward healing sexuality on a cultural level.

But we humans cling to old ways, even when they aren't serving us. As recovery increases, the presentation of sexual stimuli is also increasing. Great amounts of pornography have always been created, particularly when sexuality was more hidden, as in the Victorian Era. But today is the first time pornography is presented in women's magazines, men's maga-zines, television, and movies. The cover of *Cosmopolitan* presents us with soft porn every month at the eye level of prepubescent children.

The resulting crisis will resolve itself in one of two ways. Sexuality could again go underground as repressive influences react to the public display and reenact countless centuries of repression. The "religious right" is working in this direction. Or, if the movement toward sexual healing continues, we can change our culture in such a way that we rediscover our intuitive, spiritual understanding of sexuality and lose our reactivity to the sexual presentations. Only time will tell. In the meantime, we will experience chaos that is normal to all major social change. The old will not die easily, and the new will have to forge strongly ahead.

§ Sexual Shame Underlies Social Ills §

I walked through downtown Seattle recently, looking at people. I encountered a neighborhood with many homeless people passing time. I heard voices under the influence of drugs or alcohol and the vacant expressions of those who in the past would have lived in mental hospitals. I watched members of a volunteer organization set up a card table on the sidewalk and hand out clean syringes and condoms to anyone who wanted them. Many did. I asked myself how these people got this way. Why were they unable to create a life of value to them, to join in a community that allowed all to evolve? As I looked at their faces, I saw self-hatred and the pain of living in their bodies. I knew they had been damaged by caregivers when they were growing up, caregivers who themselves had been damaged when they were young. I wondered how the damage got started, what was the first order of damage that preceded the rest. One possibility was the shaming of sexuality—shame that was brought to the child even before birth, recorded in the brain at levels not yet available to the intellect: painful shame that made it impossible to remain aware of the body, that required psychic blindness in order to continue to live. As the original people made these choices, they became unable to perceive the needs of their children because they had abandoned the source of knowing—perceive the ability to their own wants and needs. They couldn't help damaging their children because without accurate perception of needs, mistakes are automatic. Then as their offspring were not seen, the offspring went on to damage their progeny, and so on, through centuries of generations, to the present. As we have lost sight of ourselves, we have spilled that blindness out onto a world that is suffering the consequences. Having lost ourselves, we have lost sight of the needs of our environment—except when the needs become catastrophic and unavoidable. When they do, then drastic measures, such as recycling and water rationing, are needed in an attempt to restore sound ecology.

The healing of sexuality is vastly important to a world that is in danger of extinction. Many are attempting to learn how to create a sustainable culture, but their approaches will be limited unless sexuality is healed.

§ SHAMED CHILDHOODS LEAD TO AN ARTIFICIAL WORLD §

We are conceived and grow for nine months in a body that is shame filled. All women feel shame about their bodies from countless shaming experiences throughout their lives. They have been shamed from early on for being sexual, shamed for having a body that isn't considered "sexy" by our culture through adult years, and at the same time, shamed for having a body that *is* "sexy" and receiving sexual responses from men. When a woman is pregnant, she has concerns about being sexual enough. She fears losing her sexuality as her body changes, and at the same time, fears being too sexual in ways she thinks might harm her child or are incompatible with being a mother.

Breast feeding brings on another round of shaming as the mother responds to shaming reactions of others by hardening herself, or by hiding herself and the baby when feeding. She passes shame on to the child about this natural act.

When the baby is old enough to touch his or her genitals, even the most sexually healed parent won't be able to prevent shaming of the child. Other people, including other children, will feel shame and act shamingly toward the baby.

Sexuality continues to be associated with body shame, and as the child learns how to repress the full extent of sexuality, he or she must also cut off awareness of vital information that comes from living in a body. Our intuitive understanding of other people and the needs of the world we live in is greatly diminished. We lose the ability to know exactly when to eat and what will sustain us, and we lose perception of the energy of others who are close to us. From there it is a short leap to not knowing if we are hungry or if we want sex for healthy reasons. We are forced to live by rules instead of "knowing," and we turn to "spiritual" leaders to give us "answers" instead of support for our unique path. Rules seem necessary, because it is no longer possible to gather data from within ourselves. God is seen as outside of us and is attributed characteristics that we can no longer check out for ourselves.

The great overlay of body shame resulting from the shaming of sexuality makes us feel that we are bad people because we live in sexual bodies. This feeling of badness leaves us with little self-esteem or self-respect, and so we set out to find outside-in self-esteem. We learn the rules of our culture and believe that if we can follow them we will be good/accepted/loved/safe. The rules, not surprisingly, are dominated by the belief that those who can win in competitions win the right to have self-esteem. Thus we compete in terms of income, job status, characteristics of our children, sexual performance, qualities of mates, appearance, and ability to be good to others, among countless possibilities. We join organizations, such as churches and family or community groups, that will give us rules for "goodness," and then work hard to follow them.

If we lived in a culture in which bodies weren't shamed and maintained access to the data our bodies give us, we would be able to form naturally spiritual groups that supported us in finding out who we are and how we will live in community with others, and how we will offer our contribution in ways that are consistent with our inherent purpose. Competition could take place only for fun, not to establish one's worth. We would be able to encourage each other as we discovered how to live, and when we wanted to change the way we contribute, and how we spend our time.

§ CULTURE SUPPRESSES SEXUALITY §

Very little observation is necessary to see that our culture has embedded within it the control of sexuality. From the time children are born, parents and other adults are reacting to any evidence of sexuality by ignoring it, directly shaming it, or, in the best possible scenario, merely tolerating it. Even parents who are sexual with their children follow cultural rules the rest of the time. They don't discuss sex with the child and act as if there were no sexual exchange going on.

Shame is heaped on children as they attempt to learn about the place of sexuality in their lives and as they approach certain developmental tasks. Shame is a debilitating feeling of being defective for who we are, not just what we do. It is triggered by the thought of our shameful nature as it is observed by others. Children are taught that the natural act of touching their genitals is bad and forbidden, a fact they ascertain even if no one says a word to them about it. Expressions, body language, and sounds communicate even more effectively than words. Unlike guilt, which can be lessened by changing behavior, confessing, or finding out that we haven't violated anyone, shame cannot be eliminated without deliberate intervention. In order to avoid the intense feelings of shame, people will go to great lengths, including shaming others.

Somehow each of us is supposed to figure out how to be nonsexual until he or she is married, or at least in a lasting relationship. Then we are to blossom into fully sexual people, although this is to be done in absolute isolation from anyone other than a spouse. People know, but don't know, that the couple is sexual. The sexual revolution of the 1960s and 1970s was supposed to change much of that, and it did to an extent. But the change is slight in comparison to what remains.

If cultures were successful in eradicating sexuality until marriage, it wouldn't return simply because of a formal ritual saying that it was now acceptable behavior. Even the Victorian Era and the Vatican didn't succeed in reducing the birthrate by shaming sexuality.

§ SUPPRESSED SEXUALITY BECOMES REACTIVE §

If sexuality were capable of being shamed into oblivion, our species would have perished long ago. Human beings are *compelled* to be sexual in spite of early training not to. Something has to give.

Since we as a species cannot afford to stop being sexual, all the shaming and control exercised at various times has not been able to decrease interest in sex. How has this happened? As the natural, unfolding, inside-out sexuality became overlaid with shame, it was replaced by sexual reactivity. As we were prevented from accessing real sexuality, we had to find ways to feel sexual anyway. The result is that *the sexual nature of humans has become distorted and reactive to any sexual stimuli, or stimuli that have been defined as sexual.* This reactivity prevented sexuality from being lost (as many of our other primitive human experiences have been lost). Examples of reactive sexuality fill this book. They include arousal when watching other people be sexual, whether in real life, pictures or stories; perceiving nudity and body positioning as sexual; the belief that we have a sex drive that must be stimulated and satisfied on a regular basis; the agreement that if married, a couple will be sexual (as Catholic ceremonies include promises to have children); the purchase of sexual services; the belief that some women are "whores" to be used for sex, whereas other women are to be married; the perception of childbirth and breast feeding as sexual scenes; and the use of children for sexual stimulation.

The vast majority of our sexual "responses" are actually examples of our sexuality trying to attach itself to something outside of us in order to remain alive. The perpetuation of the species requires this more of men, because they must continue arousal, penetration, and orgasm to create pregnancy. Women as a gender are more able to respond to the cultural injunction to reduce or obliterate sexuality because pregnancy is still possible, even if no arousal occurs. Women, on the other hand, must continue to express the bonding part of sexual energy in order to engage men to share with them in supporting babies. This accounts for the focus of women's reactivity on romance and marriage. As each gender clings to the requirements needed to perpetuate the species, it becomes difficult or impossible to find out how sex might gently bond people into families, prepare them to accept new life, and bring them together over and over again for many years.

Reactivity may also take the form of condemnation of sexuality, as in the father's distasteful response to his daughter as her body takes on the shape of a woman. Since he has been trained to react with sexual arousal, or at least a sexual hum, to women's body parts, he must override that reaction with a negative one to prevent himself from feeling like an incestuous child molester.

As the repress–react dichotomy takes hold in a culture, the nature of stimuli that are defined as sexual extends to many, many things that are not at all sexual. In fact, sexuality is a rather small part of our overall ability to experience life, loving, and joy. But we have confused much of our nonsexual experience with sexual experience as we search for it, seeking to find it anywhere. As a result, we are uncomfortable with things that might seem sexual, such as making noises that are similar to sexual sounds, receiving massages, sitting right next to another person, men hugging men, holding hands with friends or family members, and nudity.

Early in my relationship with my husband Rex, I found myself uncomfortable when I heard him sigh deeply after he got out of the shower or threw himself down after strenuous exercise. It sounded like the sighs he made when making love. I felt some jealousy that the sighs weren't reserved just for that special time. When I told him, he laughed and kept on doing it. He sighs when getting out of the shower, when he feels the sunshine on his skin, when he lies down to sleep, and any other time he has feelings of satisfaction and pleasure. He makes sensuous noises when I play with his hair or the cats rub against him. He uses his whole body to express his pleasure. Once I became used to it, I started letting out sounds too, when I felt satisfied or happy. It made me feel more alive and more fully in my body.

As I began to expand my repertoire of sounds, I could see that sighs coming from either of us in these nonsexual situations are different from the ones that come with sex. But I couldn't separate them from each other as long as rich, full sighing was perceived as sexual and had to be limited to that activity.

I also had to free myself from the idea that only people who are sexual partners could touch each other with affection, and allow myself to walk down the street with a woman friend with our arms around each other, sometimes touching the sides of our faces. The more I am able to reclaim my natural sexuality and discover its boundaries, the more I am able to engage in sensuous (not sexual) exchange with cats, friends, massage therapists, children, and my husband. When I receive massages, occasionally I will be rocked in a way that rubs my clitoris against other tissue and brings on mild sexual feelings. Of course, this happens. But I can know that the massage therapist isn't trying to be sexual with me, and that we aren't being sexual because of these feelings. They are just there. Prior to my sexual healing, however, I thought that many people were coming on to me when they did things that resembled sexual acts. Perhaps they were, but most likely they weren't. On the other hand, I flirted addictively and attracted people who did the same. We said that it wasn't sexual when, in fact, it was. Flirting is an integral part of finding a mate and of staying bonded once mating is complete. It is a powerful part of the bonding component of our sexuality and one that has been vastly distorted.

Breast feeding also resembles sexual activity. A baby is sucking on a breast in much the same way a partner may sexually stimulate a breast. Bodies are wired so that breast stimulation elicits reactions in the uterus and stimulates other parts of the genitals. In this reactive society, many women experience sexual arousal when breast feeding, and the reactions to this feeling are polarized. First is the La Leche League's[1] statement that arousal is normal and healthy. By giving mothers permission, they perform the important function of reducing shame. But, in fact, it is not a natural reaction. The mother is a member of a society that can make it difficult to differentiate between sexual feelings serving her adult self and the feelings that come from a baby breast feeding. Second is an intense negative reaction to the mother—a reflection of the culture's abhorrence of incest. Neither of these reactions helps a mother work toward healthy relating with her child. (This is explained in more detail in Chapter 6.)

The more shamed and controlled a person or a culture is, the more reactive he or she becomes to sexual stimuli to make sure this energy is not eliminated. Thus, in past eras of long skirts, ankles brought the same sexual charge a bikini does now. The current cultural definition of sexual "freedom" is to be able to react to any kind and amount of stimuli we choose. Real freedom will come when we don't have to react to stimuli, when we are able to allow our sexuality to emerge when it is right for it to do so.

The cultural repression of sexuality and the essential nature of procreation play upon each other, intensifying the distortions. As sexuality is repressed, reactivity increases, and as reactivity becomes more intense, the cultural desire to control it increases. Over centuries, this interplay has brought about a lack of understanding of the true nature of our vital energy.

This ancient paradigm has resulted in the vast distortions of sexual energy that prevail today, which will be the subject of the chapters to follow.

§ How It All Got Started §

Once upon a time, in ancient history, even before the Bible, it was somehow decided that sexual energy was a dangerous, powerful part of being human, and men and women began to control each other's sexuality. Perhaps a man was jealous when his wife stopped loving him and turned her sexual bonding toward another person. He might have wanted to control her instead of allowing himself to grieve and then relinquish her. His jealousy, a perfectly natural phenomenon, may have seemed like too much pain. So he shamed her sexuality, blaming her for breaking the bonds of marriage, in the hope of preventing her from leaving him. Perhaps it succeeded. She decided to stay to avoid feeling shame, or perhaps she wasn't really going to leave and it only looked like he controlled her with shame. Neverthe-less, the seed was planted that people can be shamed for being sexual, and rules can be created about how and when sex is allowed. The rules overrode the natural, intuitive understanding of monogamy. As the rules gained in authority, the individual's intuitive knowing of how to use sexuality in life-enhancing ways diminished. *Even though some of the rules were similar to intuitive knowing, when a person obeys rules, truly intuitive, inside-out understanding becomes lost.* As we could no longer "know," more and more rules became necessary to control this powerful force residing within each of us. So far we have not had a cultural climate in which the rules could be abandoned, making room for the return of intuitive understanding.

As this hypothetical couple created a family, they used this newfound control over their children to reduce feelings evoked by childish behaviors they found unpleasant. The wife controlled them even more, because she succumbed to the control of her husband—passing it on from generation to generation. As she abandoned herself to prevent feelings of shame from overtaking her, she, by nature, had to pass on the control she received to those she was in a position to dominate. If she wasn't allowed to be sexual in ways that felt intuitively right, then her children would be subject to the same restrictions.

Over time, as each child grew up and passed on the controls of their parents to the next generation, each child had more to contend with and more to resist. As centuries passed, this spread across many cultures. Each generation learned that although sexual bonding is intensely pleasurable, the breaking of a bond or even threatened break is intensely painful. And they learned that this pain can be diminished by controlling those who could bring it about.

This naturally led to adults controlling children's sexuality, and as each child grew up, he or she in turn passed on the control to arriving children. As the children were subjected to such control and the inhibition of a natural, essential part of being human, they reacted. First, they received the shaming of this vital nature. The lack of conversation about sexual feelings, sexual body parts, or sexual activities, and adults' discomfort when these subjects come up, teach children from an early age that sexuality is something that must not be revealed. A tremendous amount of energy goes into assuring adults that they aren't sexual beings, until it finally becomes believable to the child too. *When puberty arrives, the young person is caught in conflict between allowing natural human feelings to emerge and be explored and the prohibitions that have been presented to him or her since birth.* In confusion, they set out as teenagers to find out how they are going to be sexual. Through trial and error, and the unconscious expression of parents' sexual issues, they map out the form sex will take. Added to this are media messages and erroneous information passed down from one generation of teenagers to the next, untouched by truth. Most young people find it impossible to use sexual energy as a way to love a partner and to love themselves. Instead, sex becomes connected or cross-wired with proving love, feeling like a man or woman, becoming tranquilized, being reassured, redirecting attention from unpleasant feelings, and many other nonsexual elements. ("Cross-wiring" is a term I coined to refer to anything that becomes attached to sex that doesn't belong there. Chapter 14 details the ways sexual feelings are hooked up to nonsexual preferences—such as age, weight, and hair color, and the need to have specific fantasies or sexual activities in order to have an orgasm.)

§ WE ARE CHANGING §

But now it is changing. A number of factors are creating a backdrop for the discovery of healthy sexuality. For the first time in history, women and men are working on equal relationships, a necessary foundation for a healthy use of sexuality. The women's movement brought about the beginning of change in family structures, as women were no longer content with the role-prescribed relationships of the past. Equality on all levels is becoming more common and is a new model for relationships.

Financial, emotional, and social equality are necessary to discover the true nature of sexuality. Ownership and control of one gender by the other prohibits intimacy, creating, instead, a vast schism between the owned and the owners. When a woman and man are each other's equal, they open doors to understanding each other and to creating a bond free from culturally imposed differences.

The women's movement brought about the vast change in perception of the amount of sexual abuse of children that occurs. This common activity was so hidden that every woman thought she was the only one who had experienced it. (And most perpetrators thought they were the only ones doing it.) But as the women's movement allowed women to speak and great numbers of women listened to each other, women became able to begin talking about what had gone on sexually. I was a psychologist in private practice when the wave began. Because of this, I got to see that the mental health profession did not create the change—it responded to it. The power came from women in therapy who presented their memories in a way that was indisputably authentic. Soon, even when a client didn't believe what she was saying, I did. Over a span of two years, I went from having no idea how to respond to a client who talked about having sex with a parent to being able to recognize body memories and hold mirrors for women who didn't have words for the memories they felt. I had almost no training in child sexual abuse during this time. The training came from experience and being caught up in the wave that was beginning to form. The *zeitgeist,* or spirit of the times, that produced simultaneous inventions by people with no contact had taken hold. We were all affected by it. When I took continuing-education workshops and read books, I learned that I already knew what was being taught. The educators had learned it the same way I had.

Men are now beginning to follow suit, as women have created mirrors for their experience, too. But it is harder for men to establish that they were also sexually abused as children—in equal numbers, I believe. As a culture, we are willing to see men as sex addicts and women as victims of men. It is more difficult to know that 80 percent of sex addicts were sexual abuse victims.[2] I am one of many therapists who believe it is closer to

100 percent. It is even more difficult to face the fact that as many women as men abuse sexuality and are addicted to sexual feelings (when romance is included as a sexual feeling). The "men's movement" has not yet allowed men to believe themselves. Recovery from sexual addiction is a form of healing that allows men to access their memories.

It is my experience that men who have to examine their memories are suffering intense sexual despair—sex addicts, pedophiles, and those with obsessions for sexual activity that prevent loving sex with a partner. It is harder for men to know they were sexual victims, because they feel like (and some are) victimizers.

§THE FIRST SEXUAL REVOLUTION§

The sexual revolution that began in the 1960s is another reason for our culture's changing. That decade saw a greatly increased sexual activity between "consenting adults." One result was that people got to act out their sexual stories, telling through action what had happened to them in childhood and under the influence of our sexually sick culture. As the 1970s saw an expanded comfort with sexual "freedom," more and more people took for granted sexual activity with partners and casual encounters. Traditional sex therapy promoted guilt-free sex so long as the adults were consenting. The result of this change was that people were now engaged in activities that were likely to bring up memories from the past in the form of feelings and body sensations. The decrease in culturally supported monogamy and the growing loosening of sexual boundaries both told of early experiences of boundary violations. Increasingly, *sexual freedom paved the way for memories to surface.*

Masters and Johnson helped along this sexual revolution and initiated the field of sex therapy by applying for grants to study sexual activity in complete physical detail in the mid-1950s. In the early seventies, their books *Human Sexual Response*[3] and *Human Sexual Inadequacy*[4] became the underpinning for a new field of mental health services—sex therapy. As therapists became trained in the new methods, this therapy caught on quickly, popularizing to the world at large that it was now permissible to enjoy sex.

The socially accepted fields of psychotherapy and medical research increased the influence of the developing sexual freedom from the sixties by sanctifying it with professional approval. Not only did the counterculture try different sexual activities, but also the average person living a typical middle-class American life was told that it was okay to enjoy sex. Therapists now approved many of the previously taboo sexual activities, such as erotic movies and oral sex.

Women could admit they didn't have orgasms and get together to learn how. We were no longer required to act as if we weren't sexual. Instead of believing something was wrong if we had orgasms—particularly more than one—we were now required to have them. Although the new pressure to be sexually correct wasn't helpful, the openness about sex was. Now we had to think of ourselves as more than objects to attract men. Romance as the exclusive mode of sexual expression faded, replaced by self-perception as overtly sexual beings engaging in specific, adult sexual acts. This change in perception encouraged our sexuality to emerge out of repression. As this happened, the repression of other sexual experiences—abusive ones from the past—could not be as easily held back from consciousness. *The magnificent result is the proliferation of women, and now men, who are remembering what happened to them as children, who are telling therapists and support groups, and who are readying themselves to discover what is possible when the rules are lifted.*

All these factors have resulted in the potential for sexual healing at a cultural level—an essential underpinning for the healing of the culture, and, ultimately, the world.

CULTURES RESIST CHANGE

§

§ FROM GENERATION TO GENERATION §

"Culture" can be seen as the institutionalization of beliefs and practices that were introduced at points in history. Beliefs and practices that become acculturated then become "normal." Although most elements of cultures are necessary and useful in allowing communities to form and continue, many are incorporated that are damaging to individuals, and to communities. Sex is one area that is readily given to distortions that become accepted at a cultural level. Our world is filled with beliefs about sex that seem ordinary to those in the culture in which they are accepted and absurd to those in other cultures.

A particularly poignant example is the circumcision of thirty million women in some African countries.[1] Alice Walker writes of this practice in her novel *Possessing the Secret of Joy*.[2] Her story, based on actual practices, graphically illustrates how beliefs begun centuries ago influence the present in ways that seem to make no sense. The people in her African tribe believe that women must have their vulvas cut off and vaginas sewn shut in order to be sexually attractive to men. Girls are implored to go through the operation in order to get a man, because none will want her if she doesn't. Men are given the blame for this massive violation of women's bodies and sexuality, in which the clitoris is scraped off along with the labia. But would many men want to rape their wives in order to express sexuality with another person? Or have sex with someone who consents to being inflicted with severe pain?

Women perpetuate the culturally required practice. Women perform the surgery, and women counsel girls about the need for it.

Hanny Lightfoot-Klein, in her beautifully written book *Prisoners of Ritual*,[3] described three kinds of circumcision. The least invasive is the clitorectomy. Part or all of the clitoris is removed. The rest of the vulva remains intact. "Infibulation" is the sewing shut of the vagina except for a tiny opening about the size of a pierced ear hole. Urine, vaginal fluids, and menstrual blood seep out slowly. Urination can take ten to twenty minutes. A third procedure, known as "pharaonic circumcision," involves cutting off the clitoris and the inner labia, removing most of the flesh of the outer labia, and then sewing the remaining labia skin shut over the vagina, again leaving a small hole. This leaves smooth skin and scar tissue instead of moist folds of flesh.

When a woman marries, her husband must force his penis into her, tearing the skin to create an opening. This is, of course, extremely painful for the woman and can damage the man's penis. Full penetration takes days or months for couples dealing with a pharaonic circumcision. A wound is created and mustn't be allowed to heal until the vagina is opened sufficiently to allow penetration. Once this occurs and the wound heals, then intercourse can be pain free and even pleasurable. However, women who have had the most severe procedures may never have pain-free intercourse. These women often become depressed and suicidal, according to a psychiatrist interviewed by Lightfoot-Klein. Lightfoot-Klein was able to guess what kind of circumcision various women had had by their demeanor. The more extensive, the more submissive, depressed, and unhappy the woman.

Those interviewed by Lightfoot-Klein tried to explain why the practice was necessary. One spiritual leader said that he abhorred the practice and wanted it to stop—yet his own daughters had been circumcised. When Lightfoot-Klein asked him why he allowed this act that he considered a crime, he said it was because of custom. "Custom was too strong in the people. *No one* could defy custom."[4]

As Lightfoot-Klein examined several of the cultures in Africa, she learned that the rationale for circumcision varied. Some believed the surgery would enhance sexual relating, but most felt it would inhibit women's sexual feelings, which was necessary to the community. Most of her information came from many hours of living with and talking to the Sudanese, people who believe that a woman must not enjoy sex. She is not allowed to directly initiate sex but can send out a signal by perfuming her skin with oil and incense. When having sex, she must not show any interest. If she is able to have orgasms, she must not show it.

In taking a look at the influence of religion, Lightfoot-Klein points out that "Islam's stern emphasis on chastity and its general suppression of sexuality"[5] creates shameful feelings that might require extreme measures to remove. She also points out that most Islamic countries have no female circumcision and religion does not justify the practice. Apparently some Islamic communities discovered this method of responding to the religion-based shame, whereas others developed their own methods. Other religions have communities that practice it, too, including African Coptic Christians and a small sect of Ethiopian Jews. Sexual shame is not limited to any one religion, and the creativity of people in devising methods to remove the feeling of shame takes different forms.

The perception of female sexuality as shameful can provide an understanding of the origins of female circumcision and the refusal of these cultures to abandon it, even when against the law. Lightfoot-Klein quotes one of her subjects as saying, "If you refuse to do it, you will not be beautiful."[6] A groin free from folds of flesh and with greatly inhibited flow of menstrual blood and other vaginal fluids would of course be seen as beautiful by people who consider a normal vulva ugly and repulsive. *The shameful part of the body is cut off.* Shame drops because her "badness" has been removed and, as a sexless woman, she is allowed to belong to her community. Her husband begins sex with smooth skin and has to force his way through the sewn-shut tissue. He doesn't have to feel his own shame at seeing her vulva and having his penis sucked into an eager vagina. He has been raised in a culture that sees vulvas as shameful and so, of course, will be more comfortable with a bride who doesn't have one. Lightfoot-Klein describes at length the reactions of the men she interviewed. They often had difficulty staying erect when cast in the role of rapist, causing their wives pain. (But they may also have had difficulty staying erect entering a normal vagina after growing up in a culture that defines vulvas as dirty and ugly, and female sexuality as bad.)

Most circumcisions are done with no anesthetic. Several people hold the four- to six-year old child down while a midwife or other person cuts her and sews her up. She knows she will have more pain when she is married, as her husband is required to rip her skin to enter her. This pain can serve to "purify" her of her sexual "badness"—punishment has long been known to pay off debts of badness.

Shame that is seen as inherent in being female can be reduced, but the consequences are hardly worth it. Lightfoot-Klein found that the more severe the procedure, the more emotionally distressed the women were. Part of this is because the sewing shut of the vagina creates ongoing pain during intercourse and childbirth. Her vulva remains "bad," and the debt cannot be paid off.

When I speak of the practice of female circumcision, people are aghast at the thought of cutting off part of the body in order to fit in, be more beautiful, and appear less shameful. To those living in the United States, this practice seems barbaric and unacceptable—something that would never be done here. I agreed until I realized that plastic surgeons routinely cut off pieces of skin in order to make people feel more attractive, to reduce the shame that comes from aging, with loss of the acceptable body and face. Major face-lifts involve excising all of the flesh away from the face and cutting off fat and pieces of skin. As with female circumcision, it is possible to cause nerve damage, and to remove too much skin, yet thousands of people are willing to face the risk of full anesthetic and surgery in order to feel more "beautiful," and thus, more acceptable and valued— less repulsive. Our culture supports this "solution" to the shame of not looking right by perceiving the person as more attractive after the surgery. The price paid for even successful surgeries is little understood. For example, the face is limited in expressiveness.

We can cut the experience of shame from our bodies, but we cannot cut away the shame itself.

§ Mothers and Grandmothers Enforce Female Circumcision §

The mothers, and particularly grandmothers, who make the decision and control the process aren't mean people who want to maim their children. They are people who heard from their mothers and aunts and grandmothers and *all* adults that this procedure is necessary in order to lead the right adult life. For a woman to say no to the surgery means setting herself up to be a misfit, an outsider. She will be shamed for having a vulva unlike all other women. Therefore, when a girl reaches puberty, she *wants* to have it removed.

As I look at other culture's sexual distortions, I am appalled that they are unable to question practices that seem obviously unhealthy. But I am able to see these practices as damaging, because I haven't been acculturated from childhood to believe that what they do is right. I am, however, blind to many of my culture's damaging practices and am spending my career learning what they are and how to become as conscious of our fallacies as I am of those of other cultures. One purpose of this book is to bring to light those sexual practices that are as acculturated as the maiming of girls' genitals in parts of Africa.

Western cultures have something in common with these African countries. We all have sexual shame, and we all figure out how to reduce our experience of it. African methods look strange to us, and our methods probably look strange to them. For the world to be healed of sexual shame, we must all acknowledge its existence, look at how we reduce the feeling of it, then give up those methods, face the shame, and relinquish it.

§ Acculturated Practices Take On a Life of Their Own §

As Lightfoot-Klein sought out the reasons for female circumcision, she heard conflicting ideas. The original purpose was perhaps never conscious and now cannot be articulated. The excuses have become institutionalized and support the custom. She gives examples of pressure to continue the practice.

- One man who refused to have his daughter circumcised was shunned by his mother, who broke off contact for three months.
- Girls who aren't circumcised will be ridiculed by those who have been. In one community the girls refused to be circumcised, and every man refused to marry them. They finally gave in and had the surgery.
- Men who cannot penetrate the infibulated vagina are considered less than masculine. It is shameful to go to a midwife and have the vagina opened surgically, and when done, it is kept secret. He needs her to be circumcised so he can prove himself.

As I wrote the previous section, I wanted to offer an example of how U.S. culture enforces damaging beliefs. Again, I am confronted with my blindness to how our practices are enforced. Why can't people just *see* the truth when it is presented and stop requiring themselves to function according to absurd beliefs—such as how men are supposed to get and maintain an erection at will. At the same time, I know this has become internalized, so each man believes it is true even if other men are questioning it. Changing beliefs takes hours of questioning, permission to be angry, and confrontation of feelings of inadequacy that come with giving up. Most people will never fully relinquish such deeply ingrained beliefs. I know that this belief is supported by the fact that men brag about how they kept an erection all night, and by the absence of hearing men talk openly about how they didn't get or keep an erection, and by women either shaming men for losing their erection, or trying to "make it okay." Still, it is easier to see how this works in other cultures than in my own.

§ THE SEXUAL SALE OF CHILDREN §

As we in the United States, Europe, and other places learn about the sexual abuse of children and connect the damage of body, soul, and emotions with sexual activities in childhood, we can see clearly that selling children as prostitutes is harmful to them. We also know that the person who wants to pay money to have sex with a child is not healthy and should be stopped from harming the child. We have always *said* this in our culture, but, until the late 1970s we were blind to it's existence—a cultural blindness—and so we unknowingly allowed it to continue. Now that we are becoming conscious, we can see that other countries are also engaged in sexual practices that are seriously harmful. Asian countries, particularly Thailand, sell children for sex to those in their country and to tourists who go there for that purpose.[7]

Greg, who told me his story for my book *From Generation to Generation*, was a sex addict who had sex with women, men, and children. He wanted to believe that he wasn't a pedophile, just an addict who would have sex with anyone who was willing. He "fell in love with" his daughter as a baby and believed that was the cause of his sexual interest in her. But as he reflected on his purchase of children for sex when he was in Asian countries, he began to see that it was more than availability. He preferred to have sex with prepubescent girls and boys. Greg was one of many who travel to countries that offer these services. Although such sales also go on in the United States, they are so condemned that the flourishing business in Asia has not been duplicated.

In ancient Greek and Roman times, the use of prepubescent boys for anal sex was common and accepted. According to Brett

Kahr,[8] Plato and Aristotle both wrote about anal sex with boys—called pederasty. Plato believed that the boys should be shared among many men. Aristotle advocated sexual use of children, but, Kahr writes, may have been the first recorded writer to caution against sex between a man and his own son. Kahr goes on to say that the ancient Roman use of children was accepted and integrated into the culture. One example was the establishment of a public holiday for child prostitutes.

Most people who hear of the accepted sexual use of children in the past or in other cultures react with shock. It is clear to us that these children were/are being massively harmed and that such practices should be stopped. We know the children will go on to have children who will be sexually violated: It has become common knowledge that those who were molested as children are more likely to do the same. Yet until the past two decades, people in the United States did not know the magnitude of the use of children for sexual purposes, far more often by family members than by strangers.[9]

§ INDIAN CULTURE AND THE ATTACHMENT OF MOTHER AND SON §

Elisabeth Bumiller has described the centuries-old, acculturated incestuous bond between mother and son in India.[10] When a man marries, he remains bonded with his mother, which prevents the formation of a monogamous sexual bond with his wife. The new wife, who moves to her mother-in-law's home, loses in competition with the older woman. Her only recourse for finding value and self-worth—and love—is to give birth to sons. Because her marriage prohibits a loving sexual bond, she finds it with her sons. Indian culture accepts this connection, approving of her sleeping with boys until they are six or so. She cannot be expected to forego this bond, because her life would hold little or no value. But of course, she has to play out the role of the possessive mother, be unable to fully accept her daughter-in-law, and prevent her son from separating from her and bonding with his wife. She becomes like her own mother-in-law. As this cycle went on, it came to appear "normal" and is rarely questioned today.

When I lived in Madras, India, as a child, my family and other Americans criticized the Indians for practices such as women walking ten paces behind their husbands. They also looked down on the women for being controlled by their husbands and family. That was in 1958, five years before the publication of the first book that launched the most recent women's movement—*The Feminine Mystique*, in 1963.[11] After three decades of consciousness raising, we see how controlled wives are by their husbands in the United States, too. Laws, as well as mores, gave women fewer rights than men, but American women (including those I met in India) couldn't see what was wrong with the system until feminists and the media began to call attention to our practices. And, of course, there is more. Our consciousness has been greatly raised, but we have a long way to go in order to understand the reality of gender equality.

Now I understand that the wife walked behind the husband (and the spirit of his mother walking with him) and then became powerful when her son was born. Throughout life, her power came from her emotional power over him. Until other routes toward achieving self-respect become available, she will follow her assigned place in the generational process.

As I read *May You Be the Mother of a Hundred Sons*,[12] I was appalled that an entire culture supported an incestuous bond between mother and son—until I realized that American culture does the same—in ways that look different. Most of my male clients who are healing their sexuality felt incestuously bonded with their mothers. Most were left with feelings of disgust for women's bodies, disgust they overrode with lusting for body parts or sexual activity. At the same time, they felt abandoned by their mothers, their real needs not clearly seen. Although I have no statistics to support it, I believe that in our sexually addictive culture many more people than psychotherapy clients have this combination of reactions toward women.

Our culture prepares women to bond with their children in ways that don't serve the child, the mother, or the family. Couples are not supported in maintaining a powerful, loving sexual energy–enforced bond that prevents spillover of sexual energy onto other people, including children. As a result, many mothers violate their children without knowing they are doing so. Our culture encourages this and does not offer mirrors to mothers so they can see what they are doing. (This is addressed in my book *From Generation to Generation: Understanding Sexual Attraction to Children*).

I expect you, the reader, to accept what I say about Indian culture and reject what I say about ours. I can only make it clear when I am able to describe it as it is happening and those involved are able to process their feelings. This happened in a group of three couples who were friends before entering therapy together. The couples related with a good deal of sexualized energy, which I didn't point out for the first few meetings. Then one of the women came to the group exuding it, primarily toward her husband and toward me. When I described what I was seeing, she became very upset, telling me I was wrong. Other group members agreed with her. By the end of the two hours, all six understood what I was saying and began identifying their own use of it. Once they could *see* sexual energy, they could see it everywhere.

§ LEGISLATING MORALS §

The United States didn't have sexual obscenity laws until the late 1800s when a man named Anthony Comstock took it upon himself to create them. He began a personal campaign to eradicate any evidence of sexuality, including marriage manuals and information on contraception. He succeeded. The resulting Comstock Act influenced a century of thought.

Why would a man take on the enormous task of legislating the morals of his country? Comstock perpetuated the belief that he was a righteous person who wanted to help his compatriots. I believe he was motivated by an entirely different desire. In his diary, Comstock wrote that he had masturbated compulsively in his teens and had been afraid it would drive him to suicide. It appears that Comstock was a sex addict who desperately wanted to stop his compulsive sexual activities. He had no twelve-step program to help him understand the nature of his compulsion and offer him support in stopping. He had no mirror for his right to remove shame from his activities. Instead, his only option seemed to be forcing himself to no longer engage in masturbation. But, of course, the more he controlled his sexuality, the more reactive he became—and the more he wanted to control it.

Therapists working with sexual addiction and other kinds of cross-wiring of sexual arousal have heard many stories about people who were highly upset by their arousal patterns and *condemned the stimulus that brought on the arousal.* When it is not understood that the arousal is a result of faulty associations from the past, this is a natural conclusion. Prior to two decades ago, children who were abused were often held responsible for seducing the adult.[13]

Given this view, it makes sense that Comstock and others like him truly believed their misery was caused by something outside them. Beginning with this premise, the solution was to gain control over the stimulus. Comstock felt that his masturbation, and the stimuli that provoked it, were so evil that he wanted to eradicate the causes. Naturally he would believe that what provoked sexual arousal in him would do the same for all others. This conclusion would result in attempting to do our country a favor by eliminating the evil of sexual stimulation.

Comstock's reaction to his own sexual addiction and his attitude of shame toward his masturbation has had a tremendous impact on the lives of millions of people over a span of 100 years. This serves as an example of how one person, back in the beginning of an era of sexual shaming, could influence the sexuality of an entire community and for centuries thereafter. The circular effect is created first by sexual repression, which is followed by the bursting out of sexuality, which results in further repression by those like Comstock, who project their own shame onto everyone around them.

§THE CONDEMNATION OF GARY HART§

Cultures are capable of holding a value that is verbally agreed on, and at the same time, an incompatible value that is unspoken. An example is the agreement that monogamy is important, yet more than half of Americans have extramarital sex.[14] David Rutter, in *Sex in the Forbidden Zone*,[15] describes how sex between therapist and patient, although unethical and illegal, is commonly overlooked by other professionals who know it is happening. There seems to be a mixture of acceptance and refusal to tell on a respected person, as well as condemnation once the truth is out. In 1984, when Gary Hart was preparing to run for President, information about his extramarital sexual activities caused a strong negative reaction, and he withdrew. It was assumed that sexual distortions would interfere with his ability to be a good President. There is no logic in this assumption. *Having sex with other women and lying to one's spouse, although not healthy activities, are covertly accepted behaviors.* Many people who judged Gary Hart have had sex outside of marriage and lied to their spouses. These hidden activities are placed in a compartment in our minds that remains separate from publicly visible actions. Gary Hart was judged by the *stated* values of our culture. He was not accepted by those who were also unable to achieve monogamy in their marriages. Instead, their shame and self-condemnation were projected onto Hart.

§CULTURES CHANGE§

Cultures change, of course. Changes occur faster now than in history because of rapid communication and transportation. Cultures evolve in some ways while remaining stable in others.

Popular and accepted clothing is constantly changing in Western cultures, while female circumcision is unchanged in Sudan.

Cultures change in two basic ways. One way is the introduction of something new that pushes the old aside. New clothing styles render the old ones unattractive to our perception. The introduction of affordable computers and word processors has made typewriters almost obsolete. Telephones in every home and many cars have made it socially unacceptable to drop in without calling.

The second way culture changes is through increasing awareness of the harmful nature of certain practices. Child-labor laws came about as people realized that working children weren't allowed to grow up in healthy ways and were deprived of education. Limited work hours and labor unions appeared when people objected to other unhealthy work practices. Women obtained the right to vote when enough people saw that denying it was wrong. Equal pay for equal work is now understood, even though the culture hasn't brought it about. Thirty years ago, the idea seemed absurd.

In cultures in which women are becoming able to talk about sexual abuses during childhood and come to understand the damage that occurred because of it, a cultural shift is following. As the media have brought to public attention the extent of sexual abuse of children and the massive recovery from it that is underway, consciousness of the existence of this damaging practice now exists. As a result, more women and now men, too, are able to know what happened to them and talk about it.

As these people heal, they are discovering that many of the previously accepted sexual practices are not healthy, and they are stopping them. Sexual addiction has been identified, books have been written, and many people are examining their sexual activities to see what really serves them. We are becoming more conscious of what was previously hidden and are getting to have our feelings about it. As those who are healing their sexuality change their perceptions, the whole culture is confronted with the new truth. Families in the United States are in upheaval over this issue.

§ No Sexually Healthy Cultures §

I am frequently asked if any cultures have healthy sexual energy. I cannot truly answer that question without going to every country and tribe, and taking a look. But I can guess that there are no communities that have been able to fully access healthy sexuality because, according to feminist examinations of cultures, there are none with gender equality. Only a culture that welcomes both genders at birth and views them as spiritually, morally, and intellectually equal, and equally worthy to be born, has the necessary environment to allow sexuality to unfold and be expressed in optimal ways.

Two countries with massive populations, China and India, are among the many noted for the desire for sons and disappointment with daughters. Girl babies are still killed in India, even though it is illegal. Girl babies are easily adopted from China because they are abandoned by couples who, allowed only one child, prefer raising a son. Although there may be exceptions to the wish for sons only, as in some Indian families in which female children are educated and assume positions of power, even these women are affected by living in a culture where women are owned and not valued, and where they are the exception.

True acceptance of women must come before couples can use their sexual energy optimally. Women's issues are increasingly seen around the world now and are paving the way for changes in sexuality. Women are capable of healing from abuses of their sexuality and are discovering a more spiritual and healthy use of it but are still limited by cultural perceptions. Cultures change when individuals within it change, and the two arenas of change play back and forth. In decades (or centuries), we can accomplish both the acceptance of women and the discovery of healthy sexuality.

3

GROWING UP IN A HEALTHY CULTURE
§

Sexual attraction to another person is the beginning of a process that, if allowed to run its course, will lead to a monogamously bonded relationship. This relationship will persist as long as both people continue to use sex to bond and don't store up negative feelings that will drive them apart. Even when the result of such a buildup of feelings is divorce, it is tremendously painful for people to separate and begin new lives apart. The bond is a powerful one.

The purpose of sexual energy to bond humans into couples and create new families through bonding and procreation has been vastly distorted over centuries of superimposed cultural beliefs. We are not able to understand the natural evolution of sexuality for each individual within a sexually healthy culture, because we have all been raised in an unhealthy environment.

Because it is difficult for us to see how our own culture is not healthy, I would like to begin this chapter with a picture of what healthy evolution of sexuality might look like for a person born into a healthy culture. Drawing from my life, from the experiences of my clients who are recovering from an impossible use of sexuality, and from the stories of countless others I have encountered over the years, I have formed an understanding of healthy sexuality. The description that follows first appeared in my earlier book *Discovering Sexuality That Will Satisfy You Both*. You might envision yourselves growing up again in a culture that allows you to explore your sexuality without shame and on your own time schedule.

The story could begin like this: You are born fully sexual. Sexual potential and sexual feelings are a natural part of your developing sense of yourself, along with the desire to live, to be taken care of and loved.

As your mother offers a breast for nourishment, she delights in her ability to feed you from her body. Her feelings about her breasts are free from shame. When others watch her feed you, they do not have sexual thoughts about her breasts, but see them as beautiful organs for feeding a new being. Your mother hasn't had years of regarding her breasts as sexual objects for the arousal of men. She respects and understands the sexual feelings her breasts can have. She doesn't have feelings of worth based on breast size or on the power of attracting attention that she can pass on to you. She doesn't experience you as a lover because you suck on her breast. Your feelings about breasts are clean and appreciative. You meet your need for food with feelings of calm and pleasure for both of you.

Your parents focus their sexual energy into their relationship and have none left over to spill accidentally onto you. As you go through the dependent stage of life, when adults carry you everywhere and bathe and dress you, you feel safe and secure that they attend only to your needs; they do not use you for needs they're not meeting elsewhere.

§ FIRST SEXUAL FEELINGS §

When you are old enough to walk, and you see your parents being sexual with each other, which they do in many of their day-to-day interactions, you might invite yourself to join them in a hug. They could continue to have sexual feelings toward each other, but these feelings are kept separate from their feelings toward you. They can be sexual with each other without arousing your sexuality. Your arousal comes from inside of you, when you are curious about this part of being human. When your other needs are met—when you aren't hungry or sleepy or needing affection—you might explore these other feelings. One of those times might be when you see adults having sexual feelings with each other. Their use of sexual energy might make you think of yours, and if the time is right, then you might explore. You could touch your genitals and see how the feelings increase.

When you are around three, you will find that your interest in sexual feelings and in your genitals becomes stronger. Other maturational needs are pretty well taken care of now. You can walk, talking is getting easier, and you are feeling quite separate from your parents—a real individual. Now you have room to attend to your sexual self. If you are a boy, you want to show off your penis. You want others to see that it changes size and that when it is larger, it usually has more feeling in it. You want people to be delighted with you when you take off your clothes and run around with it bobbing up and down. If you are a girl, you might touch your genitals and look at them. You could rub against a parent, tipping your head while looking adoringly at him or her and smiling.

You live in a respectful home where parents and siblings understand that your sexual feelings are a delight to you. They won't see your sexual expression as an invitation for them to have their own arousal or to join you in sexual activity. They will observe and be delighted with your delight, as will the neighbors and other adults when you show yourself off to them.

Relatives will mention to you that a few people were sexually damaged as they were growing up, and they may want to be sexual with you. Your parents will calmly explain that they want to know if anyone wants to touch you in ways that don't feel right. They need only tell you briefly, because you already know when touch feels healthy and so, of course, you will know when it is intrusive. Your parents have listened to all your other distresses, so you know you can take something like this to them too, and be heard. If someone does touch you in a way that doesn't feel right, you may be frightened, but you know someone is close by to protect you. If the person who touches you intrusively is a parent, you tell another relative, who immediately protects you from further violation. You are not left alone with the parent until she or he has seen a therapist and is able to touch you in ways that are healthy.

After a time, you will become curious about this sexual relationship between your parents. It looks interesting, and you know that you, too, might want to have one when you are grown up, much as you are becoming aware that you want to do other things they do—driving a car, going to work, cooking, and having your own family. So you flirt with one of them. You put all your sexual energy into trying to attract his or her attention, to get him or her to bond with you, instead of bonding with your other parent. This is pretty serious business, like learning to walk and having to work on the balance part of it over and over until you get it right. But this turns out differently. No matter how hard you try, your parent won't break the bond with the other parent and create a monogamous bond with you. This is very frustrating. Eventually you realize that it won't work, and you give up. It becomes clear that this is like driving and going to work: You have to wait until you grow up some more before you can do it. You have a glimmer of awareness that you will bond with someone else—someone who also doesn't have a sexual bond and wants one. There's no point in trying again with someone who is already bonded.

The thought goes through your head that perhaps a sibling is available—someone who doesn't already have a bond. As soon as the thought appears, you reject it. No, not with them! But friends seem a little more interesting. You might talk to your friends about things you have seen your parents do, such as kissing and hugging. It feels good when you try it, so you go on to explore those other parts of your bodies that you already knew bring good feelings. You see what penises and vaginas and labia and testicles look like. You find out what it feels like to have them touched by someone else. You may do this with several friends, some of each sex, and find out how different genitals can look, and how different it can feel to be touched by various children. Your curiosity may focus intensely in this area of humanness for a time, before moving on to your next developmental task.

As you learn about these things over a period of months, you tell your parents all about it. They listen with interest in the same way they have about anything new you are learning. You might tell your mother that you saw Rachel's labia today, and they were much bigger than Deborah's. You might say, "Mommy, why are some labia big and others are small?" or "Why can I see my penis's head but Victor has skin over his?" Your siblings may tell what they learned when they were your age and compare stories. This is really fascinating stuff. Your parents respond in the same interested, alive way they do when you tell about learning how to read an entire book or being able to swim all the way across the pool.

When you have learned enough about all of this, it is time to move on to skills that will serve you as you become an adult. Sports are one way to learn, reading another. You may find one area that interests you more or be drawn to several at the same time. Now your life will move toward going places and doing things, and sexuality will fall into the background until it is time for it again. No one will be deliberately arousing you. Otherwise, it will be difficult to let sexual energy make its own choices as to when and where it will emerge. The people in your life know that your sexuality will unfold when it is your time. Your age-mates will not be feeling very sexual either, and those who are already reaching puberty won't see you as an interesting, potential sex partner, because it isn't time for you to join in this new process.

§ Puberty §

When you reach puberty, however, everything changes. Now the younger kids who are still in sexual latency won't be very interesting, and those who are also going through hormonal changes will become fascinating. It seems that from one day to the next, several other people around your age have become different. Instead of a person with a name and some predictable characteristics, you now see someone who intrigues you.

Actually, you see several such people and are drawn to them as if a magnet had appeared under your skin and theirs. You find that some of your interests are put on hold for a while, or at least they don't pull at you with the same strength. Your desire to explore has changed its focus.

Your teachers are prepared for this change. They mirror back to you some of your shock that previous interests seem of little value and your curiosity is now so focused on other people. School changes to meet your needs, with less direction in academic pursuits and more in the personal. In sex education, the role of intercourse in conception is made clear. Educators know it is only a matter of time until you experiment with sexual activity. They know that intercourse must no longer be connected with pregnancy, as it once was, and on the heels of puberty, because our world has changed. Now when a heterosexual couple have established themselves in their work lives and their home, they are in a better position to welcome their babies a decade later than they might have in the past. Same-sex couples don't have to worry about this. They choose when to have babies, calling on the many models for how to do this.

The next years are chaotic in some ways as you explore with others how to select a mate. You find that two things are happening: (1) You feel sexual a lot now; (2) your peers and teachers understand what is happening, because talk is open. For boys, erections seem to come unbidden, and sometimes orgasms do too. Everyone knows that when a young man has a bulge in his pants, his sexual energy is practicing for when he is ready to use the erection for sexual pleasure with a lover or self-touch. It is so common that people hardly notice it after the first few times. Those early erections are a male's initiation into his adult sexuality.

For girls, the ability to have strong sexual arousal is accompanied by the beginning of menstruation. The first flow of red is celebrated as your family and friends join in the excitement over your new status as a young woman. You have become able to use your body to invite new life. You already know there are several ways to catch the blood, because you have seen other women do so from the time you were a baby. You are familiar with the reverence around this blood, understanding that it is the food for embryos as they become babies. You feel no disgust or fear, because it is familiar. You may already have seen births.

Your community helps you discover the form you want your celebration to take. Some young women will use menstrual blood in a ceremony, while others may focus on the babies to be invited. Long before the beginning of menstruation and erection, males and females are prepared for these physical changes and for the appearance of pubic hair, changes in body shape, and emotional upheaval. Your emotional process is the same as it would be if you were twenty-six and ready to begin a family. You understand this process is inherent in being human, and you honor it. You know it would be foolish to be sexual more than a few times with a person you don't want to partner with, because you would bond together anyway. The choice to bond is not one made by the intellect.

When you find a person you feel compatible with, then you may be ready to explore sexual activity. You find that sexual energy opens you up and removes the usual boundaries of privacy and modesty. These boundaries, important in creating a sense of your separate self, are not useful now, when the task is finding out how to have oneness. You find this experience joyful and exhilarating. Your life tasks have had much to do with separating yourself from family members for many years. Now you get to return to the primitive experiences of your infancy. Naked and open, looking deeply into each other's eyes and souls, and aroused by the power of sexuality so that your skin and organs vibrate, you come into possession of a new life.

You curiously explore each other, finding out how your body works and how your partner's works. You learn how to bring on strong arousal in yourself and in your partner, and see the function this has in enhancing the opening and bonding. You discover that your bodies know exactly what to do and turn yourselves over to them. You have sex often, and you tell others about it. As you hear their stories, this new part of humanness becomes more natural. In time, being a sexual person in a relationship becomes an accepted, understandable part of your life.

You may find your mate quickly, or you may go through a series of matings, because each one of the early matches doesn't turn out to be a lifetime coupling. In this latter case, the two of you must grieve for the loss of the intense bond that sexual energy has created before you are able to move on to your next choice. This grieving process is very intense. To break the bond, it has to be equal in force to the power of sexual energy that created it. The grief is as painful as the sexual bonding was pleasurable. But you are able to complete the grief process in a few weeks, because you have complete access to your emotions and can let the anger and tears flow. You already know how they do their job, because you have had other losses to deal with, either permanent or temporary, during your earlier years.

You may find that you have periods without a partner as you return to other interests. This becomes possible as you get used to your adult sexual energy and it is no longer new and chaotic.

Masturbation might play a role in your life too. Your first explorations of how your sexual body works will include touching yourself sexually to learn about your body parts, what they do, and how orgasm happens. You may delight in making love to yourself. At the same time, you also know that this energy is designed to bond you to another person, and so your attention is usually outward. Your radar can perceive the broadcasts of those who want mates, particularly if you want one too. You may find your attention drawn more to one gender or to both genders equally.

You don't have to deal with people trying to ensnare you into a sexual relationship if you are securely bonded. If you are bonded, you will send that message out (much as you saw your parents weren't available to you because they were bonded with each other). Others who aren't bonded will know that you aren't one of the possibilities and so won't waste their sexual energies in your direction.

§ BONDING WITH YOUR MATE §

When you find a mate and everything seems to be right for being together, then sexual energy will bond you. In the beginning, perhaps the first few times you are together and using sexual energy, it will feel delightful. The bond starts to form, but your sexuality may still find other available people interesting. Neither of you feels jealous of the other's interest in another. But in a matter of several weeks you go through a change. Seemingly from one day to the next, you find that you don't want your partner to send sexual energy to someone else—flirting, implying sexual interest, dating. You want it all for yourself. Your partner is delighted with your feelings and expresses joy. At the same time, you find that your sexual interest in other people is dropping rapidly. When you meet a person who is available and with whom you had exchanged sexual energy only a few weeks before, you will find that your sexual energy is not engaged. This is information to you that you are mating, and you might feel even more joyful as you tell your partner about it. As each of you affirms how your sexuality is limiting itself to the other, your bond strengthens.

As weeks become months, your lives mingle further, and you feel like a couple. After a time, the bonding feels complete, and you find that your attention is no longer drawn so intensely to each other. Instead, your old interests and friends resurface, only now to be integrated into your mated relationship. You jostle some priorities, perhaps with some fear and jealousy as each of you is concerned with maintaining the bond. But in a few more months, you see how both the relationship and the rest of your lives can mesh to provide richness that far exceeds each facet.

Sexual activity assumes less importance in your life now. It has done its job of creating a new family. Although you still feel a sexual hum when relating intimately with your partner (with or without sexual activity), the urge to take it further has lessened. You warmly and joyfully expand into each other when the time is right, when you can dedicate yourselves to each other fully. The purpose is to rebond, a regular need that surfaces after each of you has oriented to other needs for a time. Now you have the leisure to explore each other more quietly, with less urgency. The experience of sexuality continues to expand as you learn more and more about this powerful energy. Your sexual lessons continue throughout your life. You can't learn them all right away. As the two of you go on learning, you find your-selves always curious and never knowing what lessons will appear each time. This process can never be boring, even with the same partner and similar sexual activities.

By now you have moved well into the complex process of "marrying." The wedding ceremony is only a ritual that affirms a natural process with several facets. The sexual-bonding and sexual-activity components are complete. Another component is living in the same home, and yet another is the mingling of finances. At some point during this process, you may find that you know throughout yourself that this is your life mate. Then a wedding is useful to announce to your community that you are a couple. You use the power of standing up in front of other people and stating to each other in words and gestures that you are together—perhaps for life. You find that the public statement makes you feel even more bonded. The ritual allows more of your being to know that you are together. As well, others in your community now see you as a couple and reflect this back to you, further affirming your mating. If you add children, their pres-ence further bonds you by creating a family in which the two of you are responsible.

If you should decide to break your bond, then the process reverses itself. Sexual energy is cut off so that it no longer holds you together. Intense feelings of grief replace intense feelings of joy—emotions necessary to change our perception of the past so that it corresponds to the present. You find yourself in rages, screaming out your pain of loss. At times, it may seem that life isn't worth living, because you felt half of a whole and now the other half isn't there. Other times you sob, in effect, cleansing yourself deeply. The process is intense. Your employer, friends, and family make room for it, expecting that you won't be as attentive as you usually are to other tasks and relationships. They know that if they support your grief, then it will soon pass and leave you again with plenty of energy and attention for other parts of your life. They are aware that mating is deeply significant, and the community supports it, both in the creating of the bond and in the breaking of it.

You know that while you are separating from your mate, it is not time to look for another. It isn't possible to experience the joy of new bonding fully while in the anguish of breaking the old. It isn't a conscious decision. You see that your sexual energy doesn't reemerge and trust that it will when the time is right, after the grief is complete. You may also enjoy a period of being single, exploring this lifestyle again, falling in love with yourself.

Then one morning you wake up and suddenly there are many attractive, available people around. You begin again the process of sorting, as they sort, until you find a new mate.

If your last bonding included having children, you are now in a position of parenting without a mate. As you send out your sexual energy, you find it possible to regulate it so that you do not direct it at your children or toward people who are in relationships. Actually, it never occurs to you to send your energy in these directions, because they are not areas in which you will find a mate. The only fruitful place to direct it is toward those who are also available.

Your mated friends, remembering their mating days, want to find unmated people with whom you may sort. They know that you will need to meet many people before finding the right match, and they want to help once they see you are ready. At this later time in life, most people around you are already mated, and so your community helps to bring together those who aren't. Eventually you find a person, one who is even more suited to you. You are older and know more about your needs in a mate, as your mate knows her or his needs too.

You again move into a mated state. As you settle into marriage, it feels correct. There is something right about merging your life with the life of another. You have learned how to do it without overdoing it. You sacrifice nothing of yourself to have a mate and children. Meeting responsibilities is joyful, because it is right for you. Everything you do in your life is from choice, because you can clearly see what brings you the richest life, and so all your decisions are useful ones. Even bonding and then breaking the bond make sense in the scheme of your life.

§ SEX OVER THE YEARS §

Your bonding matures over a few years, and the need for sex to rebond or to invite children becomes a normal, understandable part of life. If one of you is focused away from the relationship, the other isn't interested in sex either. When it is time to rebond, then both of you find sex compelling.

Couples have differing patterns of sexual activity over the years. Sometimes you may enjoy sexual feelings when touching but only occasionally go on to intercourse and orgasms. Other times, you have intercourse frequently. Less interest is based on many things. If you are securely bonded, then you enjoy sex together, but it isn't necessary. It is simple. Sometimes you have sex, other times you don't. There are no rules, because rules would limit the free expression of yourselves and your bonded relationship.

A ceremony is held by women when menstruation stops. You express the feelings that come up as your flow changes and grieve for the loss of fertility. Looking at yourself intently, you notice how different you appear after only a very few years. Getting acquainted with the new you and accepting yourself is assisted by the loving looks and touches you receive from your mate. Your partner's touch feels just as loving and accepting, reminding you that you are the same person. The only difference is that you are entering a new place in the life cycle, one that brings freedom from responsibilities of younger years and wisdom accumulated from living fully. Sexuality affirms your life in a changed body and your continuing bond with your mate.

Men also change during the middle years. Your body is becoming different too. You are softer and rounder as lines and wrinkles form. As your mate's body changes shape, you touch her frequently to allow your hand to know that she is the same person and to remind yourself that the bond is still there, ever maturing. As you run your hand over drier skin, notice the change in her vagina, and feel her rounded belly, you rejoice in the years you have had together and the knowledge of the years to come. You cry with her to release the attachment to both your bodies as they had been. In the middle years, your interest changes from the firm, muscled bodies of youth to the ones in which you now reside. The softness of her skin feels electric to your hands, and the years of fitting the two of you together helps you adjust to the change. Sex serves as a reminder of your love.

As the decades move you into old age, your sexual patterns may change many times, reflecting your emotional and physical states. Even when you aren't being sexual, your sexual energy flows as strongly as ever, keeping you alive and bonded. Your children and grandchildren know you are a sexual person, even if you are wrinkled and move slowly. It is expected that people will be sexual whenever they feel like it, and age does not limit the full expression of sexuality. We are sexual beings.

§ We Are Not Raised with Sexual Health §

This picture of the perfect environment, within which we can evolve in natural ways, does not yet exist. Instead, sexual feelings are distorted from the very beginning. By the time a person goes through a long childhood of sexual silence, sexual shaming, and being confused while trying to express this vital component of being human, he or she will be unable to easily integrate sexuality into the rest of life. The need to bond and be sexual will be more intense than in a healthy culture, because it must become very intense to overcome the shame surrounding it. Each person must figure it out for him- or herself, with no clear models in the home, school, or community.

The high rate of extramarital affairs is an indication that something is interfering with the bonding use of sex. Many of our cultural values support behavior that prevents complete bonding (e.g., the requirement that men respond with interest to "sexy" women, and seeing flirting—in men or women—as innocent). To make things more difficult, few of us are comfortable with intimacy after a childhood of sexual confusion and shaming, particularly when intimacy includes the use of sexual energy.

There are a number of ways people avoid the intense intimacy that accompanies full sexual bonding, including the following:

1. Partial bonding to two or more people dilutes the bond to any one person. One way to do this is to marry one person and have an affair. Another is to date two or more people.
2. Sexless affairs can serve to dilute the primary bond without forming a strong bond to the other(s) involved. Looking into each other's eyes and holding one another while having sexual or "romantic" feelings are also powerful ways of transmitting sexual energy. With no overt sex taking place, the person can do everything in the open. Few people would believe a partner's jealousy would be appropriate, because "nothing happened." These affairs can be just as intense as those with sex, because we can bond with sexual energy just as well without sex.
3. Sex addicts have sex with people (or pictures) other than their mates to bring on their sexual drug. They are not intending to bond at all. When therapy allows for exploration of the cross-wired patterns acted out by the particular behaviors chosen for the addiction, addicts find they are searching for something akin to the loving bond

with their parents that didn't go well. Early childhood experiences may prevent them from forming a naturally loving bond in adult life. And so, the sexual energy used to create such a bond can only be converted into an obscure imitation of intimate sex.

4. Leaving relationships before they have time to become fully bonded allows one to have intense sexual interest without becoming enmeshed in the bonding. Such people may be infatuation addicts, enjoying the illusion of bonding without paying the perceived price that accompanies joining in a committed way.

5. Fantasy, pornography, and other ways of depersonalizing one's partner can reduce the impact of the sexual bond by changing the experience of sex with a partner to sex with people who live in fantasies or pictures. Immediately after having sex, such people need to go to sleep or otherwise interrupt the process, so they don't accidentally feel the closeness that sex makes possible. Seeing sex as a "need" to be met helps this avoidance of intimacy and bonding. People who use these maneuvers may very much want to have a loving relationship but find the price too high.

6. Not relating sexually at all is a solution a surprising number of people elect. These people may have friends and be engaged in activities, but they are not comfortable meeting people who have the potential for a bonding relationship. Some have pushed their sexuality so far underground that it is no longer available for bonding. Others can feel sexual but only when it isn't directed toward a person.

7. Bonding with a married person serves to prevent the bond from becoming a total, committed one. The bond seems to be always just beginning. This solution can prevent fear of long-term bonding, and it can be used as a form of sex addiction by retaining the intensity of the initial period of bonding for a long time.

§ WE CAN RECLAIM SEXUAL HEALTH §

Healthy sexuality is possible, even though none of us grew up in a sexually healthy culture. We may not have been allowed to develop ourselves well in this area, but we can go back and unlearn the damaging messages and gradually improve the use of our sexuality. The next chapter addresses the nature of healthy sexuality and the process of retrieving it.

4

HEALTHY SEXUALITY

§

Looking at how sexuality might be healthy (as presented in
the previous chapter), it becomes obvious what is wrong with
the advice of sexual experts and the media, and how our
sexuality is continually abused by exposure to unhealthy stimuli
and advice. As people come to understand this in their own way,
they can begin to direct their own sexual healing.

Generations of mistruths about sex lead us to believe that
many sexual symptoms are a natural part of sexuality. This book
addresses many of these symptoms. One example, examined in
this chapter, is the vast distortion of the role of lust. Intense
sexual response to sexual stimuli or intense desire for sexual
gratification are not normal phenomena, except perhaps in early
adolescence. They are sexual symptoms.

§ LUSTLESS INTIMACY §

The experience of lust arises because from a very early age we
repress sexual feelings. When a natural part of our aliveness is
inhibited, it will find a way to be expressed—resulting in sexual
reactivity to stimuli around us—the repress–react dichotomy I
discussed in the Introduction. Women and men who have had
their sexuality abused when growing up and who were not
allowed to tell the story and have the feelings have a particularly
intense focus on sexual things.

Those of us who, in the past, lived in a state of perpetual
lust and arousal, and who have been able to relinquish it, have

found out what it is like to live lust free and yet be passionately sexual. Kenneth, a thirty-two-year-old man who has been in therapy for three years for an intense addiction to sex, told stories to the men in his therapy group about his discovery of the difference between lust and intimacy.

§ Intimacy versus Lust §

About a year and a half after beginning recovery for the sex addiction that dominated his life, Kenneth was delighted to find out what loving, intimate sex was like. Yet at the same time, he yearned for the life he had missed out on in his teen years—the life of chasing women, seducing them, and having impersonal, casual sex. And so he set out to do just that. He was aware that such activities didn't seem to be part of his recovery and would not be approved of by the twelve-step groups for sex addiction, but he had an intuitive feeling that he needed to revisit this time of life in order to learn further lessons. After watching Kenneth do just that in a number of ways, I supported this form of education.

He spent the summer with an old friend from his addiction days—a man who knew how to "find women." Early in the summer, Kenneth and Rob spent every weekend on Rob's boat. On one of these weekends, as the two were heading to the boat, Rob spied two women with "#10 bodies" in bikinis. He suggested they join the men on the boat. They did. Rob claimed his first choice, leaving the second for Kenneth.

Kenneth described this with a shy smile. This woman, whose presence said to the world that he was successful and lucky, was actually going to the boat with him. He felt like a teenager who at last had what it takes to make life complete. As they walked to the boat, he found himself aroused, wondering how long it would be before she would agree to have sex with him. When she wasn't looking at him, he looked at her breasts and the rest of her body.

Once on the boat, Rob and the other woman went to the front to maneuver out onto the lake, while Kenneth and Karen sat in the back. Kenneth strutted himself in front of her, searching for the attention he felt he had missed. As they began the seductive dance, Kenneth suggested they jump in the water. Karen refused, saying she couldn't swim for a few days. When he asked why, she hesitated, and then told him that she had just had an abortion.

As Kenneth heard her words, she transformed from a sex object into a whole person with emotions. The feeling of being puffed up by her presence subsided, and his perception of her changed from one moment to the next. He sat down next to her, asking to hear about it. He really wanted to know.

During their many hours together, Karen and Kenneth talked in depth about the subjects of relationships and male–female acculturation. Kenneth spoke every thought he had about what he was supposed to do and not do, and Karen followed his lead. At one point she sat on his lap, after explaining about the abortion and the rejection she received from her ex-boyfriend, and he comforted her. Rob came to the back of the boat, and, seeing his friend with a bikini clad woman on his lap, assumed that Kenneth was "getting somewhere." When Kenneth saw Rob's expression, he knew he would not be able to explain the real story.

Late in the day, Kenneth and Karen lay in a bunk, holding each other and discussing the usual course of this kind of physical contact. Kenneth knew he didn't want to have sex with her, because he was now fully present. He knew that sexual energy would bond them, and he couldn't know in such a short time if she was a woman with whom he wanted to bond. He guessed that she wasn't. She said that under typical circumstances, she would say "yes" to sex with a man she had spent the day with, and she was ready to have sex with Kenneth. She was surprised to be with a man under these circumstances and find that he didn't want to have sex with her. Her own sexual patterns came up; her "inner voices" said that he didn't find her attractive, which she also knew wasn't true once she spoke them. She was quite aware that she was having an unusual experience.

At the end of the day, Rob and Kenneth compared stories. Rob and his date spent the day in seductive play, using sexual energy and flirting to intensify their experience. As the day came to an end, the woman played with his penis and brought him to orgasm. But Rob didn't feel good about it. The day—a repeat of countless times like it—hadn't been much fun for him.

Two days later, when the men were again on the beach, they saw the same women. Kenneth immediately called out to Karen, and the two hugged like old friends. Rob avoided them entirely. His shame from creating a lustful, flirtatious new relation was very different from Kenneth's reaction to an honest, caring exchange. Neither man wanted to have more than the day together, but one created a day he wanted to forget, while the other created a nice memory.

Kenneth also told of trips to singles clubs—threatening to him because he had always felt out of place and unattractive, setting himself up for sure rejection. So off he went, again with Rob. After the first night of merely looking over the scene before leaving, he returned after a day in the sun that burned and blistered his lips. He believed he was sexually unattractive. In spite of this, he decided to observe the scene, believing he couldn't join in. As he sat by himself, not initiating interaction, he found that women flirted with him from across the room, inviting him with sexual body language to join them. He didn't. He was soon ready to leave. Heading toward the door, he overheard a conversation between two women about John Bradshaw's books. He stopped, listened for another minute, and then asked if he could sit with them. As he joined in the conversation, he again moved into the present and out of his childhood perception of valuable interaction. He stayed several hours, developing conversation with a number of people who joined the two women, and he had a wonderful time. One of the women called him a few days later and told him she found him really interesting. They began dating even before his mouth healed.

§ LUSTING AFTER "SEXY WOMEN" §

I have met few people who question the propensity of men to have sexual thoughts about women who are defined as "sexy." It is accepted as part of human nature. If we take a look at some of the implications of this belief, it becomes obvious that in a fully functioning society, lusting doesn't fit. I will examine four of these implications here. The first is the automatic objectification of women.

Lust Objectifies People

Men and women can have friendships that add richness to life—relationships that do not include sexual energy. Yet if the woman fits the man's definition of sexually attractive, he is conditioned to think of her sexually. She is immediately a sex object, even if they have no sexual interaction. He cannot see the whole person. On the contrary, if a man lives in a culture that respects the natural order of things, and he is already mated, he would be able to meet a woman who is considered a lust object by our current media and have no sexual thoughts. That this is possible is borne out by the experiences of people who are healing from sexual wounds—men who lusted profusely in the past and now find they can look with curiosity at women who wish to draw their sexual attention. Gary Brooks, in *The Centerfold Syndrome*,[1] tells about the men in his therapy groups who are discovering how lusting after women who look like the centerfold stereotype interferes with intimacy with women—and with other men.

Bruce came to me for help with his desire to have an affair, because he didn't want to violate his marriage. Bruce, an accountant with his own successful firm by his mid-thirties, routinely interacted sexually with women who were within the stereotyped qualifications of our culture, unaware that flirting with women was also a violation. As he talked about his activities to me and to the men's group, he realized they were not the normal behaviors that are part of being a man.

When a woman walked into his office, presenting herself as a sexually attractive person, his first thought was of sex, and he immediately began flirting with her. He often found it difficult to conduct business and usually combined business with lunch, over which he could pursue the sexualized relating. He always stopped short of sex.

As Bruce came to view this behavior as addictive and heard from other members of the men's group, he began to study what was happening. He learned that he wanted the intense attention that sexual energy brought because, along with working eighty hours a week, it prevented painful feelings about other parts of his life and past. He felt alive. He also began to see that the women he interacted with were using their sexuality to control him and feel as powerful as he was. By having his attention and the exclusivity implied by sexuality, a woman can feel power she has not otherwise been able to claim. Both of them were playing a game.

As Bruce was able to see this game as a symptom of a larger problem and a violation of his marriage, he decided he no longer wanted to play. He set out to learn about what was really going on and soon discovered that women who attracted his attention smiled at him sideways and stood closer to him than another man would. He saw that they dressed and made themselves up to obtain his response. As he became conscious of this, he was able to see that women who were interesting, and whose company he enjoyed in a nonsexual way, did not evoke sexual thoughts.

With the support of his group, Bruce began to talk with the women to whom he had responded. The first was a salesperson who visited him regularly to sell him products for his business. He arranged to see her in a meeting room, so he could end the conversation more easily than if it occurred in his office. As she walked in, smiled, and sat down, he observed. For the first time, he saw each movement and the effect it was designed to have. He didn't have his usual instant reaction. She apparently perceived his change and increased the stimulus. She touched his hand and made a soft noise appropriate to lovers' bedrooms. As Bruce found himself beginning to respond, he took his next step. He spoke the unspeakable. He told Gina that he found her attractive, but he was married and wanted to focus his sexual attention on his wife. He said he didn't want her to flirt with him anymore, and if she did, he would no longer work with her, even though he valued the services provided to his company.

To Bruce's amazement, Gina responded well. She sat back, smiled, looked relieved, and buttoned one more button on her blouse. She explained that she thought she had to flirt with him to get his business, and her own company was in the early stages of development. She was deliberately meeting the "needs" of her customers to increase sales. Once Bruce was open about what was happening and indicated that he respected her as a business person, she could be open with him too.

They went to lunch that day, and Bruce learned more. He found that she no longer appealed to him sexually. Once they had spoken openly, the spell was broken, and it was no longer possible to generate illusionary excitement. Gina was still attractive, but she had become a real, whole person. Bruce, who had intensely wanted to believe that his response to women was based on real caring, got to watch his feelings change from one moment to the next.

Bruce's next encounter in the series of confrontations didn't go nearly as well. Buoyed by the first experience, he plunged easily into the second. Laura was on the elevator when Bruce went to the coffee shop midmorning for a snack. They had often met this way, flirting over croissants. He told her he wanted to talk to her, and as they approached the shop, he was aware that she was doing what they had both done with such relish only the week before. She was flirting. Bruce found himself pulling back from her, physically as well as emotionally, wanting her to stop. She didn't respond to his body language, and so he spoke to her in the hall, not waiting until they were seated with food. His discomfort was rising, and he wanted to end it as soon as possible. He later realized that he felt like a sex object. Taking her to a corner of the hallway, he blurted out, "Laura, I'm married and I love my wife. I think you're very attractive, but I just can't flirt anymore. Can you understand? I hope we can still be friends."

Laura frowned at him, as if he were very strange. She told him with annoyance that she knew he was married, and she hadn't wanted to have sex with him.

Bruce's guilt rose as he watched her, and he prepared questions to ask me later about how to do this without hurting the other person's feelings. It was clear to him that she wasn't comfortable hearing the truth and wanted to deny it. He wanted a way to discuss flirtatious interactions that would assure that both he and the woman could continue to like each other. The group told him that his first experience was probably an unusual one, and that most people will be uncomfortable hearing the truth. They also pointed out that for his own recovery, he had to tell the truth, even if the other person had negative feelings about what he said. It had become clear to most group members that talking about what is really going on is the surest antidote to living in illusions. Once the truth is spoken, it becomes almost impossible to return to old, stylized interactions.

As Bruce continued to speak to women he had sexualized, he received a variety of responses. Some could not hear what he said, and these women he stopped interacting with altogether. If they did business with his company, he arranged for other employees to deal with them. If they were women he ran into in the course of his day, he nodded to them but refused further interaction. Some were hurt, and, although they denied the sexual nature of the relating, they changed how they responded to Bruce. He was able to continue relationships with these women.

As Bruce proceeded to examine how he had sexualized many of his interactions with women, and changed his behavior, he was amazed at how he had blindly accepted his feelings as natural to men. Each week, as he reported his experiences, he saw the smiling faces of men who had already discovered that seeing women as sex objects is not naturally male.

Lusting within Marriage Is Not Healthy

It is natural for humans to bond with sexual energy into a couple who will become the center of a new family. Sexual bonding is, by nature, exclusive of other people. This is why both sexes feel jealous when their partner shows sexual interest in someone else. *If this bond is made with clarity, and sexual energy is fully engaged in its creation, then neither partner will have sexual interest in anyone else.* But few of us are comfortable focusing our sexual interest so intensely toward one person for very long, and so we use countless culturally supported alternatives to dilute the bond.

Lusting after other people, if only from a distance, is one way to reduce some of the intensity of monogamous bonding. (It can also express anger toward the other sex and anger toward one's partner, as well as meet an acculturated requirement for a male to be a man.)

Kenneth, three years into his recovery, entered a relationship in which he learned about the pleasure of monogamous bonding. Prior to the beginning of his recovery from sexual addiction, he had learned the concept of monogamy through the church in which he was raised. His constant desire for sex with prostitutes and use of pornography for masturbation prevented him from feeling a commitment to containing sexual energy in his marriage. After his divorce and two short relationships, he fell in love with Jane. Within six months, they both found themselves committed to each other. By moving in together, they took another step in the process of marrying. (Their first was having sex. Later steps are combining possessions, having a ceremony, combining financial resources, and possibly having children.)

Kenneth continued to act out occasionally. His compulsions were increasingly unsatisfying as his experience of intimacy grew. One morning in the men's group, Kenneth was talking about his relationship with Jane. He referred to it as his marriage without realizing he had done so. The group immediately pointed it out to him. As tears came to his eyes, his face softened and emanated surprise. "I *feel* married," he said. We were all touched. He was obviously in love with Jane and deeply affected by his monogamous bond with her. Yet the next week he came to group depressed, telling us how he had acted out. His life seemed impossibly painful and out of control. As he spoke, it became clear that he was reacting to the intimacy he had felt the week before. As he saw the depth of the bond he had with Jane, it brought up fears of his parents' possessive, controlling bonds. He wanted to avoid these bonds at all costs, yet here he was letting this woman come close to him. He countered this fear by engaging in a lustful activity, whether this was with a woman he knew, with a prostitute, or with pictures of women in magazines. Kenneth knew his lusting was based on fear of becoming entrapped. The monogamous bond was the real relationship.

Daughters Are Violated

Men who are trained to lust after a particular body form find themselves responding to bodies or body parts without any conscious decision. When daughters' bodies develop into young women, fathers will see them through the filter that has been securely placed over their eyes. The result is that the father will have sexual feelings toward his daughter, or he will have to prevent himself from seeing her in ways that reveal her body or otherwise arouse sexual thoughts.

I have heard countless stories of the effect on women when their fathers rejected them as they were growing up. Men criticize their daughters' bodies and clothing as a way to prevent sexual reaction. Some shame them and call them sluts and other sexually derogatory words as they blame the child for the father's arousal. Others become cold and have no further physical contact. Messages about dress are delivered indirectly, so the girl doesn't understand that her father is trying to prevent himself from violating her. Instead, she feels rejected just as she is becoming a woman and associates the rejection with her sexuality. Still other fathers have strong sexual fantasies about their children, most of which they don't act on. Fathers with no sexual boundaries will find themselves engaging in sexual activity with their child. (Fathers who are sexually attracted to their children when they are younger than puberty age are responding to more than the acculturated conditioning described here. Their cross-wiring is not just cultural conditioning. This is also true for men who have sex with older children.)

If men grew up in a culture where they were not required to lust and were allowed to sexually unfold with peers and then with a mate, they would be able to interact with their teenage daughters with no sexual thoughts. Such a world seems more consistent with the natural order of things than one in which each father must figure out, consciously or unconsciously, and alone, how to deal with feelings he didn't bargain for and about which he feels deep guilt and shame.

Steven started therapy soon after his daughter had her twelfth birthday. He was distraught because he discovered sexual feelings emerging when he hugged her or thought of her in the shower. He had become depressed and was having difficulty functioning normally at his job. Steven knew he was in no danger of touching Kim sexually, because his cross-wired sexuality involved looking from a distance while yearning to be close to a lover. He wanted to create a romantic relationship with her. Steven had already begun a process of sexual healing prior to his daughter's becoming a young woman, and so he was aware of what was happening. After three months of depression, he began individual therapy and joined the men's group.

Some of the men in the group had difficulty hearing about a man who felt lust and romance for his young daughter. The subject of child sexual abuse is a loaded one in our culture. Even though it is common, adults who are sexual with children are seen as the most evil of people. In addition, those who have been sexually abused as children themselves, particularly those who have not recovered memories, often find themselves with intense reactions when they hear of others who are doing such things to children. People who have desires to be sexual with children, and who fight them, may also be among those with especially intense condemnation of adults who have sex with children. (For a thorough depiction of this subject, I have compassionately told the stories of many people who are recovering from sexual desire for children in *From Generation to Generation: Understanding Sexual Attraction to Children.*)

Steven pursued his recovery by searching for memories of sex during his childhood. He found out that sexual abuse of children occurred several generations back with a relative who was repeatedly thrown out of boarding schools in which he taught. As the doors opened to new information, Steven was also able to retrieve memories of early sexual interaction with both of his parents.

When we began working together, Steven believed that as long as he didn't act on his feelings, his family wouldn't know what was going on in his head and his daughter would not be harmed. As we explored the ways he acted when having sexual feelings, it became clear to him that, indeed, his entire family was affected. His romantic attraction to Kim showed up in family pictures he brought to my office. The facial expressions and body posturing in pictures with her were similar to those of lovers. These same expressions were not present in pictures of Steven with his wife. Once I named what I saw, then Steven could see too. When he saw the romantic looks, he knew that his wife perceived them as well, although perhaps not on a conscious level. His knowledge of family systems filled in the gaps, and he became aware that his sexual attraction for his daughter was creating family dynamics that were not healthy for anyone in the family.

Steven observed another example of the visibility of his obsession. As he walked toward the bathroom door to see if he could view Kim through the crack, he heard his younger daughter at the bottom of the stairs. Guiltily, he turned and rushed down the stairs. She had just seen him go up and asked him why he hurried up and then back down. He offered a nonsensical answer, saying that he liked to get his exercise, then laughed as if it were a joke. At the time, his distorted thinking allowed him to believe that this way of dealing with the situation could really prevent her from knowing what was going on. Although she didn't know the details, he could see that she was picking up that something was wrong with her father's humorless joke. She knew on some level that he was lying to her.

As Steven became aware that he was damaging his family with his sexual attraction for his daughter, he reached the place where he knew he had to tell them about it. We found a therapist with experience helping families with such issues, and Steven and his wife have been meeting with her regularly. The result is a major change in the family dynamics. Steven is feeling increasingly sexually bonded to his wife and able to see clearly when he has feelings toward his daughter that are not healthy.

The Man Who Lusts Is Violated

A man who lusts for a female body or body part leaves himself. Lust is not a feeling that enhances being alive. It is a narrowing-down, distracting feeling that overrides a more natural experience. Instead of experiencing sexual energy only in an appropriate time, alone or with an appropriate person, men have been set up to lust. From an early age, they were shamed for evidence of sexuality—they were frowned upon when erections appeared and shamed for masturbating. They were told they would suffer shameful effects if they continued, such as insanity or hairy palms. But at the same time, they have been required to be sexual. They must be able to have erections at will and maintain them. In other words, they must have complete control over their penises. Almost all men choose to be sexual in secret, so sex takes on a hidden, forbidden quality. Men will react to the combination of repressed sexual energy and the requirement to be sexual to be a man by lusting after "sexy" women. They cannot help doing so unless they have somehow avoided the influence of our culture or if, as adults, they have been able to undo the effects.

Kenneth describes the difference between lusting for a woman and the gentle, inside-out unfolding of sexual energy with his partner. When he lusts, whether for a partner, a prostitute, or a picture in a magazine, he feels small. His body is tight and hard, and feels as if it were preparing for battle. If he were to make noises, the sound would feel as if it were pushing him forward in pursuit. In contrast, when he is with Jane and the two of them find sexual energy emerging from their loving, his experience is expansive. He opens and softens, and when the blood fills his genitals, skin, and the floor of his pelvis, he feels his pelvis releasing into an open state. During intercourse, he feels as if he is releasing his *self* into all of her, not just putting his penis into a vagina. He feels huge, as if he were filling the room with his being, and his passion is immense—very different from the hard, driving power of lustful sex.

When I hear Kenneth's and other's descriptions and think of my own experiences over ten years of sexual recovery, the very idea that lusting for another—including our partner—is natural to healthy sexuality becomes absurd.

§ Goals and Healthy Sex Are Incompatible §

We live in a goal-directed, competitive society in which sex is influenced by our tendency to put everything into a hierarchy. The evaluation of worth through accomplishments and productivity, through making money and getting degrees, has influenced our way of perceiving our humanness. Sex has been cast into the arena of performance, of success and failure, of quantifying, of starting and finishing. As a result, it has made sense that sex has a definable beginning and ending, and that some of our personal evaluation is based on accomplishing goals.

This approach, however, is opposed to what will allow the real nature of sex to emerge in our lives. By abandoning all consciously created goals in sexual activity, we can open ourselves to the much larger experience of what sex can be. Some of the goals to abandon are frequency, orgasms, maintaining erections for their own sake, maintaining arousal because "once you start you can't stop" until orgasm, maintaining your body as a desirable sex object, and doing sex "right."

What follows are some qualities of sexual energy that emerge from the experience of sex as a non-goal-directed activity.

§ WE DON'T HAVE A "SEX DRIVE" §

One of the greatest myths introduced into our culture is the idea that we have a physiological need for sex, commonly called a "sex drive." Instead, we have sexual potential that is always available and contributes to our feeling of aliveness. We are also drawn intensely to use sexual energy to bond with a mate as we create new families. The experience of "drive" comes from the repression of sex, resulting in an intense push for expression. Belief in a sex drive is also supported by a competitive, goal-driven culture that encourages sexual addiction. If we were allowed to develop freely during childhood, we would have a more comfortable relationship with our sexuality. We would be neither driven by it nor abandoned by it. (See Chapter 15 for more on this.)

§ WE CAN CHOOSE WHEN TO FEEL SEXUAL §

I remember the first time I heard the idea that we can choose when to feel sexual. At the time, it seemed like an intriguing idea that made sense only on some vague, intuitive level. I was still susceptible to the sexual stimuli I was bombarded with and to intense sexual desire for a new lover. It didn't seem as if I had any choice at all about when I would feel sexual. I was preprogrammed to respond or not respond at any given time.

As I uncover my past and find out how my sexuality has been damaged, and have the feelings that have long been repressed, my sexual reactivity diminishes and choices regarding when I will have sexual feelings increase.

Just knowing that we can choose isn't enough. Our sexual programming is deeply ingrained and automatic until we confront the source of the conditioning. But knowing that we can choose allows us to look at sexuality differently. Instead of believing that we are stuck with it the way it is now, we can look at the differences between how we are and how we can be. This leads to finding the sources of cross-wiring and brings about change.

§ SEX DOESN'T ALWAYS END WITH ORGASM §

Our goal-directed society holds the pervasive belief that sex is complete when orgasm has occurred. Sex without orgasm is given a special name in East Indian culture, as if it were a rare thing that only exists within a particular spiritual practice. As usual, in our Western culture, we must have new goals in order to let go of old ones—this time the goal is not having orgasm. It is possible, instead, to allow our intuitive selves to decide if we will have orgasms.

Rex and I "had sex" the other morning before he left for work. I was standing at the sink combing my hair when he came up to me. We looked at each other with love and hugged warmly. Sexual energy emerged for both of us while we continued kissing and looking at each other. Then smiling at me, he said, "We just had sex," and left for work.

In years past, I would have called this interaction "fooling around." It would have felt incomplete, and I might have looked forward to the evening when we could "finish what we started." But now I see sexuality as a bonding energy that reinforces our exclusive, committed relationship. I experienced this five minutes as a full sexual interaction. By staying in the present and not thinking of our exchange as only the *beginning of something else*, I get to have a continuous feeling of completion as I move from one activity to another during my day.

When I recommend to the members of my Reclaiming Healthy Sexual Energy classes that they give up goal-directed sex and replace it with the commitment to address every feeling and thought that comes up, I receive puzzled looks and downright disbelief from most of the members, even those who easily agree with the rest of the principles. Our society is so goal directed, and sex has been no exception, that it is difficult for people to think of sex as something that can be interrupted for just any old reason. This interruption and expression of the "voices" and the feelings that come along with them are necessary to relinquish the old kind of sex and discover the new.

§ OUR BODIES TELL US WHAT TO DO §

Once we let go of programming our sexual interaction, we become able to respect that our bodies and intuition can direct the sexual interaction to meet the needs of the moment. If the need for bonding and intimacy is great, then perhaps we need an hour or two of sex, in contrast to a shorter time, for a delightful restatement of our commitment to coupling. Or perhaps we need sex to prepare for the creation of a new life, when orgasm truly is the purpose. But these decisions are not ones for our intellect to make—our cerebral cortex is only for limited functions. Instead, our instinctive, animal nature "understands" the purpose of sex and, if given the freedom to do so, will make perfect decisions. (In the meantime, we do need to use intellect to decide when to conceive, and when to use birth control. Most of us will never be sufficiently free from emotional damage to allow our spirits to make that decision.)

When our bodies have the freedom to determine what will happen sexually, then arousal goes up and down based on unobservable phenomena. When it goes up, it means that we are to follow sexual activities as they unfold. When it goes back down, with or without orgasm, then sex is complete for that time. Rex and I have observed our sexual energy communicating back and forth between our pelvises, deciding together when it is time for arousal to build to orgasm, and when it is time to prolong intercourse in the service of unfolding with each other.

As we relinquish the need to follow rules and the need to perform properly, we are uncovering this instinctive communication cleverly directed by our bodies.

§ Jealousy—A Useful Feeling §

Jealousy has been maligned. It is an absolutely necessary source of information for couples. When it has been overlaid by cross-wiring so that it no longer expresses accurate feelings, then it becomes a sickness instead of an asset. The next chapter addresses the function of jealousy in monogamous bonding and the ways culture can distort it.

5

THE PURPOSE OF JEALOUSY

§

Healthy jealousy is a searing pain, an outwardly directed, angry emotion whose function is to alert you to a threat to your monogamous bond. Your mate's behavior triggers this feeling, alerting you to the possibility that your mate may be sending sexual energy toward someone else and diluting the bond with you. This could entail having an affair with full use of sexual activity, or it might be indicated by flirting. Wearing sexy clothing to gain attention, laughing seductively, crossing physical boundaries by touching a person when the relationship doesn't call for it, commenting on a person's sexiness, holding eye contact longer than appropriate to the exchange, and making sexual noises are examples of how we communicate sexually. In addition are relationships based on that something extra that is not inherently part of a nonsexual relationship. Many of these behaviors that are acceptable to our culture are sexual communications designed to enhance relating. Flirting is considered "innocent," and "charisma" is revered when it is usually based on sexual energy. Sometimes a group of friends will exchange flirtatiousness as part of their standard relating, not knowing it is sexual until it is pointed out to them. It may take the form of a stylized charm.

In a healthy culture, your mate would see your jealous reaction when he or she flirts with someone else and assess what was going on. Your mate might find that some unconscious pattern, or fear of intimacy, was directing the "unbonding" acts, and your expression of jealousy would bring him or her back to focusing sexual energy on the bond with you. Or your mate might find that the bond with you isn't an appropriate one.

Sending sexual energy out to others serves as an indicator. In this case, you and your mate would work on breaking your bond so that both of you are free to find new mates. Then your jealousy would turn into anger over the loss and form a vital part of grieving.

In order for jealousy to do its job, we have to have access to another naturally human faculty—honesty. People in healthy human relationships tell each other about all feelings and activities that reveal who they are. Most of us are afraid of total honesty with our mates, because they may misuse information to shame us, control us, and judge what we do. The price for dishonesty is that it prevents us from creating truly intimate, clean, bonded relationships. Instead, we create imitations and then expect them to provide the real thing. They cannot.

If you decide to engage in an honest relationship, then jealousy is an important source of information. This might be particularly true when honesty has not been natural, and you are using it to learn how to form a committed relationship.

Rex and I committed to honesty before we were aware that we wanted sexual bonding. We had both yearned to find others who would be willing to speak the truth, regardless of resulting pain. We wanted others who would persist through truth telling so we could find out what was actually true of the other person, and what were old patterns from our earlier experiences. So when jealousy started to appear several weeks after we began sexual bonding, we had a context in which to address it.

I raged that he had shared his sexual energy with other people! Rex had given me permission to read all his journals and letters—as he could read mine—and a few months after we were married, I went through them systematically over a period of weeks. I knew I had nothing to be jealous about, because he was clearly bonded to me and committed to our marriage. Yet here were the feelings.

I soon realized that these feelings had two functions. One was declaring that I want all his sexual energy in our relationship. He loved hearing this jealousy, even though I spoke angrily. I was expressing how much I wanted him, matching his feelings for me. The second function was to clean out the old "jealousy patterns" from my past. I began remembering all those times when my partners had hidden feelings from me, or when I was supposed to believe that they were not expressing sexual energy, when, in fact, they were. I had spent years feeling crazy for having jealous feelings, even though I knew my partner wasn't going to have sex with someone else.

§ FLIRTING BLINDNESS §

Years before, I sat on an airplane beside a man with whom I was in a lengthy relationship. He flew often on company business. A flight attendant approached him with warmth beyond that required for her job, asking why he wasn't sitting in first class. He didn't explain that he was sitting with me, who only flew coach. In fact, he didn't even indicate he was with me, although I listened attentively to their conversation. After some banter, she told him, in a conspiratorial tone, that she was going to bring him a drink from first class at no charge—he was obviously a prime customer who flew first class on business.

He had his drink while I sat there on the other side of a very thick wall, wondering about the nature of his relationship with her. I can only guess, because I couldn't ask back then.

At that time, I didn't understand jealousy and thought I was responding not to the present, but to my ancient patterns of possessiveness. I could do no more than observe and feel terrible, wanting to yell at him to tell her that he was with me, his life mate, and he didn't want this kind of attention. But I would have felt absurd and inappropriate to have done any more than ask him in a calm, unemotional voice how he knew her. And accept his answer that she was the attendant on many of his flights out, and they had gotten to know each other. My ancient patterns were not about jealousy, they were about not being able to see my rights and responsibilities in a love relationship.

Our weekend in another city was marred by my rage, which I thought I could not express. I did manage to mention what I'd seen, but I directed my anger toward the flight attendant. I went on and on about how she was seducing him into flying first class. I didn't let myself see that he supported what she did, and did not stop the threat to our bond. I believed that most of the people on that plane would have felt that rage was not appropriate. Perhaps annoyance toward her might have been allowed. It was years before I could know that he had a strong desire to use sexual energy flirtatiously with many women, creating relationships intensified with sexuality, and that if he had been aware of the nature of monogamous bonding, he would have been delighted with my anger. Instead, much of his self-worth was tied up with the sexualized attention of attractive women.

My feelings were from two sources. First, a man who was having sex with me and stated that he was in a monogamous relationship was being sexual with someone else. Second, a lie was being lived out. He said one thing when, in fact, another was happening. He didn't know he was lying. He had the support of our culture in believing that as long as he didn't touch another woman in a sexual way, he was monogamous. This man also frequented clubs where women took off clothing to sexually stimulate men, had conversations with women who worked there, and expected me to listen to these experiences without jealousy or anger. He was so believable that I complied. He said he wasn't sexually aroused, and perhaps he wasn't. All this took place before I learned that I had a tendency to mate with sex addicts of various sorts, without knowing consciously that they were.

§ Recognizing Sexual Energy §

From this confusing history, when Rex and I got together, I thought I must not be trusting him when I began to look suspiciously at other women. But soon I could differentiate between old, patterned feelings of jealousy—unexpressed from past relationships and from my childhood—and reactions to Rex's behaviors that actually violated our monogamous bond.

After pointing out to him several times that he was responding to flirtations of women, I could see by his response that he had no idea. Blinded by our culture to think that sexual energy is just "being friendly," he had responded inadvertently. This triggered my intuitive, instinctive, jealous feelings. In the beginning, I attributed my feelings to "jealousy patterns" and began to work on why I was having this intense reaction when Rex was not doing anything that should offend me. As this work progressed, I became increasingly able to perceive sexual energy and could see that these women weren't just being friendly. They were using sexual energy in ways that let another person know he was of particular interest, ways that belong to those who are searching for a mate, or, if mated, used only with one's mate.

Early in our marriage, I went to meet Rex at a shopping mall. He told me where he would be, and as I glanced around the area he named, I didn't see him. But I did see a woman standing a few feet from a man seated on a short wall with his back to me. She was in a pose that looked obviously sexual. Her legs were spread, and she smiled at him with her head tilted sideways and her chin raised. With her eyes sparkling, she looked as if she were about to laugh as her arms floated out from her sides. I stopped and stared because I was taken by how obviously she was sending out flirtatious energy. I was amazed that she was willing to be so obvious about it in public.

In another moment I realized the male object of her attention was Rex! I hadn't expected him to be sitting down, but there he was. As I saw the entire scene—this woman putting out obvious sexual energy toward *my husband*—I felt rage wash over me. I wanted to scream at her to leave my man alone, and I also wanted to push him off the stand onto the floor. However, due to decades of training not to make scenes and to disbelieve my perceptions, I refrained. Instead, I walked within Rex's line of sight. He immediately smiled lovingly at me and introduced me to the woman. She appeared to be just delighted to meet me, shook my hand, and gushed with pleasure. I nodded coldly and said nothing. Her training not to see was as strong as mine, because she didn't react to my rudeness.

Rex noticed my feelings but didn't understand what caused them. He thought perhaps I was angry because I had to drive twenty minutes to bring him a key, so he could get his car open. It wasn't until we were away from the woman and out on the street that we began to process what had just happened. I yelled at him, "Didn't you see how she was looking at you? You let her flirt with you, and I'm your wife. I'm the only one you should do that with!" As I continued, he looked at me with shock, unable to comprehend what I was saying. As I noticed his face, my anger wound down, because it seemed absurd to yell at someone who had no idea what I was talking about. So I asked him, "Didn't you see her facial expression? And the way she was standing? She was flirting with you."

Rex shook his head in disbelief. He truly didn't know she was sending sexual energy, and he spent the next few minutes asking me for details about how I knew. As we walked down the street, I pointed out when people were emitting sexual energy, people who were turning their heads sideways with bright-eyed smiles, and who positioned their bodies in sexually suggestive ways. He gradually caught on. I asked him what he thought of the woman looking at him that way, and he said she looked stupid. Smiling vacantly with her head turned sideways and standing in a position that was very bad for her posture, she had looked like a person who didn't care much for herself. He had been uncomfortable with her and was glad I arrived to rescue him. She was a student at the massage school where he taught and apparently transferred sexual energy onto the authority figure he had become to her.

As we pieced the picture together, we could see what was happening. Rex had felt uncomfortable with her adoring focus on him and responded to his own childhood training to be polite by smiling back. He felt anxious but didn't know why. He thought it was because he sometimes was shy or awkward when an attractive woman spoke to him. We guessed that his uncomfortable smile was interpreted by her as a response to her flirting and encouraged her to do it more. Then when I arrived, she turned her attention on me to assure me that she wasn't trying to take my husband away. (Many men's lovers become good friends with the wife.) We don't know if this woman was seriously interested in engaging in a sexual relationship with Rex, or if she was interacting typically with men she considered to be of value. It doesn't matter. Either way, she was using sexual energy in a way that can be disruptive to bonded relationships and will not help her move toward one of her own.

§ MEN AND WOMEN FLIRT WITH MEN AND WOMEN §

The previous examples are of women flirting with men and the man's partner experiencing jealousy. Men flirt too, of course, and their female partners may be jealous. But men flirt with men, and women flirt with women too, whether the flirters are heterosexual or homosexual. For example, Kenneth, whose stories have been presented in earlier chapters, flirted with men and women. He is heterosexual when choosing sex partners, but he exchanges sexual energy with other men who value sex-laced exchanges. His partners have had to choose between feeling jealous, which didn't make sense to them because they knew he wasn't going to have sex with the man, and joining in the flirtation in order to not feel jealous. In his therapy group, Kenneth told of meeting a charismatic spiritual leader and how he came to see that the charisma was actually charming sexual energy. Kenneth was in his element as the object of this man's attention and returned the sexualized interest. I asked how his fiancée felt about his exchanges, and he described how she was as charmed by this man as Kenneth, and all three felt loving and close. Kenneth, a longtime sex addict, recognized the feelings as sexual and was relieved that his mate didn't object. He was willing to share the man in order to have the exchange run smoothly. When I later spoke with Kenneth's fiancée, Janice, she told me that she wasn't comfortable in the beginning when, at the party they were attending, she observed Kenneth and the man. But as she walked up to them, and they turned together, smiling at her, she felt reassured. This man wasn't a threat to her, because he was willing to flirt equally with each of them.

Many heterosexual women flirt with each other too. They get to be safe from expectations of having sex and still be able to highlight the interaction. Our culture tells us that they are just being friendly, that it isn't sexual. My therapy groups learn what really is sexual and become able to see when someone is flirting with them and denying it.

Gay men and women knowingly flirt with the same sex, of course, as do heterosexuals. The gay-male culture has tried to incorporate lusting and flirting into everyday exchanges, which functions to reduce feelings of jealousy. In addition, monogamy is so rare in long-term relationships that gay men have had to learn how to suspend jealous feelings or choose not to have relationships. This is accomplished by engaging in extramarital sex too, or by joining the mate in lusting for other men.

Both heterosexual and homosexual people use another method of reducing feelings of jealousy—using it for sexual arousal. One of my clients took his wife to orgies and chose men for her to have sex with. He became aroused at the thought of his wife having sex with someone else and watching her do so. But he came to therapy when she wouldn't follow the rules, and his jealousy got out of hand. She went with a man to a private room, leaving her husband in the main room, unable to observe. And she met a man privately for sex, telling her husband what she was doing. His jealousy escalated, and he felt crazy with rage. She was puzzled, because she thought he wanted this. She didn't know he wasn't without jealousy as he had said and that in order to avoid it, she had to allow him to decide what she could and could not do.

The women I have encountered who attempt to minimize jealousy do so differently from the man I just described. They use the jealousy to fuel a sexual interest in the woman their husband is sexual with, sometimes inviting three-way sex or becoming close friends with the woman, excluding the man. None of these methods work for very long, and they easily get out of control.

§ HONESTY PERMITS HEALTHY JEALOUSY §

The innate desire for monogamous bonding is so strong that it requires the intense emotions of anger and jealousy to maintain the bond. This is because in our crazy culture, the constant threats from countless directions make it extremely difficult to have a sexual relationship that isn't filled with misunderstanding and confusion about perfectly normal feelings. The dishonesty built into our cultural perception of relationships makes it difficult to use jealousy for its inherent purpose.

It is possible to access healthy jealousy, however, through a commitment to complete honesty with our mate. This is a complex and difficult task involving several steps. The first step is to define honesty. Honesty does not mean revealing everything and answering any question asked. On the contrary, being honest means saying things such as, "I'm not comfortable with your question," or "I'm not ready to talk about that yet." Setting boundaries is necessary before it is possible to safely reveal oneself.

Second, each person examines patterns created from the past and takes responsibility for accompanying feelings. For example, when I found myself raging in jealousy toward Rex, I was willing to see why I was feeling this way rather than blame him. My partner on the plane did not "cause" my feelings either. My blindness to what was happening and our cultural belief that flirting is innocent blinded me to our nonmonogamous bond. He had never agreed to stop flirting with other women. I assumed it to be based on the intense bond that had formed between us. My anger was trying to alert me to the truth, which I could have then dealt with. Once I could see, then my anger subsided.

Third, allow plenty of time for processing truths as you begin to reveal all those things that have been secret. The two of you may be surprised again and again by each other as you discover how to be honest with words and actions. Intimate time can help you integrate the perpetual changes.

Fourth, see truth finding as a lifelong task. We have been trained by our families and culture to be unaware of what we are feeling and thinking, what others are feeling and thinking, and the complicated dynamics that go on in relationships. A commitment of honesty can allow you to begin unraveling these complexities. This can be an invigorating process that can enhance love and intimacy throughout the life of a relationship.

The Beginning of Bodily Shame

§

Pregnancy, Birth, and Breast Feeding

Sexual and other types of body shame begin during gestation, are intensified during birth, and compounded further when breast feeding—or bottle feeding—begin. Sexual shame doesn't begin at puberty. This chapter looks at the role of mothers and caregivers in creating sexual shame in babies before and after birth.

Given our culture's idealization of mothers and the requirement that they be perfect, you might find the information here difficult to receive. To make it easier, you could focus on your breathing as you read, and notice if you feel shame, anger, or other responses. Your feelings can be a source of information about the cultural stereotypes you have absorbed. They can also be "feeling memories" from your experiences, whether as a mother or an infant.

§ Parental Guilt Prevents Seeing §

Parenting is the most difficult job to do well. Our dysfunctional culture provides few models of how to be with children in ways that permit natural development. At the same time, it requires that parents meet every need of their children in optimal ways. Even though this is impossible, most parents hold themselves personally responsible for their inadequacy. The result is an ever-accumulating blanket of guilt.

Books and classes add to the guilt by "helping" parents become better at parenting. An unhealthy culture severely limits the effectiveness of this help, resulting in further guilt.

Mothers are generally the primary parent and receive the largest portion of this guilt. Fathers are allowed to pay some of theirs off by providing well for their children's physical needs. Both, however, feel guilt and shame when they treat their children in ways they find unacceptable. These feelings accumulate over the years of child rearing, piling layer upon layer, because there are no avenues for removal.

The guilt and shame from harming dependent children are so intense, particularly for parents, that defense mechanisms are employed to avoid these painful feelings. It is possible to remove events entirely from conscious memory, and with them, the debilitating shame.

This shame, even when felt, does not help parents to be better parents. On the contrary, it actually causes worse parenting. Parents respond to their shame with a variety of maneuvers that take them away from their intuitive understanding of the child's needs and lead them to abuse the child in ways they were abused. For example, seeing the child as the one to "blame" reduces the parent's feelings of blame. If a mother were able to examine her behavior, she would automatically change in ways that are advantageous to her child's health. Instead, she lives in a culture that produces useless shame, and she has to spend tremendous time and energy figuring out how to manage these feelings. In the process, the child is less *seen,* because the parent must sacrifice awareness of the child in order to reduce the deadly feeling of shame.

When parents gather together in therapy groups with the purpose of *reducing* shame for ways in which they've abused their children, they find themselves increasingly able to see their children's needs and meet them. In contrast to our culture's beliefs, shame increases abuse, whereas lessening shame actually decreases abuse of all kinds. (See Chapter 2 in *From Generation to Generation: Understanding Sexual Attraction to Children* for information about mothers' shame when even thinking about sexual-boundary difficulties with their children.)

§ SHAME BEGINS BEFORE BIRTH §

Although we view pregnancy as wonderful, the language our society has applied to this condition would lead us to think otherwise. For instance, when a single woman is pregnant, she is said to be "knocked up," a term that sounds like rape. In the past, women were kept "in confinement" during the months they were "showing." In the early years, television didn't allow pregnancy to be shown or mentioned. We said about a pregnant woman that she was "in a family way" or "she's expecting." Actual evidence that a child resided within a woman's body was considered shameful. Maternity clothes are designed to hide the developing bulge as well as make room for it.

When "She's pregnant" is spoken with a shaming tone regarding a woman who isn't married, it conveys to children that there is something shameful about pregnancy itself. The child later learns it is acceptable for a woman if she's married, but the emotional connections between pregnancy and shame have already been made.

In the present time, with its emphasis on reducing population and limiting use of our earth's resources, many frown on a pregnant woman with two or more children. No longer does she receive smiles reflecting the delight of friends and strangers.

The body shape of pregnant women is shamed by terms such as "beached whale." Women who are "showing" are no longer "sexy" by our culture's standards. Many women view the last months of pregnancy as a time when they are undesirable women. Self-esteem based on "sexual attractiveness" will drop during this time and for the months following, until the body resumes its prepregnancy contours. Even if a particular woman does not respond to this definition of female worth, the people around her do.

Given our culture's attitudes toward pregnancy, each woman will have a mix of feelings, even if she deliberately becomes pregnant, with the desire to raise a child. She will feel shame projected onto her, as well as the shame she has internalized prior to her pregnancy.

With this backdrop, the baby she carries inside her will receive her feelings of shame and intuit that it has to do with his or her presence inside her body. Even before the baby enters the outside world, the baby's little body is receiving messages. The fetus knows in its way that the very physical nature of its existence is not entirely well received by the mother, the family, or the community into which she or he will emerge. If the mother hates pregnancy, doesn't want a baby, is afraid of giving birth, and/or has incest memories awakened by pregnancy and delivery, then the feelings she transmits will be even more shaming of her child.

§ BIRTH IS NOT SEXUAL §

The process of giving birth is not a sexual experience. It is painful and very intense. Women describe it as enormously satisfying and fulfilling, but at the same time, it is one of the most stressful, emotional events one can go through. When it is seen as sexual by caregivers, the father, or others present, the baby perceives its passage through the birth canal as sexually arousing. The beginnings of life are met with a sexual response. This event, and the parents' blindness to it, provide the infant with shameful feelings about his or her emergence into the world.

In Western culture, which is prone to confuse things that seem sexual with actual sexuality, some professionals have decided that birth is sexual. They make this assumption because they themselves have sexual feelings during the birth, and so have decided that this is evidence that the event is a sexual one.

The body parts are the same as those used in sex, and the physiology of the mother resembles the physiological process that goes on during sex. The mother's vulva is uncovered and swollen, as in sex. If she is in the hospital, she is lying on her back with her legs up. If she is at home, she is naked from the waist down, perhaps entirely naked. These things usually happen only when a woman is being sexual. She is making noises of strain, and her face shows the intensity of her experience. Human flesh moves out of her vagina. But here the similarities end. She is not aroused. She doesn't have an orgasm.

Those who think this experience is sexual are responding to their cross-wiring. Because all of us have grown up without clear sexual boundaries and are reactive to sexual-seeming stimuli, watching a mother give birth can seem like a sexual experience. Those who have responded sexually felt shame until sex therapists gave permission to see it as a sexual situation unworthy of shame. As in other aspects of sex therapy (see Chapter 16 for more information on the drawbacks of sex therapy), therapists give permission to have any kind of sexual experience between consenting adults in order to reduce shame around sexuality. Although reducing shame is a necessary first step, they don't know that it is possible to go further than accepting what people are now experiencing. This is dramatically revealed in the area of childbirth. Although having sexual feelings when observing or attending a birth are not experiences we should be shamed for, they are a symptom of the repress–react dichotomy. When we can see that, it becomes possible to heal and relinquish the cross-wiring.

Sheila Kitzinger is a prominent teacher and writer in the area of childbirth education, midwifery, and breast feeding. She is responsible for the promulgation of the idea that birth is a sexual experience. Many have followed her lead, because no one has a real understanding of what is going on in this very physical and emotional time for mother, mate, and caregivers, and Kitzinger was willing to express her beliefs.

Childbirth professionals have been able to acknowledge their feelings of arousal during birth, because her writing has taken away some of the shame for having such a reaction. But, as with traditional sex therapists, she doesn't know that sexual response while watching a birth is not part of healthy sexuality. It is a symptom of a sexually repressed culture. As with pornography and other stimuli that elicit sexual responses that do not come from the inside out, the scenes of birthing can trigger sexual feelings. The similarities between birth and sex make differentiation difficult for those who do not have clear sexual boundaries. And lack of clear boundaries is a symptom of living in this culture.

One of Kitzinger's books[1] has a ten-page section called "The Sexuality of Birth." She draws parallels between the physiology of sex and the physiology of birth. She says that "the energy flowing through the body in childbirth, the pressure of contracting muscles, the downward movement of the baby and the fanning open of soft tissues, can be powerfully erotic." She prefaces this by saying that the sensations of labor have nothing to do with being "sexually titillated," but it isn't clear how she differentiates "titillation" from "sexual." She likens the end of each contraction to orgasm, comparing the breathing patterns of mammals in birth to the patterns of breathing during orgasm. Orgasm is also compared to the culmination of birth.

Perhaps Kitzinger doesn't really mean sexual experience as sexual in the sense of having sex or bonding energy. But by using the word *sexual*, she has paved the way for others to see it as sexual in the everyday sense. A woman who saw birth as truly sexual presented a workshop to childbirth educators in Seattle on the subject of birth as a sexual experience. She gave an example of a husband whose wife had just given birth. He was invited by the midwife to hold the baby, but he chose to stay in his seat next to his wife. It later came out that he had an erection and was embarrassed to stand up and let it be seen. The presenter treated his ability to allow his sexual feelings to come up as positive. She didn't see that he was triggered by the similarities between sex and birth by his cross-wiring, and that his decision to stay in his chair was in the best interests of the baby. The child was spared the connection between passing down the birth canal and his father's sexual arousal at seeing his child as a sexual stimulus. I wonder how many people begin their lives in the outer world welcomed by women and men who see the child as having sexual contact with their mothers.

Kitzinger's descriptions of birth appear to be a romanticized version of a sexual experience. Her poetic descriptions may match the experience of the caregiver but are impossible from the point of view of the birthing mother who is working with her pain. The following are some excerpts:

> The second stage can become an intense sexual experience. . . . She feels the extraordinary and intensely sexual sensations as the baby's head presses first against her anus and then down through the concertina-like folds of her vagina until it feels like a hard bud in the middle of a great, open peony. . . . Suddenly she is full, stretched to her upmost, as if she is a seed pod bursting. There is a moment of waiting, of awe, of a kind of tension which occurs just before orgasm and then suddenly the baby passes through. . . . A peak sexual experience, the birth passion, becomes the welcoming of a new person into life. All the intense sexual feelings of labor and delivery have culminated in the passion, the hunger and the fulfillment of a mother with her newborn baby.

Prior to reading this information, I had thought that perhaps only a small handful of people found the birth experience to be sexual. At the same time, I had had several clients inform me, while doing guided imagery about what life was like when they were young babies, that people around them were including the baby in their sexual exchange. Some "remembered" their parents feeling sexual together when the baby breast-fed. I had doubts about the validity of these memories and received them as information about something that remained perhaps nameless. But after learning that many childbirth educators and midwives feel sexual and openly acknowledge it, I can see that my clients were retrieving valid information about what was really going on.

Brad, a Seattle therapist, told me about learning from his mother that she had an orgasm when he was born. He felt repulsed when hearing this, as if he had been "incested on." He said it felt like she began the sexualized bond between them by having a sexual experience at his birth.

No Reason for Shame

If you are one of the people who have felt sexual when you or someone else was having a baby, please don't take on shameful feelings. Even though what you experienced was not healthy—for you, for the mother, and for the baby—it is not your choice to be cross-wired to sexual response in this situation. Instead, you might use this information to take a look at how you have been conditioned to feel sexual in situations that aren't inherently sexual. Perhaps it is the body positioning or the moans and other expressions of feeling. Or the focus on the vulva—touching it, or seeing other people touch it. Perhaps the openness of the female body feels inviting, or the intensity of the mother's experience is one that you associate with a sex partner. If she (and you and others) don't express your physical sensations freely, this scene might seem to belong only to the sexual realm of life. You might also be cross-wired to pain and bondage—a common experience in our controlling culture. If you feel shame about your reasons for arousal, you won't be able to take a look in order to begin healing from that kind of cross-wiring.

I talked with naturopathic physician Cathy Rogers, who was a midwife for four years in the early 1980s. Cathy was willing to share with me her experience of sexual arousal that came from watching births. She didn't feel the arousal at the time, but found herself going home to her partner and having sex, a desire stimulated by the birth.

Cathy told me about a time when she was with a mother who had to be taken to a hospital, because circumstances didn't make it safe to birth at home, as planned. The woman, however, continued with labor as she had at home. She got down on all fours and rocked and moaned. Cathy said it looked and sounded like a sexual experience. The mother was aware of the similarity, because when a male student came in and left, she commented that he really got an eyeful.

As I listened, I expected Cathy to quote from Kitzinger, because she was the one who told me about her books. But Cathy had discovered something more than Kitzinger. After helping with many births, she realized that she had been lacking in sexual boundaries when she responded sexually. Over time, she was able to differentiate her sexuality from the triggering scene and to see that, indeed, feeling sexual from such an experience was much like responding to pornography or becoming aroused when identifying with characters in movies or books. The arousal doesn't come from within the person, natural to the timing of that person's life. It is kick-started by a stimulus that allows our sexuality to attach itself to something not inherently sexual in order to survive. In time, Cathy was able to differentiate between her own sexuality that resided within her boundaries and that stimulated by something external.

Cathy talked about the relationship between boundary deficiencies and the manner in which caregivers help with birth. In most countries, including ours, caregivers play an active role in telling the mother what to do, and in intervening. In other words, they move past the usual boundaries of the mother, physically and emotionally. The opportunity for confusion of sexual boundaries becomes greater. In contrast, she told me of a naturopathic student who attended births around the world and discovered that in the Netherlands, caregivers remain apart from the mother, allowing her to birth her child as she chooses, following her intuition. The people present are there to help when she asks them to, or if problems arise that she isn't equipped to deal with. This "boundaried" presence of the caregivers can be expected to elicit less sexual confusion.

§ SEXUAL-ABUSE SURVIVORS AND BIRTH §

To gather more information about the experiences of caregivers during birth, I spoke with Penny Simkin, the author of several books, including *When Survivors Give Birth*, which will be published in late 1997.[2] Penny is the foremost person in the United

States in the field of childbirth education, because she has made innovations that other professionals want to learn.

During the course of attending hundreds of births over three decades, Penny began to discover a cause of some of the differences in the ways mothers approached birth. She herself had suffered postpartum depression years before and was curious about the difference between women who handled birth in a healthy, powerful way and those who had a number of reactions that made the experience distressing and traumatic. One factor was the kind of treatment given in the hospital where the birth took place, which has changed greatly due to the influence of Kitzinger and Simkin, among others. But Penny saw that there was more to these reactions. Even in a situation in which the caregivers were not violating the mother and she received ample support from her husband and *doula* (a trained, supportive woman there to explain what is happening and help in whatever ways arise), strange feelings and disruptive body phenomena occurred.

Penny's first clue came from observing that mothers who had a difficult time with birth described the experience in the language of rape. This suggested that they had been violated in the past, and the birth reawakened feelings contained in the body.

The second clue emerged when Penny took a look at possible unconscious reasoning that prevented women from completing a vaginal birth. For example, sometimes the cervix will not dilate fully, preventing the baby from being pushed out. Other women, who dilate fully, are not able to push at the time most women find it impossible not to push.

Penny told me about a mother who insisted on having her facial makeup available and attended to her heavily made up face as labor progressed. Penny saw this as a sign of her need to be attractive to the strangers—nurses and doctors—who were caring for her, a desire not to be seen as she really looks when in pain or under stress. But her labor stopped, perhaps because of an unconscious need to protect her vagina by not allowing the baby to pass through it. She finally had a cesarean section when her doctor was unable to get labor to continue.

When Penny talked with the mother later, she learned that she had been repeatedly abused by neighbor boys who put things in her vagina. Although this was abusive to her sexuality and her body, she also experienced deep feelings of shame and unacceptability when they stopped being sexual with her and turned instead to her younger sister. Penny believes that the use of makeup at the time she was exposing her vagina to all kinds of intrusions might have been an attempt to remain "attractive," as she felt she hadn't with the abusing boys.

From here, it was a logical step to interviewing women about a possible history of sexual abuse prior to delivery and discovering that, indeed, there were connections between the kind of abuses experienced in childhood and the nature of the difficulties that occurred in labor and delivery.

Penny lectures across the country on the findings of her research and how to interview mothers before birth to ascertain if it is possible that childhood sexual abuse may create difficulties for them. If this is the case, she uses counseling strategies she has developed to help the mother identify and move past the obstacles. If therapy is needed, she refers clients to a qualified psychotherapist. Penny's role is specifically to help the mother bypass the effects of past abuses in order to enhance birthing. Penny has found that when mothers can do this, they are able to have a truly positive, healing experience that can also help remove the stored effects of earlier sexual abuses. Her work and lecturing is helping the childbirth community become aware of the importance of this connection, and changes are coming about. In the past, doctors didn't know what to do with "difficult" mothers and used methods familiar to our culture— cajoling or control. Now there are growing numbers of childbirth educators, *doulas,* and psychotherapists who can help with this specific symptom of childhood sexual abuse.

Penny pointed out that professionals can do anything they want to a woman in labor. She is vulnerable, because she can't get up and leave, her genitals are exposed, she can't stop the process, and she needs assistance. In this culture, most women truly don't know what is medically needed and what is the result of hospital convenience, doctor convenience, understaffing, or emotionally insensitive caregivers. In the past, and in some hospitals today, this has resulted in women's hands and legs being tied down in the name of sterility. The similarity between rape and birth was not seen, or not named, and not respected.

Into this fragile environment came people like Kitzinger with the statement that birth is a sexual experience. Such statements can confuse mothers who already view the experience as rapelike and compound the potential damage from a violating experience of birth.

§ THE COMMUNICATION OF TOUCH §

Our perception of touch develops very early, perhaps before birth, and we know if we are being touched with love, fear, or resentment and if the person is in tune with our experience or responding to our bodies as objects on which to perform a task. Some parents who are sexual with very young children believe children don't know what is going on and that they won't be harmed as long as there isn't penetration or physical hurt. The truth is that we are capable of perceiving what is happening to us long before we acquire language or "picture memories."

The physical experience of trust and security, and the capacity to enjoy it are available to us at birth. Being touched in a healthy way is an important element to an infant's development. Conversely, being touched in an unhealthy way—whether sexually, or with pent-up anger, or with obliviousness to the child's experience—is damaging. I can see this today in my own experience. I have known body workers who view bodies mainly as objects to manipulate. I feel unseen by their hands and violated by their touch. Those who have "intuitive hands" enable my body to feel safe and relaxed. After being with many body workers, including Rolfers, Trager Practitioners, craniosacral therapists, and others, I can tell when a new person first puts a hand on me what kind of touch to expect. When I am with a really good body worker, I can feel like a small child, curled safely in a mother's arms. This professional knows how to tap into my experience and meet my needs. Our intimate, nonverbal contact energizes and uplifts us both. The infant, however, cannot get up off the table if the caregiver isn't able to provide a safe, intimate exchange. (See Chapter 8 in *Discovering Sexuality That Will Satisfy You Both* for information on how to access your ability to perceive body communications, both yours and the person you touch.)

§ BREAST FEEDING §

After the baby emerges into the larger world, the offer of a breast or bottle for nourishment becomes the next major source of body shame. The mother's feelings about her breasts, our culture's attitudes toward breasts, and the mother's feelings about sexuality will influence the child's developing attitude toward its own body.

When a mother feeds her baby, she transmits her feelings. If she is comfortable, then she and the baby may connect in a deeply intimate way. However, if she is feeling shame or anger or impatience, the child experiences these responses too; it's as if the mother isn't really there—she doesn't perceive the infant's needs. This is a form of abandonment.

Mothers offer their breasts to infants with a number of possible feelings. The ideal, in a perfect culture, is to feel no shame, to hold her breast out to the infant to pull into its mouth for nourishment. The mother will feel deep pleasure as the infant expresses the satisfaction of two of its most basic needs—food and bonding.

Many mothers, however, offer their breasts in ways that are not helpful to the child's growing sense of itself and its environment. If a mother pushes her breast into the baby's mouth, as if to make her child eat, the experience can be overwhelming.

During the first weeks of an infant's life, the mother's breast—which grows greatly in size during pregnancy—can be as large or larger than the baby's head. The baby sees a mass of flesh directed its way, with the nipple forced into its mouth. If the baby doesn't feel in control of wanting, exploring, and then taking the breast, this experience can be frightening.

Another approach to nursing is tentative and fearful, when the mother worries that the child won't be fed adequately. One of the reasons women give for abandoning breast feeding is concern that the baby isn't getting enough nourishment. The baby experiences a worried mother, who fears she is inadequate in taking care of the infant's needs. The baby may grow up to become an adult who worries over the needs of others or fears that his or her needs may not be adequately met.

When a mother feels angry and resentful about having a baby, or about feeding from her body, the baby will perceive this. Not being welcomed into the world or fed with joy, the baby could translate this as either visiting an alien world, or as having done something so wrong that the mother cannot love her or him. When these negative feelings are transmitted in the personal act of nursing, the effects on the baby are powerful.

Breast Feeding May Appear Sexual

The bond between mothers and infants comes from an energy that resembles that which bonds adult lovers. However, the nature of the connection is not the same. If we lived in a healthy world, we could easily tell which is which, but in our sexually mixed-up, confused culture, it is not always easy.

I will describe the differences, but before I do, I want to emphasize that *when our adult feelings for children are not healthy, we cannot choose to feel differently.* We were cross-wired in an earlier time of life, and those feelings will be stimulated until we heal sufficiently to turn them off. The shame that comes from knowing we may have harmed our children is excruciating and can block us from seeing what happened. Breathing deeply and letting the shame feelings flow can help us to look.

§ PARENT–INFANT BONDING IS NOT EXCLUSIVE §

The energy bonding between an infant and parent is not exclusive. It is possible for parents to have many such bonds—one with each child. None of these parent–infant bonds has to disrupt or replace the monogamous bond between the parents. The parents' bond, in contrast, is supposed to be exclusive. When two adults bond with sexual energy, the purpose is to create a new family. Neither adult uses sexual energy to bond with other adults, keeping the unit intact. However, to create a family means adding children and bonding with each with the same intensity. The nature of the connection makes room for bonding with all the children that arrive.

The father can use the same energy to bond with his babies. As our culture changes, fathers are increasingly able to do this. They are now welcome at the birth and may help deliver the infant. Skin-to-skin contact, so conducive to bonding, is encouraged. Long periods of contact and eye-to-eye communication with babies are possible for the father as well as the mother. Indeed, grandparents and other relatives also can bond with the infant. Bonding is available to anyone who takes time to relate intimately. The bond will vary in quality and intensity depending on the amount of time and nature of contact.

As the child grows older, the need for an intense bond gradually diminishes. The child slowly separates from the merger with parents and others. The final grieving for the close relationship can allow the newly adult person to leave home, prepared for the new bonds of adult life. Although the family bonds can remain important and special, they will never equal the intensity they engendered during the weeks and months after birth. The adult can now form such intensity with his or her own partner and arriving children.

Breast Feeding Disgusts Some Women

Some women find the idea of allowing a child to suck on their breasts disgusting and repulsive. This reaction can come from cultural shaming of breast feeding, from the fear of responding sexually, or from some kinds of sexual abuse during the mother's childhood. Since the survival of the human race was once dependent on breast feeding, it is obviously a normal function, more likely to bring pleasure than disgust. If it creates negative feelings, we can guess that something occurred earlier in life to create unpleasant associations with breast feeding.

That was the case with me. When I was pregnant in 1970 and my doctor asked if I wanted to breast- or bottle-feed, I chose the bottle. Recently, after years of retrieving memories of sexual abuse during my early life, I have come to see that I was afraid I would unknowingly sexually abuse my son. I knew I couldn't have a person suck on my breast without sexual arousal, and I believed that I mustn't allow myself to have this feeling with my own child.

Deciding not to breast-feed a baby communicates the shame or fear that the mother associates with the process. An infant intuitively perceives that the mother is making a choice not to offer her body to him or her, as well as the feelings behind her decision. Although this can have a negative effect, each mother has to decide which choice is best for her.

Because I had not been able to make the changes necessary to breast-feed in a healthy way, my son was better off with the bottle. I could feed him with joy and commitment, without needing to withdraw to prevent sexual feelings. The decision not to breast-feed is a valid one. If it isn't possible to work through the feelings of revulsion around breast feeding, then both the mother and baby may do better with the bottle. This alternative can provide a less shameful introduction to the world. There are a number of reasons mothers make this decision. The following are five of the reasons mothers choose not to breast-feed:

1. *Childhood sexual abuse can make breast feeding sexually stimulating.* As in my own experience, mothers who were sexually abused in early childhood may have learned to associate babies with sexual arousal and find this connection totally unacceptable. In my case, I wasn't conscious of the feelings, but I protected myself and my son from them anyway.

2. *Women can be uncomfortable feeding in public with "sex objects."* Our culture views breasts as objects of male lust. The larger the breast, accompanied by the appropriately thin body, the more lustful attention men are supposed to give. Some women find this kind of attention painful even when they are not nursing infants, but find it even more distressing when they want to see their breasts as nonsexual when feeding their child. The confusion can be too great and not breast-feeding the easiest solution.

3. *Sexual feelings may arise when a mother begins feeding.* Mothers who have sexual feelings when the child sucks on their breasts might be so appalled by this that they cannot comfortably continue. This subject will be addressed more fully later in the chapter.

4. *Breast feeding may make the mother feel consumed by the child.* Sheila Kitzinger describes the experiences of mothers who feel consumed by the baby as it feeds. This is a frightening feeling, one that intensifies the already heightened nature of the bond between mother and child. If a mother is not able to come to terms with it, she will communicate her underlying aversion. As the baby sucks, it will at the same time ingest her negative feeling. More than abandonment through neglect, this baby will feel rejected by its mother and likely interpret her rejection in personal terms. A baby has no context yet to understand that the mother has issues from her own childhood that make breast feeding stressful for her. Nor does the baby have any other experience in which the greedy desire for food is reflected as healthful and wonderful.

The mother may imply that something is wrong with the infant for even wanting to feed. As she converts her own discomfort into criticism of the baby's desire to feed, she may communicate that the child is greedy, selfish, uncaring of the mother's feelings, disgusting, sexual, and even sexually abusive to the mother.

5. *A mother may want to prevent the father's distress when she feeds.* Many men have feelings that are the counterpart of the women's described above. A variety of feelings may emerge, such as ownership of his mate's breast, not wanting to share her breasts with another, not wanting others to see her breasts while feeding, as well as shame associated with evidence of sexuality, disgust with the animal nature of breast feeding, and sexual arousal, among others. Some men may try to influence their mates against breast feeding, and others may agree to it while still having negative feelings. Either way, the baby receives messages that the other important adult in its life does not like it at feeding time. In addition, the mother's anxiety about the father's feelings will also transmit. The baby will receive confusing messages that include its mother's pleasure and her distress.

The Mother Is Seen as the One with the "Problem"

Mothers who don't want to breast-feed in front of other people, or who feel uncomfortable about revealing their genitals during childbirth, are seen as prudish. Women are told that obstetricians have seen thousands of genitals and have none of the usual reaction of the average person. I hope that this is true for many, if not most, but Kitzinger's writing lets us know that mothers really are subjected to sexual reactions when they expose their vulvae and bodies.

Effects of Breast-Feeding Distortions on Adult Life

Combining the entire source of food with shame or with sexual arousal prepares the infant to associate food with the attitudes of the mother, associations that will carry into adult life. For example, the mother who is sexually stimulated by her child's need for food prepares him or her to search for sexual interest as a way to meet needs. Some sex addicts can trace their compulsive search for a person who will respond to them with sexual arousal to the search for their mother to feed them in their early months. The mother's sexual arousal can become associated with life-giving food, and come to feel life saving.

Eating disorders can be initiated at this time too. For example, if food only comes with sexual arousal, a child can choose to eat as little as possible to maintain life, resulting in the aversion to food in adult life. Or sex and food may seem to meet the same need and be used interchangeably.

Adult attitudes toward money may also be shaped by early experiences of breast feeding. Money meets many essential needs in adult life and can carry the associations with meeting essential needs in infancy. For example, people who, as children, never knew when their next meal would come might have difficulty understanding that money is an accounting system for what we give out (spend) and what we can bring in (earn). Attitudes such as never being able to get enough or having to use it when you have it equate with feelings about breast milk that is not freely given in response to the needs of the baby.

One Mother's Experience

Susan knew she wanted to breast-feed her daughter long before she was born. Giving birth for the first time at age thirty-three, she considered herself a "militant" breast feeder, angry about the encouragement to use bottles by the makers of baby formulas. She felt rebellious, angrily reclaiming her body for its original purpose. Susan hadn't yet begun to reclaim memories of her father's coming into her room at night to be sexual with her. She was therefore unaware that when she refused to let others tell her what to do with her body, she was expressing anger partly directed toward him. She fed her baby in public, openly, even if those around her didn't approve. In fact, she rather enjoyed their disapproval, dismissing it as "their problem."

Susan found both pregnancy and breast-feeding powerfully affirming, feeling proud and complete. She enjoyed the self-sufficiency of carrying her child's food with her.

By the time Susan's second child arrived five years later, Susan had uncovered the incest in her childhood. She also lived more fully in her body; the therapy had freed her cells of some of the inhibiting memory. The result was that Susan was no longer able to fend off feelings of shame with militant anger. Yet she hadn't completed the incest-recovery work. Because she hadn't removed the shame that was deeply imbedded in her, breast feeding became unpleasant. She now had difficulty touching her breasts or having someone else touch them, and she found it shameful that she even had breasts. Preparing to feed was the most shameful time, when it was more likely that someone would see her breast. She was only comfortable in the presence of her husband and older daughter. In contrast to the loving, warm experience she'd had with her first child, she didn't like the feeling of the second one sucking on her breast. It tickled and wasn't comfortable. Her child received the message that feeding her was a duty.

Susan, along with many women, did not want her breasts touched sexually during the months she was breast feeding. She could not make the transition from good, healthy, motherly use of her breasts to using her breasts for sexual arousal. She found it too confusing, and was unable to separate the compartments so that sex belonged in the shame compartment and breast feeding in the healthy, child-loving one. To do so might have allowed her to feel sexual excitement when feeding, and she couldn't tolerate the shame that would accompany such associations.

Some of the same feelings created by ownership and use of Susan's body by her father generalized to her feelings of obligation toward her daughter. This child was affected by the sexual activities of a grandfather she never met. Her mother was prevented from being fully in her body and soul when feeding her child—an experience they deserved. We can only guess what happened in Susan's father's history that led him to believe that he could use her body for sex in the context of being loving and playful. We do know from examining our culture that he believed he owned her body because she was his child. He was a well-respected doctor who loved Susan and provided her with a great deal of real nurturing in addition to violating her sexuality. If Susan were not examining her sexual history and working to change her relationships with her daughters, she would pass on to the next generation the abuse of her sexuality, although in a form different from the one her father employed. Susan's willingness to examine her sexual feelings and sexual history, in spite of tremendous shame that accompanies both, will break the intergenerational pattern.

Unavoidable Shame

Even when a mother wants to feed her baby from her breast, she suffers the effects of a culture in which sexuality and body parts are contaminated with shame. *Mothers who feel good in their bodies and take joy in feeding their precious child still transmit our culture's shame.* These mothers cover their breasts and the baby when feeding in public, because they know there will be people who will react in unhealthy ways. Some will shame her for feeding in public and for showing her naked breast. Others will feel sexual arousal and assign blame to her for it. Still others will want to be aroused by looking. As the mother protects her infant and herself from such intrusions, she communicates to the baby that there is something dangerous about the feeding process. These events also evoke the mother's shame about her body, which she transmits to the child.

Susan described a situation when she was sightseeing in a foreign city with her family and had difficulty finding places to sit down and feed. She went into a restaurant and sat at the very back to avoid people watching, but even then, she became aware that two men were staring at her. She felt as if she were lying naked on the table in their eyes. A friend who read an early draft of this chapter wanted to know why she didn't go into a restroom to avoid this situation. This reaction is typical in our culture. The woman is made responsible for avoiding peoples' reactions, even to the extent of trying to feed her child in a room designed for elimination. In addition, few rest rooms are equipped for a mother to sit down to feed a child. If she sits on the floor or on a toilet, further shame is being attached to the child's views of breasts and of feeding. My friend had no children and hadn't thought through the difficulties involved in trying to manage normal, healthy child care while in public.

If the mother chooses to feed from a bottle to avoid these contaminating influences, she communicates that there is something amiss. *There is no way to entirely avoid communicating to an infant that there is something wrong with bodies, with breasts, and with feeding from the body of another.*

Some Mothers Use Breast Feeding for Sexual Arousal

Breast-feeding is a major area of confusion. Breasts are designed for feeding babies. At the same time, stimulation of breasts by oneself or another can bring sexual arousal. In our repressed–reactive culture, these two experiences become confused so that many mothers become sexually aroused when they feed. Some take this a step further and use the stimulation of their breasts for sexual pleasure, sometimes masturbating to orgasm. If we were to grow up in sexually healthy cultures, mothers would be able to differentiate between sexual feelings and the feelings that come with the very physical, satisfying, intimate experience of feeding a child from their bodies. But we don't. Instead, all of us grow up with strange combinations of associations with breasts, and these are likely to appear. In addition, our culture shames women overtly or covertly when they feed from their breasts.

Mothers need not feel shame for sexual feelings. But it isn't possible to simply decide to change the way you are programmed. A healing process takes time and requires help. As with childbirth, mothers can use this information to learn about themselves, asking why they are cross-wired to breast feeding as a sexual stimulus.

Sheila Kitzinger has written about this subject too, not only condoning sexual feelings, but describing breast feeding as a sexual experience. In *Women's Experience of Sex*,[3] she shows us a full-page picture of a woman with glamorously arranged hair breast-feeding two babies lying on pillows, while she and her husband are kissing erotically. The caption reads: "Breast feeding can be a highly sexual experience, not only for the mother but also for the father and the baby." I was shocked that incest was presented as not only normal, but also actually healthy and desirable. The imagery memories of my clients who experienced their parents being sexual when they were feeding from the breast do not suggest that this was a valuable experience. On the contrary, the parents are introducing their sexuality to the babies, stimulating them in a way that does not respect the natural development of the child's sexuality. This is overt sexual abuse. Again, Kitzinger is influential and her beliefs are accepted as truth because no one else offers a picture to the contrary. She, and many traditional sex therapists, sanction their own experience so they do not have to feel the shame that comes with knowing they are harming children. She does not know that we can heal. I offer an alternative: It is possible to know what we are doing and not feel shame for it. Instead, we can use it for change.

I showed this picture to therapy groups. The members concluded that it was pornography. It elicited cross-wired sexual arousal from those who had been the object of both parents' sexual energy, among others. Some found it arousing, and others found it disgusting.

I knew a man, Rob, who was addicted to affairs during his marriage of more than thirty years. He remembered that when he was five, his mother held him lovingly and put her breast in his mouth. He sucked on it while she spoke to him and stroked his hair. Murmuring endearments, she communicated her pain and "love." During his affairs, he murmured these same endearments and wanted his hair stroked as he sucked his lovers' breasts. In addition, he wanted them to wear clothing out of which they would bare a breast, as his mother had done. The nature of the affairs reproduced the element of a love triangle that had originated with his mother and father and himself. He was profoundly gratified when he could arrange to have his lover and his wife together for an evening. The lover knew of the triangle, of course, but his wife didn't—at least not consciously.

§ SOME MOTHERS HAVE AN "AFFAIR" WITH THEIR CHILD §

Other women create a sexual affair with their child but do not recognize it as such. When in their presence while they are nursing, I feel as if I have just entered the bedroom of a couple making love. They somehow communicate the exclusive nature of the sexual bonding.

When a mother creates an exclusive bond with her baby, she will automatically break the bond with the older child and also with her husband. Such a relationship seriously disrupts family intrabonding, and the disconnection of the parents threatens the security of the children. Each baby with such a mother begins life with an intense, exclusive bond, and then loses its mother to the next child. This dynamic creates feelings of sibling rivalry and competition.

It is difficult for most people to consider that a mother could use breast feeding as a way to have a sexual relationship. But given the nature of many cultures' dealings with female sexuality, it makes sense. Women, until recently, have not been allowed to be fully sexual. Sex is hidden and cannot take its place in the normal functioning of life. Although it may be inhibited from normal expression, sexuality will not disappear entirely.

One possibility for its expression is in having babies. Such a choice allows a woman to live a sexual life without identifying it as such. The naturally intense bond between mother and child, which society glorifies, serves to mask what underlies her behavior. She is given *carte blanche* to create a sexual relationship. She does not have a mirror to reflect the difference between the natural, boundaried sexual feelings that go with a mother–infant bond and the use of these feelings to permit a sex life and "love life" with her baby.

When a man offers a baby his penis to suck on, he is labeled the worst kind of pervert and may be put in jail. Women can unknowingly do a comparable thing and be supported.

It is excruciatingly painful for a mother to let herself know that she has used sexual energy in this manner. Mothers don't want to harm their children, and our culture gravely condemns adults who use children for sexual pleasure. Yet for a woman to be able to discover healthy sexual energy, it is necessary for her to see what she is doing. Our cultural abhorrence of using children for sexual purposes makes her position untenable. It contributes to her inability to know, just as sexual arousal by babies can remain out of the awareness of men.

§ MONOGAMOUS SEXUAL BONDING WITH BABIES §

Women and men can use their bond with an infant as a lover relationship. Overt sexual arousal may not take place. The lover relationship is a way of using sexual energy to bond into a couple in a way that excludes bonding with others. This engages the baby in a relationship that is not healthy. The baby needs to have intense bonding with a parent to feel secure during the helpless years, but the nature of infant sexuality must be expressed according to the needs of the child, not the adult.

If the infant is being required to bond with only one adult, there can be no deeply sustaining, nurturing bonds with others. The baby is more vulnerable than if bonded with two or more adults.

If one parent is bonded exclusively to the child, and two parents are in the home, the child becomes part of a destructive triangle. The excluded parent may blame the child, without understanding that it isn't the child's doing. Jealousy that might be natural in an adult lover relationship and appropriately directed at the "other woman" or "other man" is now dangerously directed at the child. The other parent and the child both lose, but the child is particularly vulnerable, being dependent on the care of its parents. (See Chapter 7 in *From Generation to Generation* for an example of a mother who bonded sexually with her daughter, excluding her husband, who came to hate the girl. Their recovery allowed them to form a balanced, loving family.)

Relationships with siblings are also affected. The parent's "lover" is the chosen child, creating natural jealousy in brothers and sisters. The child is given power in the eyes of the rest of the family—power that isn't real—and results in deprivation of loving, bonded relationships.

Mothers can use breast-feeding to enhance the power of this kind of sexual bond. However, fathers can also create exclusive bonds from early in the baby's life, even without sexual interaction or arousal.

Early sexual bonding with a parent creates difficulties in adult life. The story of childhood will be retold in adult relationships. The chosen child may bond with a person who is married and anticipate the jealous reaction of the spouse.

Garth had been the chosen child of his mother and felt powerful in winning her away from his father and brothers. As an adult, he engaged in numerous sexless affairs with married women, never able to form a bond with an available person. Part of his pleasure came from being friends with the women's husbands, creating a scene in which he appeared innocent while bonded to their wives with sexual energy.

§ No Sexual Activity §

Healthy bonding energy between an adult and child will not lead to sexual activity. Two adults will often find themselves using and intensifying their sexual arousal to enhance their bond. They take their lovemaking to a room by themselves, invite no one else, and allow their sexual relationship to evolve.

7

HOW SEXUAL SHAME INHIBITS US AND HOW WE AVOID IT

§

The subject of sexual shame comes up often in this book. I would like to summarize here how sexual shame inhibits sexual loving, and why it is the first priority for sexual healing.

If evidence of our sexuality had not been shamed, and we emerged from the bodies of women who loved their bodies and lived in a culture where sexuality was not shamed, we would therefore grow up to discover the real nature of sexuality on our own time schedule. We would find out its purpose and use it for that, and we could learn through trial and error, without admonishments from others. But we aren't born into such an environment. Instead, shame is focused on sexuality more than any other human quality.

The shaming that accompanies most expressions of sexuality becomes attached to it, so that when we are sexual, we evoke shame too. This puts into motion distortions of sexual expression in both universal and unique ways.

§ HOW WE ARE SHAMED §

Chapter 6 explains how we can pick up shame even before we are born, and how birth and breast feeding convey sexual shaming. This is followed in early months and years, when we

101

become able to touch our genitals and receive a number of possible reactions from others. Silence conveys shame. Parents respond to almost everything the child does with reflections of the child's experience, except sexual stimulation and feelings. Many people think they are seen as sexual only after they marry, and even then may feel uncomfortable knowing that other people now know. Avoidance of the subject is pervasively shaming of a natural human quality. Some adults avidly tell children not to touch themselves, that they are bad for doing so, and some even threaten bodily harm if it continues. Sexual activity with an adult unavoidably intertwines shame with sexuality.

After more than a decade of sexual shaming, the child's hormones change, and a number of things happen. Sexual feelings become stronger, and bodies change to look more and more adult. These changes are almost never met with helpful responses from adults.

Occasionally I get to see a healthy response to a child's sexuality. I watched a boy about three run naked to the end of a long swimming pool at a resort in Mexico and stand there, holding his penis out to be admired. People smiled and chuckled, affirming the rightness of a child this age taking delight in his body, appropriate to his developmental task. Although some people might fear that this could be the root of sexual exhibitionism, instead, he was completing his developmental task, so that he would not need to show off his penis to strangers as an adult. Those who are not shamed or prevented from doing what this child did are more likely to continue to meet the need appropriate to that age.

§ Our Culture Believes Sex Is Bad §

Our culture has developed the belief that sex is sinful, even while we know it must take place in order to perpetuate the species. We have difficulty seeing that our culture holds such negativity toward sex because at the same time, we are bombarded by sexual stimuli that are considered acceptable.

Through working with people who have been sexually shamed as children, I have seen that some of the resulting confusion about sexuality comes from the fact that sex and shame become associated. It isn't possible for a child to see that sexuality as a whole is good, although some uses of it are vastly harmful. It is parallel to our culture's views of anger. We generalize from the harmful use of anger that violates another's body or possessions to all uses of anger, including very healthy expressions. Sexuality is even more confusing, because it is secret.

Viewing one aspect of our nature as bad contaminates the rest of our view of ourselves. And, as I have made clear, overt sexual abuse is not necessary for a person to view the sexual self as bad.

§ PUBERTY: FIRST BRAS AND MENSTRUATION §

When girls become young women, their mothers' shame makes it difficult for them to help—an example of distresses passed down from generation to generation. Few mothers had good models in their own puberties. Women in my workshops and groups have told me their stories. Few have good ones. The most common experience I hear is that the child is not comfortable telling her mother that she has begun to menstruate. Ruthie, who was born in the early fifties and is now a successful attorney, had older sisters and was thus able to hide her bleeding by using pads that had been purchased for her sisters. Months later, her mother noticed the absence of pads and figured it out. She was concerned that Ruthie hadn't told her, and was sincerely interested in helping Ruthie. But the shame she felt had been transmitted to her children, and Ruthie had picked up her discomfort. By keeping menstruation a secret, Ruthie avoided both her own and her mother's shame.

Sherry, another group member, wanted to keep the secret so badly she burned her underpants when they were bloodstained. It was months before her mother figured it out. Most girls must tell their mothers, because they cannot hide the evidence.

In talking with mothers in the women's group, stepmothers had an easier time than natural mothers. Somehow the absence of a maternal bond seems to make it easier to talk about becoming a sexual person.

Purchases of the first bra were also fraught with discomfort. These two experiences are the significant steps from childhood into young adulthood, and into becoming a sexual person. For a mother, looking at her daughter's breasts and talking with her about the need for a bra are direct interactions about this forbidden subject. To know that a daughter is capable of having sex and conceiving is as well. Menstruation is about having sex and conceiving babies, and no matter how much a mother doesn't want to talk about this, it is a fact.

Maggie, a thirty-five-year-old mother of three and a good psychotherapist, was a member of the women's group when her daughter reached the age at which she needed a bra. She told us about it, afraid that she had damaged her daughter's feelings about her breasts. But the story she told reflected her increasing level of sexual boundaries and decreasing shame. She had been able to openly talk about bras, and she had allowed her daughter to try on the bra without going in the dressing room with her—the opposite of her own experience with her mother. As Maggie recounted this experience, the group told her she had done much better than she thought. At the same time, we knew that her shame still inhibited her daughter, and was communicated even without Maggie's awareness. We suggested that she talk with her daughter again and tell about her shame and her own experience with her first bra. This way the shame is spoken, which may reduce the transmission to her daughter—the next generation.

My own mother was so uncomfortable with the subject of menstruation that she didn't want me to go to the movie shown at school, and when I first bled, she denied that it was menstruation—she said it was nothing. Throughout my teen years, I was uncomfortable telling her when I needed pads and was relieved when I discovered tampons and began buying them with my allowance. She never asked why I didn't need more pads. When she discovered that I was using tampons, she was upset, but unable to say why, leaving me with the feeling that I was doing something wrong.

My mother never bought me a bra. She took me to the store to do so once, but after some initial frustration over finding one, we went home. I was unable to express how important it was to have one like the other girls. Some time later, some used bras of a friend of hers appeared on my dresser, and the subject was never brought up again. I saved my allowance and bought my own.

§ Puberty: First Masturbation §

Although most girls masturbate, it doesn't usually have the driving force behind it that it does for boys—perhaps because of the need for erections and ejaculations for procreation. Most boys masturbate soon after puberty, and with it invariably comes shame. In spite of the greatly increased societal permission to be sexual, masturbation isn't included. My clients who can talk with relative comfort about having sex with a partner have difficulty talking about masturbation. Many clients have talked about knowing before puberty that masturbation was considered to be wrong but are unable to tell me how they found this out. This reflects the nonverbal nature of this programming. But when the hormones changed, and erections came unbidden, masturbation was soon discovered. However, because of the shame attached, many boys felt bad about themselves for it. The increased shame about being a sexual person intensifies the pain of living. If a boy thought he was bad before puberty, discovering that he is sexual, and that he wants to be, will add greatly to this belief. For those with a tendency to become addicted to sexual feelings, this is a natural time for that addiction to begin or strengthen in order to reduce feelings of shame.

The Shame of Masturbation

Masturbation has been heavily associated with shame from childhood experiences and cultural communication. It is hard to imagine where the idea was introduced into history that touching part of one's own body in a way that brings up sexual arousal and orgasm could be seen as harmful, particularly since most people do so. As the men in the men's therapy group began to tell about their experiences masturbating, one mentioned the Christian view of it as "self-abuse." We looked masturbation up in the dictionary and found out that the word is based on "self-mutilation!" Although our culture is becoming more verbally accepting of masturbation, particularly after the advent of sex therapy in the 1960s, shame is still attached to it for both sexes. People still do it only when no one else will know, and few people talk openly with their partners about when and where and how they touch themselves sexually.

This association of shame with masturbation means that most people feel more shameful once they reach puberty and begin masturbating to orgasm and ejaculation. The men in the men's therapy group didn't believe they had much shame as they went around the room telling about it. Two even moved their hands in a gesture that represented stroking their penises. However, when I brought in a three-by-five-foot watercolor of several penises in differing stages of erection, and all of them ejaculating, the latent shameful feelings emerged. These penises were beautiful ones in bright colors, representing recovery. They were portrayed as wonderful organs that are lovely to look at. In spite of the healthy nature of the picture (very different from those shown in "erotic art" or pornography), the men had reactions of embarrassment (a form of shame) and discomfort. Although all of them had been exposed to pornography at some length, it was a first for them to sit with other men (and me), speaking openly about sexual organs and masturbation. This time, as the men spoke, they were unable to talk about penises without discharging strong feelings. The painting broke through shame barriers and allowed the men to talk about shameful things in a way that didn't make them feel bad. Each man was able to shed some shame, and by the end of the two-hour meeting, the picture was just a decoration on the wall— no longer a shame stimulus. (I showed this picture to the women's support group, creating equally intense but different reactions, and they also shed the feelings sufficiently, so that by the end of an hour, the picture was no more than a colorful decoration.)

I suggest that students of my Healthy Sexual Energy class make love to themselves, and come back the next day to tell about it, if they choose. I explain in detail that this means no fantasy, no pornography, and no vibrators or other sexual apparatus (no outside-in stimulation). They are to abandon goals of arousal or orgasm, and instead just explore their bodies and sexual arousal, if it comes. (This is explained in detail in Chapter 9 of *Discovering Sexuality That Will Satisfy You Both*). Typically, less than half the class is able even to attempt it, and among those who do, few find themselves aroused. This affirms that people must use shame-reducing arousal maneuvers to even have arousal when masturbating. The cultural change in perception of masturbation has not filtered into the individual unconscious.

With the experience of sex so shame laden, it is amazing that we are even able to experience a desire for it. Those who have learned methods to overcome the shame, such as the use of pornography or intense need for emotional reassurance, can continue to have sex without feeling shame. For others, it is easier to forego sex. In any case, a "sex drive" is not the fuel for these choices. It is more likely that the need to couple and a push to keep our sexual selves alive are the motivators, along with the addictive function that sex serves by operating as a drug that will easily remove unpleasant feelings.

§ BEING A SEXUAL PERSON IS UNPLEASANT §

As long as shame is attached to sexuality, then sexual activity or awareness of oneself as a sexual person will bring unpleasant feelings. It is natural for us to want to avoid shame, but the obvious solution of refraining from sexual activity and divorcing oneself from sexuality cannot be taken. We must be sexual people for our species to continue, and for us to feel whole.

§ THE SHAME COMPARTMENT §

Each of us learns a variety of maneuvers to continue being sexual and, at the same time, not feel shame. These maneuvers do not *remove* the shame from sex, but will allow a person to feel sexual *without awareness of the shame*. Most of these solutions are built into our culture, because the problem has become an almost universal one. Others are specific to a particular childhood experience.

The use of pornography and sexual fantasy, for example, prevent the feeling of shame because they elicit an intense, cross-wired arousal. Lusting for strangers who look "sexy" has the same effect, allowing a person to elicit arousal and then find a partner with whom to have sex. Romantic fantasies and activities serve the same purpose. It makes sex into something more than what it is—the love of a lifetime. Romantic feeling in the body will set shame aside for a time, allowing sexual activity to appear to be the completion of a great relationship.

Individual cross-wiring will also serve to *temporarily* eliminate shame. Examples include searching (for a prostitute, one-night stand, one's lover, an affair), being sought after, intense sexual charge from specific sexual activities, going into particular fantasies to become aroused, and myriad of other possibilities. The nature of the activities is determined by a number of things, including childhood sexual abuses, adult abuses, our culture's definition of "sexy," and observation of sexual activity during formative years. But whatever the original cause, those behaviors that can override shame become necessary to reduce the feeling of shame, so that sexual activity is possible.

The "shame compartment" is a term I invented to indicate the emotional place where one can be congruent with the shame. When in the compartment, we feel like sexual/shameful people, and so can be sexual. But if something comes along and elicits the shame, then it becomes difficult to be sexual. For example, if your mother knocks on the door, do you invite her in and ask her to wait in the living room for twenty minutes until you are through with sex? Unlikely. Instead, our culture tells you to stop sex, and pretend you weren't being sexual.

Those who are able to transform shame into sexual arousal will want to have sex where they might get caught. Shaming one or both partners as part of arousal activities can help to allow sexual activity in spite of the shame. One way or another, we must learn how to have sex in spite of the shame that has been attached to it.

Drugs and alcohol are great tools to get into the shame compartment. Both can prevent the feelings of shame and fear. However, "the morning after," the shame returns and can increase the feeling of being a bad person when one remembers what happened when under the influence.

The frequently proposed idea that sex can become boring, or needs spice, comes from the effect of shame. It can be hard to get started and not very interesting, if we can't use workable methods. Sex becomes "too much work." Long-term relationships are likely to elicit disinterest, because it becomes increasingly difficult to use cross-wired stimulators in a "normal" situation. Women's magazines have articles almost every month about how to spice up sex, reflecting the pervasiveness of disinterest. None seriously address the reasons behind it.

Sexual Relationships Produce Shame

Sexually bonded relationships are, by definition, sexual. If sex equates to shame, then being in a sexual relationship will bring up shame. Getting married announces to the world that sex is involved. When people are still "dating" (not living together or married), sex isn't talked about openly, and it becomes possible for others to know and not to know at the same time that sex is part of the relationship. Because sex isn't openly talked about, shame can be kept at bay. But once certain thresholds are crossed, such as a marriage ceremony, living together, or pregnancy, "knowing" becomes more public. The agreement "not to know" lessens.

During the early 1960s, when I was sexual before marriage, no one talked about it. Many of us in the college dorm were having sex but acted as if we weren't. Each of us felt alone with our choices and highly shamed by the need for keeping a secret, and the belief that we were the only one who chose to do the unacceptable. Pregnancies were secret, and were either terminated illegally, or the baby was born in secret, or the couple got married, and everyone was surprised that the baby came early. Gossip communicated the truth with further shameful secrecy.

In any case, sexual activity attached more shame to sex. Even the girls who were "good" and didn't have sex were shaming their sexuality. This vital part of themselves was declared bad and withheld from direct expression.

Marriage was supposed to make sex acceptable, but it didn't. Sexual activity was still hidden, although now everyone knew.

American sexuality appears different now, but I believe the same amount of shame remains attached. Shame has lessened around the ways we get into the shame compartment. Traditional sex therapy has given permission for the use of pornography, sexual fantasy, and other stimulating sexual activities to override the shame.

Long-term relationships create the most difficult arena in which to be sexual. Figuring out how to avoid shame while *in* a relationship is more difficult than when involved in one-night stands and short-term affairs, because it is more difficult to stay in the shame compartment with a loved one who is part of "normal" life than in a situation that is defined as shameful.

Frustration typically evolves, because each partner usually has different ways of getting into the shame compartment. For example, women typically feel violated by a man's desire for her to wear sexy clothes or use porn with him. She is shamed. Her reaction brings on his shame. Men feel violated by a woman's desire to be romanced to avoid shame. He feels pressured to lie. His reaction brings on her false belief that all he wants is sex, and that he doesn't really care about her. (My book, *Discovering Sexuality That Will Satisfy You Both: When Couples Want Differing Amounts and Different Kinds of Sex* tells more about the resulting differences and confusion for couples.)

Our culture seems to be sexually permissive, but little real shame has been removed. We do have in place, however, changes that can remove shame. Natural childbirth, the introduction of labor-support people, and attending to the mother's emotional issues that create shame for her (and thus for her baby) are allowing babies to enter the world with less shame attached to their bodies and sexuality. The millions of people who are recovering from childhood sexual abuse are creating a cultural shift, and the result will be less sexual shame. Sex addiction has been defined, allowing people to identify the results of sexual damage, and offers a route to healing. As these and other phenomena evolve, we will see the result in our cultural views of sexuality.

Coupling Distresses Result from Sexual Shame

Couples may not be aware of feeling sexual shame that increases as the relationship progresses, because our culture does not provide them with language for it. The result is unnameable distresses. A man cannot say he is angry with his wife for triggering his sexual interest, when he knows she is supposed to do just that. A woman cannot expect her partner to stop initiating sex, so her sexual shame isn't triggered, and thus she has a hard time naming her distress. These and countless other conflicts resulting from sexual shame can result in couples picking fights and trying to find nameable reasons they are angry with their mate. Few couples get to bond with sexual energy and then allow it to pull them into rebonding over and over in a way that is comfortable and life enhancing. Most couples struggle over the differences between what they want, what our culture says they should do, and what they want to avoid. When a person can name the feeling as sexual shame, it is often assumed that that person was sexually abused as a child or has something else amiss, when, in fact, he or she may be experiencing the effects of living in our culture.

People can choose not to be in relationships to avoid shame. This is more practical now than in past decades, because more women are able to support themselves. They do not need to find a man to live well, and men are less obligated to support "helpless" women. The added shame that accompanies homosexual partnering has made the partnerless option more common for homosexual than for heterosexual people. Our culture consistently shames gay men and lesbian women, in contrast to the mixed messages given to heterosexual people.

§ Sex Can Drive Us Apart §

I have heard countless descriptions of the ways sexual shame creates difficulty for couples. One of the most obvious is the supposed "goddess–whore" dichotomy, in which a man is able to have sex with the "whore" but reveres his mate as a "goddess" and is not able to have sex with her. We can take another look at this through the filter of the man who feels sexual shame unless he is in his shame compartment. His shame is so strong that he is unable to have intimate sex with a women he loves. Instead, he needs a woman who will join him in the shame compartment in order to override his shame. He needs her to be lustful, "talk dirty," and use drugs and alcohol to join him. Other shame overrides can occur if he is forbidden or engages in sexual acts that trigger his cross-wired reactions, or engage his sexual addiction. He must have strong arousal in order to be sexual in spite of shame. This man could work to *remove* the shame, even though it is a painful process. He could then be available to his mate in an intimate way. She (or he) would have to address her (or his) own shame so that she (or he) could join him in the same way.

Women avoid their shame too. Some women don't want to have sex and do so infrequently. Or they have sex because they are "supposed to." Or they put sex in the hands of the partner, letting him (or her) make the decision. Or they feel "swept off their feet" in order to override shame with romance and "love." Some women become the "whores," valuing the power that comes with being able to service men. This includes prostitutes, sexual dancers, and strippers, as well as women who have sex with a series of men because it doesn't make sense not to do so.

§ Homosexual Shame §

I had a conversation with a homosexual friend I will call Jim, who had not been able to sustain sexual relationships even into his late thirties. He pointed out that for a man to be sexual with men is one of the most shamed forms of sex. As a result, he was able to be sexual when acting out addictively, because that was the only way to provide enough sexual stimulus to get into his shame compartment. But once he became interested in a man, and they began to date, he found himself the object of our culture's worst shaming. If he went to the beach with a potential lover, or out to dinner, they were forced to hide their affection or go only to places frequented by gay men. Either way, both men would be forced to feel shaming from our culture, as well as their own internalized shame. *Gay men and lesbian women have few ways to feel normal and have a sense of belonging to our culture when they are in homosexual relationships.*

Jim went on to explain that if he had sex with a man he found interesting, then his shame became even stronger. To have sex when he felt loving made it more difficult to get into the lustful shame compartment that allowed him to act out addictively. He attached the shameful feelings to the man with whom he had sex and then wanted nothing more to do with him. This pattern continued until Jim was able to begin the process of extricating shame from sex and take a look at the shaming coming from our culture.

As Jim explained this to me, it made sense. I could see his shame and how it had been given to him by living in this culture. Making the bridge to my own shame, or to that of the "average" person, seemed more difficult, because I live within the culture. But the principles are the same. The shaming that has been placed on sexuality in general, supplemented by the personal childhood experiences each of us have had, has resulted in this barrier to intimate sex. Every one of us has feelings that prevent us from fully experiencing our sexual selves.

§ "BEING A GOOD PERSON" AS A SOLUTION TO SHAME §

Our culture offers an antidote to shame—becoming a good person, an upstanding member of the community, a good Christian, a family person, or any of the many phrases that affirm one's goodness.

Most religions offer a set of rules to follow and so appeal to people who feel shameful. The rules are difficult to follow, however, and failure results in more shame at a deep level. Religions don't offer methods to remove the shame, which is necessary in order to discover from the inside-out the healthy, loving, community-supporting, life-enhancing ways to live. Religious communities have higher levels of sexual abuse of children and other sexual acting out, which might be supported by the inability of these organizations to help people access their goodness, instead, offering only a set of rules to those who feel worthless in their struggle with sexual and other kinds of shame. The listing of religious rules and the use of shame to enforce them has become institutionalized, which inhibits the healthy use of spiritual teachings and community. When teachings can be used for consciousness-raising and as models for how to move from this state to a more life-enhancing one, and when community can be used for its powerful effect of pooled energy working toward the same ends, then religion can serve a powerful function.

I have a friend who was sexually abused by his older brother when he was about six. The brother, Jerry, was probably acting out what had happened to him when he was younger. At present, he belongs to a cult that controls his life and is raising his children within that community. He writes sentimental letters to my friend, letters that sound loving and committed to family. Most people in our culture would view these letters as coming from a sensitive, caring man who knows the value of family. Yet he has isolated himself from his family of origin, has little contact, and when he does, it takes a romanticized form. Jerry hasn't been able to release his shame through the help of the cult. Instead, he follows the rules and remains locked into his shame-based life.

A client was a member of a Christian cult for years as he sought to belong to a group with strong values that dictated how to behave. His recovery from sexual addiction didn't begin until he was able to leave this group.

Rules about how to behave, people in authority who will enforce the rules, and a community that adheres to a hierarchic structure will not remove shame from one's view of oneself. It will only further reinforce it. Even when a person does "good" things, he or she will know there is another self underneath that is not visible, and not removed by accolades. Many clients have described themselves as frauds waiting to be found out, because the whole truth isn't known. Facing shame, talking about it, revealing acts that have been harmful to others without being shamed about them, are the only ways to *release* shame. Pasting a new person on top of the shameful view of ourselves does not succeed.

§ Shaming Others as a Solution to Shame §

Shaming comments are built into our culture and, unless they are intense, are considered normal. As we shame others, we reduce our own experience of shame. But as each of us uses shame this way, we are also the recipients of it, creating a circular effect that results in all of us experiencing more shame. Learning to recognize when we are shaming others, so we can stop, and when others are shaming us, so we can refuse to take it in, can lead to sexual and all kinds of emotional healing.

I recently watched several daytime talk shows and observed that most of them invited the audience to shame the people on the stage. For example, two episodes dealt with men who "cheated" on their partners. The men were scoffed at, and the women pitied. Millions of viewers (mostly female) enjoyed watching someone who was "worse" (more shameful) than they were, and felt powerful as they shook their heads over "these" people. When we are shame-loaded, it is less painful to shame someone else than to be the object of shaming. In a shame-based culture like ours, these two feeling states are the only choices— unless we work to remove our shame. When we do, these talk shows will be boring.

When parents set limits, shame usually accompanies the limit. Firmness, even anger, need not carry shaming. "Stop it" and "Don't do that again" can be said in a tone that sets a limit but does not imply that the child is bad. When the parent shames the child, the parent takes the position of one who knows what is right and would never stoop to such shameful behavior. Shaming children is an effective way to avoid our own shame.

"Friendly" responses can shame, such as the recent addition to our vocabulary, "Duh," used when a person doesn't know something they "should" or states the obvious. When done in a congenial manner, it suggests an invitation to join together in the shame compartment. "Yes, I'm (you're) stupid, but, what can I say, this is just the way it is." Such an approach is not good for either the one who says it or the one who receives it.

Attempts to prevent another person from feeling shame also add shame to them. The teacher of a yoga class frequently said things such as "Jean, put your *other* right hand on the floor" when people used the wrong hand. Jean is supposed to chuckle, acknowledging her stupidity, and make a joke of the shame. If she doesn't laugh, she will feel shamed.

§ SHAMEFUL SEX AND LOVING BONDING CAN BE INCOMPATIBLE §

Paul spent thirty years struggling with how to have loving bonding and shameful sex. He thought his wife was the most beautiful woman in the world, and he knew deep within him that he wanted to live with her and have children. But once the time came for intercourse after the wedding, he found that he couldn't maintain sexual interest. Even with fantasy and pornography, he couldn't get over feelings of being asexual when with her.

A year or so into the marriage, Paul had his first affair. He was relieved to find that he could have erections and intercourse, and that he enjoyed sex with a woman. Even though this affair ended, he decided to continue having sex with other women— forbidden women who were married and would not interrupt his marriage with Alecia. Throughout almost three decades of affairs, he was never tempted to leave his wife. He wanted only to express himself sexually.

Soon after beginning therapy, Paul was able to see that he had developed a strong connection between shame and sexuality. He grew up in a place where prostitution was legal, and "real men" were not monogamous. He was filled with ideas about how good women don't like sex, and men hurt them with their penises. He didn't want to be that kind of man with his bride, and so his unconscious mind refused to allow him to become aroused sufficiently to have the shameful interactions that are associated with male badness. He could not switch into the shame place of sexuality, even by conscious choice. He could do this easily, however, with women who were willing to reveal their badness by having sex with him when they were married to other men.

Alecia was deeply pained by the lack of sex with her husband. She adopted two children when it became obvious that she could not conceive with her husband. After a decade or so, she had her own affair that lasted for many years. She was relieved to find that she was attractive to a man who enjoyed being sexual with her. She, like Paul, knew that Paul was the man she wanted to be married to and so never ended the marriage to be with someone else. Now in their fifties, they enjoy their relationship and are glad that the sexual difficulties didn't drive them apart.

Alecia also sought help from therapists prior to and after the introduction of traditional sex therapy. She was counseled by all of them to make herself into the kind of woman Paul found sexually attractive. She did. Seeing herself as a bland, mousy woman, she set out to become glamorous, sexy, and interesting. She succeeded. She went back to school to study interior design and created a profession in which she knew many interesting people and developed activities she valued. Paul supported her changes and also felt threatened by them, but his disinclination to be sexual with her didn't change. She could not solve the problem by becoming his sex object. To him she remained the "good" woman.

Late in their more than thirty years of marriage, they found a sex therapist who was able to help them discover ways they could be sexual in a loving way. Paul was able to reduce his shame sufficiently to experiment with oral and manual stimulation, and Alecia became more satisfied with their sexual relating. But still she felt there was something wrong.

Finally introduced to the ideas of sex addiction, cross-wiring, and sexual shame, both Paul and Alecia could see that there was more to their problems than whether she was sexually attractive to him. As we mapped out his past that resulted in sexual shaming of intercourse with a good woman, he could see that his feelings had nothing to do with loving his wife, or with his being a bad person. Alecia was quickly able to see the same thing and gradually reduce her anger with him. She could see that he was programmed not to be sexual with her, and that his reactions had nothing to do with her sexual desirability or his love for her. Both got to work on their issues, knowing they had many more years of their marriage to work toward sexual health.

Women's socialization allows them to abandon sexual expression more easily than does men's. If Paul had stopped having sex, his self-esteem might have dropped even more than it did by having affairs. Particularly given his background, he had learned that men have sex, and those who don't aren't men. He was supported by uncles and cousins to have prostitutes and affairs, and these people kept the secret for him.

Women, on the other hand, are encouraged to stop being sexual in order to avoid the shame. For a woman, particularly a mother, sexual shame is a very bad experience. We don't have mechanisms built in to have sex by moving into the shame arena of life, as men do. Instead, we are revered as pure and holy. With this cultural prescription, it is more difficult for married women to have affairs or engage in sexual activities that bring up feelings of shame. There is no sanctioned place to have shameful sex.

For women, abandoning sexual activity or pleasure is a solution that allows them to experience themselves as consistent within the eyes of society. As shame grows from the inability to mother well, the desire not deliberately to engage in the shame associated with sex becomes even stronger.

Women are allowed, by our acculturated values, to focus on the coupling bond. Sexual energy can feed this bond even without sexual activity. In past times when young people were chaperoned on dates, they were still able to use sexual energy to bond by looking deeply into each other's eyes and expressing sexual energy in a touch of the hand or a kiss on the cheek. A woman needn't feel shameful about this form of sexual energy—it had cultural approval. But once she married and was required to have sex, then she often had difficulties engaging in this shamed activity to "meet her husband's needs" and to have children.

As sexuality for women has changed in recent decades, women are permitted to express themselves with sexual activity. However, much confusion has arisen over this change, because now women are required to integrate the shameful "whore" in the bedroom with the idealized mother during the day. Although women's magazines support the idea that it is possible, the task is far more complex than giving permission to use pornography, fantasize about other men, and wear sexy clothing to turn yourself and your man on. There is another step in here that has to do with removing shame from sexual activity, so that it can be engaged in openly and delightedly. The women's therapy group is making this possible by pulling the shame off of sex.

§ SEXUAL HEALING IN GROUPS §

The cultural shaming of sexuality requires group conversations in order to bring sex into the arena of normal, everyday human behaviors. When we can go to work and talk about sex as one of the interactions we had the night before, or when telling about our weekend, and not have to get in the shame compartment in telling or hearing someone else tell, then we will be able to have sex in a manner that doesn't require separating ourselves from the rest of life to avoid shame.

This is difficult to do. Cultural prescriptions are hard to break. Even in my long-standing women's and men's groups, members find it embarrassing to talk in detail about sex. Some cannot listen, because they are in danger of being triggered into their addiction. For these people, sex is still so shameful that they are unable to listen without moving into a state that will allow them to know about sexual things—a state of such intense sexual arousal that they can no longer feel shame. But most group members have done sufficient shame work that they are able to feel the shame that comes up when they or another person talks openly about sexual activities.

Jan, a college student in her fifties, made a *papier mâché* vulva for one of her classes. It was about four feet long and lifelike. After her class presentation went well, she brought it to the women's group, which had been meeting for over four years. These women, who could no longer avoid their shame, felt more shame than Jan's class members. Even Susan, a midwife who had spent years looking at women's vulvas while they gave birth, had uncomfortable reactions when seeing the vulva in this setting. The women used the opportunity to let the shame emerge, and wash out—a practice with which they have become very familiar.

Sexual arousal is one way we prevent ourselves from feeling shame, and so addiction to sexual arousal is encouraged. If addiction is defined as altering one's mood to avoid unpleasant feelings, shame being a major feeling to avoid, then sexual arousal becomes a likely candidate when sexuality begins to elicit sexual shame. It is an instant solution, supported by our culture. We assume that if someone talks about sex, it is natural to become aroused. This belief has come out of centuries of shaming of sexuality, and the result is seen as normal instead of a creative solution to a conflict.

§ Shame Generates Shame §

Parents who feel shame about their bodies and their ways of dealing with the shame cannot adequately see their own child's needs. Their hurt and rage spills onto the child, as it might everywhere in their lives. The child is hurt by the passing on of shaming and then grows up to do the same, perpetuating it from generation to generation.

Our culture shames us for many reasons—lack of intelligence, being "too smart for your own britches"; not making enough money, making too much money; losing competitions, "bragging" when we win; being sexy, being a slut, being sexless; being homosexual, being heterosexual at the wrong times; being too young to understand and too old to be attractive; farting and burping, harming our digestive systems by holding it back; expressing delight and aliveness through laughter, song, and dance, being a depressed stick in the mud; interrupting when someone is talking, not listening, being bored or uninterested, pretending to be interested; being too tall, too short, too fat and too thin; being too white, being too brown. We have a narrow margin within which we are expected to live a full life. It isn't possible until we can relinquish socially approved methods of feeling acceptable.

As shame is dropped from sexuality, these previously shameful components of our nature no longer provoke shame. In my own recovery, I have seen repeatedly that as I remove a layer of sexual shame, I am able to move more freely in the world, being who I am with less fear of how others are going to judge me.

8

Don't Talk About Sex—Except in Jokes
§

As we have seen, sex in our culture is laden with shame. Throughout childhood we are bombarded with information that associates sex with shame and secrecy, and with what's forbidden and evil. In spite of the sexual revolution of the 1960s, and the AIDS panic of the 1980s and 1990s, our culture has not allowed us to talk in ways that would remove shame from sexuality. Only when we are able to talk openly and without shame will we be able to heal from the sexual damage we have received from body shaming, sexual abuse, sexual triangulation, cultural prescriptions to be male or female, addictive use of sexual energy, cultural myths about how we must be sexual, and more.

When we can't regard sex with a partner or alone (masturbation) as the ordinary activities they are, then we have to enter a separate place in our awareness and create what I have described as the shame compartment. Without mirrors for the sexual part of us, we cannot easily know whether we are being truly intimate with ourselves or our partner, or whether we are using sex to distract or tranquilize ourselves, to search for love, or to barter for something else we want. *We can't even begin looking at sex until we can view it within the context of normal life.* This is not easy to do.

§ Breaking the No-Talk Rule §

I formed the women's therapy group (described earlier) specifically to address this issue. We met for six months before the women were able to talk explicitly about sexual activities and welcome the feelings that arose. It seemed so simple—to describe what sex was like, to say how a penis feels to the touch or how sexual arousal fills the body. When we finally did, most of the women had intense feelings of shame for several days. However, we discovered that *in talking openly in a safe environment, we could bring out our shame, see it more clearly, and experience it for what it is.*

We had previously avoided shame the same way everyone in our culture does: by not talking about sex or by bringing up sex only in jokes, innuendoes, and with stereotypical language. One result of not talking or of submerging sex in culturally sanctioned "talk" is to cover the shame with a kind of blanket. Our group removed this blanket. We talked openly, because we had created a new environment where we were able to view sexuality without shame. We exposed the shame but didn't really feel it till afterward—once we returned to the regular world. Outside our group, the culture's rules again took over, and shame emerged, because in this society, sexuality is inextricable from shame.

Not talking directly about sex allows us to avoid feeling the shame. By allocating sexuality to one compartment of our lives and our goodness to another, we are able to continue to be sexual and also to feel like good people. Most of us deal with these opposing facets by going into an altered state when being sexual. We flip a switch from the side of us that we consider "respectable," to the "bad," sexual side. By compartmentalizing our sexuality, we give it expression. If we don't separate the two parts, then feelings of shame emerge. Shame is so painful that most people will not choose to continue an activity that evokes it. By moving into the altered state, we can be sexual and not feel shame.

This maneuver became apparent in my own life when I was looking at pornography with Rex, in order to learn more about our cross-wiring. The idea of going to the adult bookstore with him to get it filled me with shame, and so did looking at it. I was surprised that it didn't burn a hole through the kitchen counter where Rex left the magazines. Finally looking at the pictures and experiencing my remaining cross-wired feelings, I was acutely aware of how the shame flowed out and freed me further from the cross-wiring.

I told my women's therapy group about this, feeling the shame all over again as I recounted the process of getting and looking at the pornography. Later in the meeting, I remembered that when I was in my first marriage, I often read stories and looked at pictures in *Playboy* in order to become aroused so that I could meet the marital requirement to have sex. (I was not able to have sex without arousal, as many women are.) I felt no shame about doing that, either at the time or now. And yet in the present, with ten years of sexual recovery behind me, I felt deep shame for doing the same thing in the service of further healing.

I had been able to keep my use of pornography to myself and away from the triggers of shame, because our culture does not permit us to do the very thing that will elicit shame—talk. If sexual practices were a normal subject of conversation, I would not have been able to isolate the use of pornography from the rest of my life. As it was, I didn't even have to think about hiding it; I automatically did. No one around me would have brought it up. If I had offered to share, I would have been met with discomfort, shaming, or "naughty," sexual conversation.

§ Don't Talk about Sex §

Silence and shame go hand in hand. Shame is triggered by the awareness that, in someone else's eyes, we have done something "wrong." We avoid this excruciating feeling by making sure that no one knows. Sex is perhaps the most secret area of our life. Bladder and bowel functioning follow closely behind, with finances in a distant third place. Each of us wants to remain silent because of the shame attached to sex. And our culture requires silence. If we are sexual in public, frowns and other nonverbal communication will shame us. Observing healthy sexual arousal, for example, a man's erection, is unacceptable.

Yet, we are constantly bombarded by sexual stimuli. When people on TV or in movies are overtly sexual, we must pretend to be unaffected. Advertisements drawing on the power of "sexy" bodies are seen as normal. To engage temporarily in the sexual world, we step outside our selves. Although others may be present while this happens, it is a solitary experience that can only be shared by entering the shame compartment with a partner.

My husband Rex told a story about the time one of his sculptures was waiting to be fired in the pottery studio at a college. Occupying the same space during the day was a workshop on learning how to repair aquariums. The students were all women. Rex's sculpture was of a large penis and testicles, about fourteen inches across and eighteen inches to the end of the penis. This piece sat in the middle of a large table with the women gathered around. The woman who was preparing to fire the sculpture later told Rex that every person acted as if it weren't there. No one even looked at it. I can imagine the discomfort these women felt going to a classroom to learn about fixing their aquariums, sitting face to face with an object that was impossible to discuss.

This particular group wasn't even able to engage in the kind of dialogue our culture permits when we view sex in the context of art. They didn't wonder about the artist, question if the sculpture was erotic art, or acknowledge with humor the size of the genitals. No one was able to break the ice and allow some conversation, although we can guess their pulses and blood pressure were elevated. To talk would be to admit they knew what penises looked like and had feelings about this one in front of them. We know, of course, they were familiar with male genitals, but they wanted to keep this information separate from workshops on aquariums.

We generally act as though no one is sexual, and just like everyone else, we think we are the only ones with a sexual component. When stereotyped exchanges or jokes or flirting are the ways that others deal with sex, we have no mirrors for healthy modes. As a result, each of us feels separate and different. In fact, openness about our sexuality could allow us to experience our membership in the human race.

Still, our culture does permit conversation that prevents sexuality from disappearing entirely. To counter the repressive forces, we become reactive to sexual stimuli and joking conversation. But to operate in this mode, we must shift over to being "naughty."

When my son Austin was thirteen, I received a lesson in communicating to children what is shameful. I had an intense reaction to Austin's presence when the man I was with, who was driving, almost sideswiped a car. He shouted, "Fuck!" I was awash with shame. As the feeling subsided, and I could look at what was happening, I began talking about it. I explained to Austin that although I used this word, and I was sure he did, too, the rules were that he and I were not supposed to let each other know this, and certainly not use the word when we were together. As I could reach the point of laughing about it, I felt great relief that neither of us had to live up to this requirement of sexual secrecy. At the same time, I saw that we had both learned a rule without knowing how. I hadn't told Austin that profanity was not acceptable, because I didn't believe it. Yet, he had picked it up, and I had indirectly reinforced it. I had to actively work on my shame in order for it to be okay for all of us to use profanity in each other's presence.

Over the remainder of his teen years, whenever Austin introduced me to a new friend, he used the word "fuck" within the first ten minutes. His friends invariably reacted with shock. They thought he was being disrespectful to his mother, and they worried how I would react. They were even more shocked when I laughed. After we had both released our shame about profanity, we could easily break the rules.

This freedom allowed us years later to take a trip to the store to buy him condoms. The condom shopping was made easier by Rex's presence, because the rules are different for parents than for stepparents who have recently entered the family. Rex, as a stepfather, took over and directed our shopping, while Austin and I looked on with some embarrassment. By the time we had undergone Rex's instruction on the different kinds of condoms and the usefulness of lubricant for masturbation as well as intercourse, we had all removed a great deal of shame. Our self-conscious laughter helped.

§ WE BELIEVE NO ONE IS SEXUAL, WHEREAS EVERYTHING AROUND US IS §

Our culture teaches us to pretend that we are not sexual beings. "Public displays" of affection are frowned on. Men and women both lust after and condemn everything that reveals the body. Evidence that a couple is experiencing sexual arousal causes people to walk the other way and avoid them. As a result, none of us gets to see acceptable sexual expression. Young people are told that when they fall in love and get married, sex in the privacy of the bedroom will be wonderful. But no one has experience that could give rise to this myth. We cannot separate the years of being bombarded by sexual badness from the rule that sex is acceptable under certain circumstances, particularly when there is no way to observe it in action.

I am not suggesting that parents should have sex in front of their children. However, I do believe that to offer a mirror of sexual health, children need to observe parents interacting with each other from a sexually bonded place. By seeing the sexual, monogamous bond between parents, even if they feel left out, children can grow up understanding one vital facet of marriage. The expression of the bond might take the form of the parents' hugging with sexual arousal, looking deeply into each other's eyes, or planning a special time for just the two of them. The children can absorb the fact that this parental bond is primary.

When we are aware that sexual energy unites our parents, as well as love and a marriage contract, then we know our sexuality doesn't belong in a relationship with either of them. We realize we can form the same kind of bond in our adult lives. We have to see all this to believe it. When we don't see the bond of sexual energy, because it's hidden by an illusion of nonsexuality, we cannot believe that what accompanies sex is good. *Because we do not have natural information about sex, we are forced to replace it with false, media representations that usually reflect cross-wired or addictive sexuality and bonding. Cultural silence has made it impossible to observe healthy sexual energy.*

Nevertheless, we are bombarded by sexual stimuli in movies, television, advertising, and by people who want to elicit admiring sexual responses. The repression of sexuality makes us hyperreactive to sexual stimuli, because our sexuality is trying to make itself known. The proliferation of such stimuli makes it seem as if we, as a culture, are open about sex. To the contrary, the kind of sexuality that is omnipresent and the way we respond to it is cross-wired. Our spark plugs are ignited at a time, and in a way, that has nothing to do with our inside-out sexual feelings and arousal. Advertisers use our repression by jolting us into paying attention to their product—a product that may be nothing we value. (See Chapter 12 for more about how advertisers exploit unhealthy sexual attitudes.)

§ Sexual Silence §

Many of us believe that we are the only ones feeling sexual energy vibrate in our bodies and genitals. During our teen years, after puberty unleashes sexual hormones, most of us feel alone with this part of our humanness, one that is deeply associated with shame. I remember feeling like an alien who didn't fit in with the rest of our culture, even though I was aware that other people were having sex. I had no mirrors to tell me that my sexual nature was the same as other people's, and that what I was experiencing was what they were experiencing. When I began to have sex at seventeen, the feelings I associated with the act were different from those I had carried with me. I lost the connection between my sexual nature (experienced as "shameful") and sexual activity. As it was, sex itself felt more acceptable, because I knew others were doing it. The feelings of sexual energy coursing through my body felt foreign for many more years.

A recent experience showed me what it might be like for teenagers in a healthy culture. During sex one night, I had remained particularly conscious of the electric waves issuing between Rex and me, and the physical uniting of our bodies and lives. The next morning, we stopped by a grocery store on our way to the office. As I walked past people, I could "see" their sexual energy. I saw their bodies as fully sexual and their flesh as capable of merging with the flesh of their mates. Some pulsated sexually more than others. None of these people would be considered "sexy" by our culture's definitions. Instead, I knew about their sexual nature because I fully knew my own. One person is not more "sexy" than another. We are all sexual.

§ HEALING REQUIRES TALKING §

Our culture, not just our particular childhoods, sets us up for the silent, shaming attitude that we pass on from generation to generation. Sexual shame is not the fault of mothers or the fault of men. It is something that evolved over a long period of time and has been perpetuated over countless centuries. We were all taught that sexuality is shameful, and we all teach the same thing to the next generation. Those of us who are retrieving some healthy sexual energy are able to see more and to interrupt some of it. But we, too, are passing shame along in unconscious ways—some we cannot see, and some we can see but cannot stop. We will continue to do so until we can talk and until we can see.

§ SEXUAL SHAMING FOR WOMEN §

The women's therapy group has become a forum for women to tell stories about their sexual histories. As each story is told in the shame-free, accepting environment, each person gets to see how distressing the experiences really were. Sarah's story depicts the role of sexual shaming, followed by secrecy, in the lives of many American women.

At the age of eighteen, Sarah's feelings about her sexual self were so devastated that she put a shotgun to her stomach and pulled the trigger. She is alive because the bullets did not hit vital areas. She lost part of her stomach and some intestine. Now that she is forty, we can reconstruct the events that led her to the belief that ending her life was the only appropriate action for her to take.

In her early childhood, Sarah lived with a father who shamed her mother about her small breasts and large buttocks. As Sarah reached puberty, he tormented her with sexual comments about her body and, at the same time, forbade her to date, so she could not be sexual with boys. His many abuses included calling her a slut and asking her if she were "acting like she was married" when he caught her wearing her boyfriend's ring. His overbearing, sexualized manner provided her first picture of sexuality. Although Sarah has no memories of her father touching her sexually, this kind of "emotional sexual abuse" is damaging to a child's sexuality in ways that are similar to overt touch.

Sarah's childhood with a father who made his own rules and forced her to follow them left her believing she had no right to control any part of her life, including her sexual interactions with men. His control was supported by our cultural belief that parents own their children and have authority over their bodies. He, along with countless others, have taken that to mean he could control his children's sexuality, both by using them for his sadistic behaviors and forbidding them to develop sexual relationships with others.

Sarah as a child had no choice but to receive her father's view of her body and believe that she had no right to physical and sexual boundaries. This early history, combined with our culture's labeling of women without sexual boundaries as "bad," or as whores, or the worst of womanhood, set her up to see herself as absolutely worthless. With an entire culture agreeing with these premises and not a single mirror for the lies she was taught, Sarah couldn't help but see herself as useful only for the sexual satisfaction of men and feel that she might as well be dead.

Cultural rules about sex prevented Sarah from seeing that her father was wrong, and that he was abusing her sexuality in many ways. Once she began to have sex, she found herself following rules for sexual adults—we all seem to know these rules, even though it is difficult to discern how they are transmitted. One such rule is that once we begin sex we cannot stop. A second is that when we have agreed to an activity with a partner, we cannot say no to that activity in the future. Once Sarah was not a virgin, she believed she could no longer say no to sex.

Sarah fully believed that from the time she first had intercourse, she could no longer be a "good girl." After that she viewed herself as a "bad girl," no longer worthy of respect. With her self-esteem severely deteriorating, she could see no reason to create boundaries—it was not possible to regain virginity and self-worth.

As her teen years went on, she began to use alcohol and drugs to deaden her view of herself as a terrible person, terrible in the eyes of not just her father, but also our entire culture. Bad girls are hopeless. They are used as a comparison for the rest of us to make us feel we have some worth on which to base our self-esteem. But the effect on the "bad girls" is devastating. Worthlessness based on sexual badness feels like a reason to give up life itself.

Ironically, men are expected to have sex anytime it is offered, in order to feel like real men. Their self-worth is supposedly enhanced by the same behaviors that, when carried out by a woman, can drive her to drug and alcohol addiction, and suicide.

The incident that pushed Sarah over the edge began when her boyfriend left the house for the evening. A male housemate, whose wife was not home, approached her for sex. She tried to talk him out of it but knew that if he insisted she would not refuse. He insisted. When her boyfriend came home, she became desperately sick, knowing that she had to tell him. She took his shotgun into the bathroom, put it to her stomach, and managed to pull the trigger. She was rushed to the hospital for hours of surgery.

Our culture's perception of women who have sex with many men leaves such women with hateful feelings toward themselves—the same view our culture holds. As they hate themselves, they have no reason to change their behavior in a way that allows them to feel worthy of self-respect. Once the definition of "bad" is in place, there is nothing that can reverse it. Such women are not helped by well-meaning counselors, who encourage them to change their behavior to conform to the cultural definition of "good." Sarah and women like her have only been helped by entering addiction-recovery programs, followed by therapy, in order to learn the causes of their behavior and their shameful attitudes toward themselves. As they are able to change the causes, it becomes possible—in spite of past behaviors—to regain self-respect.

The wife of the man who coerced Sarah to have sex with him wasn't so fortunate. She later turned a shotgun on herself and died.

§ SEXUALITY AND SELF-WORTH §

Another woman attending the women's support group with Sarah told a similar story. Rose used alcohol and drugs to avoid knowing how desperately she clung to life in the face of self-hate. After permitting coercive sex by the husband of a couple she lived with during her mid-teens, she attempted to kill herself in a car crash. After two weeks in the hospital, she returned home to find the man again coming to her bed the very first night back. Her despair was so intense, and the choice to die so repugnant, that she reached out for help. She called a man she knew from AA and was taken from the home.

Rose went through three rounds of treatment for chemical dependency before she was able to stay sober. Eleven years later, she is in therapy, learning about the causes of her original sexual choices.

These woman are only two of countless people who grow up with abused sexuality, who feel shameful and worthless because of it, their resulting adult behaviors further increasing their self-hate. They are candidates for addiction to drugs and alcohol because a conscious life is too full of pain.

Both women have had significant therapy that reveals the history that led them to their sexual choices. However, such work isn't enough. They also need to tell their stories in supportive groups where people won't shame them. Their disastrous histories aren't the result only of particularly bad childhoods but are also the consequence of living with this culture's bizarre rules about sexuality and self-worth. If either woman had succeeded in ending her life, the guilt would belong to society. Their parents, too, were victims of our culture's admonitions not to talk. They did not intend to harm their children but could not help transmitting abuses from their own childhoods onto their daughters.

Mothers in the women's group worry about how they are passing on to their children the abuses that have been inflicted on them. And they are, except that these women are learning how to talk about sexuality. As they violate the cultural admonition not to speak directly, they can allow their children to be conscious of the subject. Thus, their children will not have to "forget" that they have a right to respect their bodies and sexual selves.

It is too easy for people to react with a "Well, why didn't she just say no to sex? She could have raised her self-esteem by refusing to go along." The truth is, neither Rose nor Sarah *could* say no, because of their history. This simplistic approach to self-esteem is based on the belief that following the rules defining a "good person" will make one feel good about oneself. It is not based on what is right for the individual, nor will it let the person make legitimate and appropriate choices.

§ The "Good Girl" Loses Too §

Meg grew up as "lily white," a label of purity she came to despise. People were uncomfortable being around her, because they feared she would judge them. She became her mother's "good girl" as a way of coping with sexuality. She was required to wear high-necked dresses, instead of clothing more popular among her peers. Boys thought she was attractive and the kind of girl they would marry, but few asked her out on dates. She was just as isolated from healthy sexuality as were Sarah and Rose. She received society's approval, but the outside-in self-esteem she derived from it did not make her feel good about herself.

Meg entered therapy because she and her husband were having sexual problems. She was unable to tell him what she liked, and he didn't know if she received pleasure from sex, because she showed no reaction. Intercourse was painful, even though her physician found no physical problems. Eventually her husband stopped having sex with her, finding her unresponsive.

Meg's parents had done such a thorough job of eliminating her sexuality by defining her as a good girl that she was unable to change this when she married. As with Sarah and Rose, her parents' influence was only part of the story. Our culture supports the notion that children can be nonsexual beings until they reach an age or maturity to be able to handle sex, at which time they are supposed to make a miraculous switch. It doesn't work that way.

Meg had no more good feelings about sex than did Sarah and Rose. By living up to the good-girl image, Meg could either eliminate her sexuality or condemn it, while trying to see herself as good. She was required to live a lie. If she felt sexual, she had to see herself as "bad."

Our culture suggests, through movies and other media, that only a small percentage of us are sexual. These people are between eighteen and about thirty-five, thin, and "sexually attractive." They are looking for a lover, in a new relationship, or

recently married. Anyone who has been married over two or
three years no longer seems sexual, even though we know in our
conscious mind that they are. Most of us believe, in spite of the
existence of their offspring, that our parents aren't sexual. We
"know" they are, but the information doesn't register at an
emotional level, because our parents hide the evidence and act
embarrassed when it leaks out. We pick up from their responses
that we are to regard them as sexless. It is also difficult for us
when we are children to imagine our parents engaging in
shameful behavior.

With this cultural backdrop, it is easy for women like Meg to
believe they should be sexless until the "right" time, and that if
they do have sexual feelings, they are one of the bad girls.

§ WE DON'T TALK OPENLY ABOUT SEX §

People disagree with me when I say we don't talk about sex.
Women point out that men talk about it a great deal and have
permission from our culture to do so. Indeed, members of the
men's therapy group were able to discuss sex and masturbation
with little overt discomfort, even gesturing as if masturbating.
On the surface, it appeared that they did not associate shame
with this discussion.

The next week, however, I brought to the men's group a
drawing of several large penises in various stages of erection and
ejaculation. This was not pornographic or "erotic art." It was a
celebration of male sexuality, emerging from Rex's sexual deshaming. These same men were taken aback. Some could not
look, and one man was enraged. As they spent the next hour
looking and talking, it became apparent that this picture of
something sexually forbidden, introduced into an environment
without shame, allowed most of the men to get in touch with the
deep shame that is embedded in their sexuality. As they talked
and heard the others talk about their feelings, the shame loos-
ened up, and they could discharge it. One man did not see that

the penises were ejaculating. He perceived the large, white drops as background, not related to the picture. For him, shame was mostly associated with ejaculation, and so his unconscious mind blocked that out.

In the past, these same men had all used pornography to become aroused and had not felt shame when looking at penises engaged in sexual acts. In this shame-free context, however, where each had permission to be aroused if that happened, and to observe it, they could not relegate their shame to a separate compartment.

§ INVITING SEXUAL SHAME §

Sexual shame can be elicited by speaking directly about sex instead of using jokes, innuendoes, and other socially acceptable, shame-based expressions. Even in my office, people coming for help with sexual issues are embarrassed when I ask direct questions about sexual activities. They are bound by the strong rule that precludes us from speaking directly. If we can't talk, then we can't feel the shame. Releasing it means feeling it first.

When Rolfing clients, Rex occasionally asks which hand they masturbate with, as he determines why a shoulder is not healing properly. (Sometimes lengthy and forceful masturbation can throw a body out of alignment.) Invariably, when Rex explains why they might change their masturbation style to ease a physical symptom, his client feels embarrassed.

I asked a psychotherapist friend if she would like to hear about the "yellow" orgasm I had the night before, and she looked away with discomfort. Once her shame passed, she could listen with interest. This is a woman who routinely listens to stories of sexual abuse in her therapy practice.

I ask people in my classes to remember the last time they had sex. Then I ask them to imagine telling their partner about it. They report little discomfort. When I ask how it would feel to tell their boss, a stranger in the mall, or their mothers, the reactions are strong. This is an absolute violation of socially agreed-upon rules, and it brings up old sexual shame.

§ SEX JOKES: THE REAL SEX EDUCATION §

The repression of sexuality through law, religious rules, and societal "convention" has for centuries pushed direct expression of sexuality underground. A powerful force of human nature, it will not stay there. Sex jokes have become one permissible way to converse about sex. The storyteller and listener have an agreement to enter the sexual-shame compartment. The joke teller assumes a facial expression and voice quality that alerts the listener to the introduction of the shameful subject of sex. If both are in agreement, a form of sexual conversation can take place. (If the listener isn't, the initiator feels shame and possibly anger.)

Jokes become the substitute for natural education about sexuality, an education that doesn't occur easily for most families. Formal sex education in the schools, only recently introduced, is usually superficial and unbelievable to young people, who are picking up conflicting sexual information. Jokes continue to be one of the few ways we transmit information about our sexual culture.

When people talk about a nonsexual subject and at the same time communicate about sex, it allows conversation about sexual things in an indirect manner.

In the past I found such jokes amusing. My energy level would increase as sexual energy was introduced. I would no longer be aware of minor difficulties or emotional inertia as I basked in a feeling of pleasure and companionship. Now, I am no longer entertained. I am out of my shame compartment and can talk about sexuality openly in most contexts. As a result, I no longer need this mode of expression in order to acknowledge that I am a sexual person, and I know that others are as well. Now that it is replaced with real communication, the indirect form is no longer interesting. Instead, my feelings are the same as those that would be expected if people said the content of the joke outright, rather than as a joke. Now my discomfort comes from not laughing, knowing that will trigger the joke teller's shame because he or she can't get into the shame compartment if I don't go there too.

Jokes Can Express Hidden Attitudes and Feelings

Sex jokes permit the expression of feelings and attitudes when direct expression is not possible. Some of these feelings and attitudes include men's anger toward women; women's anger toward men; and the desire to shame, humiliate, and control, or be shamed, humiliated, and controlled.

Women's anger at men is expressed in the cartoon a colleague sent to me when I was working on my first book on sexuality. The woman tells the man that women are writing books about it, and men can't even talk about it. The man says, "It?" and the woman looks exasperated. My friend sent the cartoon as a compliment that I was doing something of worth. She didn't see that the cartoon made men look stupid and inferior. During my male-hating days, I would have found this very funny, not understanding that finding humor in putting down a group of people will encourage separation of them from us.

When the cartoon arrived, I wanted to laugh in order to have that feeling of camaraderie with my friend who had gone to the trouble of cutting it out and sending it to me. As I heard the sound of Rex's office door opening, I went to show him the cartoon. As I turned toward him, and saw that he was a man, I stopped breathing for a moment. He is one of the people this cartoon presented as stupid. In that moment, I grasped that this is wrong. I also saw that my willingness to see him like that for the sake of female bonding was harmful to him, to me, and to male–female relationships.

§ Pornography Educates §

Pornography is also a source of sex education for teenagers. People are not allowed to see the developing bodies of the opposite sex, producing great curiosity as this natural desire is thwarted. One alternative is magazines with pictures of women with no clothing, who sometimes show their genitals. This education is distorted, of course, because these are not ordinary female bodies. They are chosen and posed to elicit sexual arousal.

One of my clients, who removed shame from his pornography use, was able to articulate his feelings about these pictures. Once he became conscious and out of the shame compartment, he rarely became aroused. Instead, he noticed that he was curious and meeting a need that was thwarted and shamed during childhood. He also noticed that he enjoyed looking at all parts of the women—hands, arms, and feet. He studied their vulvae and, once he could speak without shame, he explained how he had seen girls' vulvae from age three through about eight, when children show each other these parts that aren't yet private. But once genitals became off-limits, he didn't find out what girls' looked like once they had changed through puberty. He remembers the first time he saw a picture of a woman's vulva. He was shocked. He expected pubic hair because of his own but wasn't prepared for the other changes that maturation brought. Similarly, women aren't aware of exactly how their vulvae change, because we aren't allowed to look. Men who look at pictures of women's genitals know more than women do about the differences in vulvae and exactly what they look like.

Bill also talked about how difficult it was, the first time, to find out from a woman the position of her clitoris. He described his search for this very small organ with the light off, as required by his lover, and not being allowed to ask for directions. He pointed out how much easier it would have been to have the light on, and have his lover show him exactly where everything was. As he spoke, I was pleased that he could even think about this as a possibility, because it is outside the norm of how people first become sexual.

This man's intense, childhood sexual abuse by his mother made it difficult for him to have sex with women, adding another reason for looking at pictures. Doing so allowed him to see women's skin in a way that felt safe. He also became aware that the bodies didn't need to be perfect tens—seemingly necessary for male arousal. Although his adult experience isn't typical, his desire to look at a woman safely, with no fear of being shamed or punished, is typical for our shaming culture.

§ MISLEADING INFORMATION §

A serious problem with the use of jokes and pornography as sex education is the vast amount of incorrect information that is presented. Sexual shame prevents people from asking about the veracity of a joke's content.

The comic strip "For Better or For Worse" presents a mother of a young teen finding an X-rated book on his chest where he has fallen asleep while reading. She screams and wakes him, and he is terrified, which, I assume, is the humor. The misinformation lies in the early panels, where we watch him falling asleep while reading this book. In truth, a pubescent boy would not fall asleep when stimulated by the contents of a book called Erotic Lust. He would read the book to stimulate himself, masturbate, then hide the book and fall asleep. This comic omits the reason pornography is created and lends truth to the idea that there is a purpose for it other than creating arousal leading to orgasm.

This comic supports the acculturated belief that pornography is wrong and a mother should rightfully go into a fit of rage when finding out that her son is using it. She startles him out of a sound sleep, yelling and red in the face. Yet we know that most adults have watched videos of sex acts. Perhaps she has too, but separates out child sexuality from the adult variety. Whatever the cartoonist intended, the result is support of behavior that damages the sexuality of young people. This young man was shamed for reading pornography and will be more careful to hide it, increasing his association of shame and sex. The walls of his shame compartment are strengthened.

§ ANATOMICALLY CORRECT LANGUAGE §

Using anatomically correct terms for sexual parts can bring a person out of the shame compartment and consequently elicit feelings of shame. Without an understanding of the shame compartment, it doesn't make sense to my clients why they should have intense reactions to the words *penis* and *vulva*. They find it more comfortable to use words they have long used—*dick, prick,* and *cock,* instead of *penis; pussy,* instead of *vulva* or *vagina*—words that belong in the shame compartment.

When sexual slang predominates and the use of standard language brings discomfort, children sense that there is something wrong with sexual parts and activities.

Intercourse is called *it, some,* and *any*. Oral sex is called *giving head, blow job,* and *going down on* someone. Having orgasm is called *getting off* or *coming*. Masturbation (for men) has many names, including *jerking off, beating off, jacking off,* and *whacking off*. There are no slang words for female masturbation. Although we have many nicknames for typical human activities, I believe that sex is the main area in which standard language can be painful to use. Elimination perhaps comes in second, although it is easier for people to say bowel movement and urinate than to say vulva and penis.

§ SEX EDUCATION §

How did you learn the rule that if you are married, you must have sex? Or that women must let the man make love to them, or that you cannot stay out of the shame compartment while making love to your own body?

We aren't born seeing other people as sex objects, and we don't automatically do so when we reach puberty. Instead, we hear others make comments from early in our lives, and we accept what we hear as an accurate reflection of the shamefulness of sexuality. In turn, we use the same expressions to move into the shame compartment, so we can talk about sex.

Phrases that children and young people overhear that shape their shame compartments include the following:

Did you get some last night?
You (he, she) just need to get laid.
She (he) won't give it to me.
Look at that pair o' tits (ass, legs, mouth, walk).
He got into her.
She's begging for it.
I have an itch that needs to be scratched.
I'm horny.
We did it five times last night.
She (he) hasn't given me any for a month.
I did it to her (in gay male comments, "I did it to him").

Women's indirect communications about sexual things differ from those allowed for men. Women are socialized to focus on romance, rather than sexual activity, and are allowed to shame men for their perceived interest in sex. Such comments include the following:

He just won't leave me alone.
He goes right for the main event.
He can't get enough of me.
He doesn't take long enough.
He bought me a _____.

In recent years women have focused verbally on sexuality as well. Examples include the following:

I get wet when he looks at me.
He can really satisfy me.

He's built right.
He has a big (small) dick.
He's got a cute butt.

Members of the men's therapy group tell their stories in a way that permits shame to emerge, so it can be discharged. However, the tendency to move into the shame compartment and isolate shameful stories from the rest of life is so strong that telling a story can feel like the first time all over again. They open that door, walk through for a brief time in a safe environment, and then walk back out, closing the door behind them. It can take many such visits before the door begins to disappear, the compartment loses its shame, and sexuality integrates with the rest of life.

§ SILENCE AND SECRECY CREATE FALSE BOUNDARIES §

The repression that has gone on for centuries has resulted in sexual leakage where it doesn't belong. Since the healthy nature of sexuality wasn't understood, obvious methods of suppressing or inhibiting sexuality were devised. Keeping sex hidden is one powerful way to create some controls or boundaries. Cultures are fraught with the results of suppressing this powerful energy—from people flirting with someone else's partner to engaging sexually with children. These pieces of evidence should alert us to the need for change.

Cultures do not trust that allowing sexuality to flow where and when it will is the route to healthy sexuality, and they are correct regarding adults who have already been damaged. Sex addicts will find their sexuality spilling out in compulsive ways. Such unrestrained, harmful use of sexual energy makes it seem as though controls are necessary. Consequently, setting up rules that require no meaningful conversation about sexual matters (the kind that would allow people to deal with shame) only *appears* to be helpful in inhibiting the spread of rape and other detrimental behaviors. The antidote is talking openly in ways that bring sex out of the shame compartment. As we allow sexual energy to become healthy, then outside-in boundaries become unnecessary. They will be replaced by a natural lack of response to outside stimuli.

§ ACCULTURATED HOMOSEXUAL SHAME §

Sexual shaming and secrecy prevent us from accepting others' activities, particularly when it comes to homosexuality. People who have sex with partners of the same sex are required to *live* in the shame compartment. The rest of us visit there on occasion. Those who have sex with same-sex partners are labeled "gays" or "lesbians," and their very identity is defined by their sexual partner. We don't have a common word for couples differing in age by more than twenty-five years, or of different races. These choices are not acceptable to our culture, either, but those who make them are not categorized as separate from the rest of "normal" humanity. (For more on homosexuality in our culture, see Chapter 11, Homosexuality Oppression: The Shaming of All of Us.)

All of us are interested in learning about sex with the same sex, because it is one obvious possibility. We are not allowed to explore this option openly and then accept or reject it. Those who do explore become loaded with shame and misconceptions about their sexual nature. I have heard many stories from men and women who were sexual with someone of the same sex when they were children or just past puberty, and who believed, because they enjoyed it, that they must be homosexual. They did not have an environment in which they could discuss their experiences and explore their responses to different kinds of people of both sexes. They could not learn from the inside out about choosing a mate. Instead, when they experienced sexual arousal with one of the same sex, it brought them great shame, followed by the desire to conceal it.

The shaming of same-gender sex perpetuates itself, creating a spiral of ever-increasing shame. As each person discovers sexual curiosity about the same gender (a normal occurrence), he or she is also bound to feel the cultural shaming of this interest. To deflect this feeling of shame away from oneself, a person will direct the shame toward the object of desire. Thus a man might say homosexual men are "unnatural" or "sick," or that they brought AIDS upon themselves. This kind of displacement is similar to what Sarah's father did, and what many men do when they see their suddenly pubescent and very attractive daughter dressing up for a date; they will call her a "whore" or a "tramp." Instead of looking into their own responses, they will shame the person they see as causing it. The process is unconscious.

Some men, who are afraid of being homosexual, express their shame by having sex with gay men while claiming they are heterosexual and merely using the homosexual man to "get off." A gay man told me that when hitchhiking, he was raped by two men traveling together. These men believed they were heterosexual, yet both had sex with a man. They also had sex with each other by being sexual together.

Men are sexual with each other when they go out together in a sexual context, such as picking up women or going to bars where they pay women to arouse them. Teens can be sexual with each other in "circle jerks," masturbating together. They can enter the shame compartment, share their sexuality, and not elicit the shame associated with homosexuality. They can feel accepting of their sexuality in spite of the inextricable shame.

§ SEXUAL "COMPARTMENTALIZING" PREVENTS FREE USE OF SEXUAL ENERGY §

When we relegate sexuality to a compartment that we must move into and out of, we have difficulty in making healthy decisions about sexual activity. When two people are capable of healthy sexual energy, it is irrelevant who does the initiating. Either both want to be sexual or neither does. It is simple. But if each one must first move over into the shame compartment, it can become a lot of work.

A woman makes the move into the shame compartment and feels ready to be sexual. Then how does she entice her partner to join her on the other side of the wall? He won't automatically be there, because he must do something to move from nonshame to shame. If he doesn't want to make the effort of moving over, then he won't be interested in taking on shame just to be available for her interest. But if he does want to cross over, then he has a number of ways, depending on his particular cross-wiring. He can look at her naked body (forbidden), fantasize that she is someone else, or see her as his whore, ready to be used by him. Or he can convert his shame into intense desire to make love to a woman who makes him feel loved and valued. She can dress in "sexy" clothing that can help him over the wall by triggering his sexual associations.

If he wants sex and she isn't in the shame compartment, he might lure her there with culturally approved maneuvers, such as taking her out to dinner, invoking romance in some manner he knows she will respond to, or engaging in "loving," non-sexual touch until she is seduced over the wall. Each sex may also use maneuvers associated with the other sex. For example, a man may show off his erect penis to his lover, knowing she will be pulled over the wall by her interest. Or some women know their male partner may respond to a candlelight dinner more than he will to overt touching of his genitals.

Once both people are safely into the shame zone, they must stay there. If one loses arousal during sex, it becomes easy to move back over the wall. This leaves the other in the compartment by him- or herself—an unpleasant place to be. Rules have been made and transmitted about the need to satisfy one's partner by remaining aroused until both are satisfied. This leads women to faking arousal and orgasm and creates performance anxiety in men. Both sexes learn how to maintain arousal by forcing it when they might prefer to naturally let it go. Forcing arousal can only be accomplished by cross-wired sexual associations, preventing access to healthy sexual energy.

People having sex rarely share orgasms in a bonding way. Most people become unaware of their partner when reaching their sexual climax. Energy is cut off from the other, instead of being allowed to envelop the other and intensify bonding. Some have difficulty allowing orgasms to happen at all. For people who must be in the shame compartment to be sexual, this isolation of orgasm from intimacy serves to prevent the vulnerability that orgasm engenders. This vulnerability is dangerous so long as sex is intertwined with "badness." *Orgasm, with its full potential for merging two people sexually, emotionally, and spiritually, is only safe if no shame or other negative feelings accompany it.*

The shame compartment can influence the time after orgasm too. Once the arousal is gone, it is difficult to stay in the compartment. As one moves back over the wall, the shame is more available to see. Some people want to roll over and go to sleep or leave the bed in order to speed up the transition from shame to "good person."

Increased negative feelings toward partners may result from repeated joining in the shame compartment. The other person becomes associated with shame. In new relationships, the need to bond overrides shame, but once the bond is complete, it can become more difficult to move into the shame compartment.

§ Children's Genitals Are Denied §

Our cultural blindness to sexuality results in many parents and other adults holding children in ways that don't respect their genitals. Children are held by their crotch with a hand fully covering genitals, and they are given rides on legs and on shoulders in ways that sexually stimulate. This is not sexual abuse if the adult isn't intending to stimulate the child, or use the child for her or his own pleasure. However, it is damaging to sexuality as the child sees him- or herself in a mirror that reflects the face and body, but no genitals. The child develops the perception that parts of the body that bring sexual feelings do not exist to adults except in very limited ways, thus beginning the process of relegating sexuality to a separate compartment.

§ THE DESHAMING OF SEXUALITY §

Progress in talking and deshaming sex is being made on some college campuses. The state universities in California prepare an outline for conversations on sexual activity for students that are to be led by students. They are very explicit. Students ask each other questions about what women like and what men like, and they talk openly about sexual activity. Even though these conversations and preferences continue to express our culture's attitudes, sexual activity is brought out of the shame compartment in a way that can allow real communication. The college sanction further removes shame. The fact that the student conversations are led by peers creates an environment quite different from those associated with shame-laced talk. As these men and women remove shame by speaking openly, it becomes possible for them to discover what healthy sexuality is. They can talk about sex with their lovers, free of the culture-laden rules that govern sexual behavior and prevent intimacy.

I interviewed a student advisor who coled one of these conversations, and he said that students stayed in the meeting hall long after the official time ended, continuing to ask each other questions. They didn't flirt or act as if the openness were a suggestion of sexual activity. The shame-free nature of the exchange seems to have kept it separate from the shame-based, sexual conversation popular among college students. Because this student advisor is comfortable with his own sexuality, he was capable of presenting information in a way that doesn't invite shame. He was able to model healthy conversation taking place outside of the shame compartment, and the other students eagerly followed.

I find this story immensely hopeful. As our students are breaking the cultural rules, they are becoming the first genera-tion to be able to openly and shamelessly talk about sex. They may be able to talk openly and without shame with their children, who may then be able to avoid some of the disastrous influences.

Members of my men's and women's groups are involved in a long-term process of removing shame from sexuality by talking. They realize they must talk about sexual activities, including addiction and other misuses. In doing so, they became familiar with the deeply embedded fear and shame. But once they can let these unpleasant feelings flow out of them, talking becomes easier, and the results are surprisingly delightful.

Kenneth, whose story is in Chapter 4, found that he could talk about sex in open, clean ways with many people, including women he dated. When the men's group began, Kenneth was the only member who had experience in being open with more than one person, and so he set an example. As he spoke the first day, telling about his addictive activities, I watched the faces of the other men. Shock, curiosity, and awe radiated from them, along with fear. The room's temperature and humidity rose noticeably in the first hour.

Yet each man was encouraged by Kenneth's calm, forthright manner, and as they took turns, truths came out that might have taken weeks to emerge. The truths and the intense feelings resulted in rapid bonding of the men into a community that provided the safety they needed to continue looking even more deeply. Because people everywhere are yearning to talk without being shamed, creating a therapy group, support group, or student discussion in which only one person models a different way can result in rapid change for the others. We are all ready to embrace sexuality in a shame-free way, but we need models and safe environments. These are beginning to appear.

Allen had been in the men's group for several months when he decided to take the Healthy Sexual Energy class. When telling about his "homework" (described in *Discovering Sexuality That Will Satisfy You Both*), which consisted of making love to himself with no fantasy, pornography, or other distractions, he mentioned that he rubbed his anus. He had become comfortable telling his experiences in the men's group, but the rest of the room vibrated with discomfort. Bodies became rigid, and several people looked as if they had pushed themselves deeply into their chairs. Still, as others took turns talking, two more men said that they too had massaged their anuses and found it pleasurable. They had received permission by Allen's openness to do the same.

Sarah told the story of her sexual activities and suicide attempt to the women's therapy group and to her general therapy group. The first time, group members were shocked and expressed disbelief and deep compassion. Sarah had little feeling as she recited the facts, but she was able to see the members' reactions. The second time was entirely different. She was able to feel the horror and despair she went through at the time and remember how alone she felt when her family was disgusted with her. As she became able to have feelings about her prior sex life, she was also able to feel her discomfort with her current lover and express her limits to him. As a result, he also entered therapy, and the two worked on how to love each other, sexually and in other ways. He saw her changes as clearly valuable to her growing self-esteem. Although he felt pressured to change, at the same time he was relieved to find it was possible to make his life richer by taking her seriously.

Susan is in couples' therapy as well as the women's sexuality group. The group is her most valuable source of change as she talks about sex in ways that were previously forbidden. Susan was sexually attracted to her daughter, feelings she had contained by making sure no sexual contact was possible. When the feelings came up, she would automatically go into a bad mood or create distance from the child. After talking about this in group and shedding the shame, she was able to play with her daughter comfortably and see that she was clear in her limits about sexual contact. Until she could openly talk about it, she had only one way to deal with her cloudy awareness of the attraction, and that was to force herself to avoid acting on it. Once it was out in the open, she knew she wouldn't violate her daughter and so became freer to love her physically.

Stepping out of the shame compartment while talking about sex or being sexual will bring up shame. Yet once the shame is expressed and discharged, then awareness of the truth about sexuality can surface. These are only a few examples of what happens when people break the no-talking rule and shed the shame long intertwined with sexuality. (See Chapter 19 for information on recovery.)

9

OUR SEXUALLY ADDICTIVE
CULTURE

§

The concept of addiction to sexual feelings is new. It grew out of an understanding of addiction in general. The purpose of addiction is to avoid feelings or awareness. True addiction is characterized by compulsions that are out of control, threaten jobs and relationships, and make life unmanageable. Sexual energy can be used to induce a "drug trance" similar to that caused by alcohol or drugs. If it continues unchecked, it can lead to compulsions that are out of control.

Prior to the late 1980s, when the first book on sex addiction, *Out of the Shadows*[1] became widely known, people who lusted, who had affairs, who flirted in the presence of their partners, who collected and used pornography, who bought prostitutes, and who masturbated compulsively, were perceived as "bad boys" if they were men, and "sluts" if they were women. Psychotherapists viewed male sex addicts as symptoms of our culture, and women's behaviors were seen as symptoms of other issues. Therapists condoned compulsive masturbation and other addictive behaviors, reassuring clients by saying that masturbation is healthy. Although it is true that loving oneself sexually can be entirely healthy, most masturbation is not. The enormous culturewide association of shame with masturbation prevents almost all people from touching themselves in loving, sexual ways. Instead of helping a person learn about an unhealthy use of sexual energy, therapists could do no more than remove some of the intense shame associated with it. Until the mid 1980s, I felt helpful when I told clients that masturbation was normal and regarded an extramarital affair as an individual's choice of nonmonogamy. Until I read *Out of the Shadows*, I was unable to hear that my clients were suffering from a shame-ridden, addictive use of sexuality and needed help.

Most psychotherapists and the rest of society have so far been unable to see sex addiction for what it is. This is because our culture supports sex addiction with constant references to its symptoms as "normal."

§ CULTURAL SHAME CREATES CULTURAL ADDICTION §

Sexual energy is used addictively whenever it is used to change one's mood, prevent one from thinking certain thoughts, or in any way to avoid something. Thus one can't be entirely present with oneself and/or one's partner.

Tony gave the men's group a good example of the pressure to become and stay a sex addict. He and another group member worked in the fishing industry, a business that is fraught with sexual acting out and competition to establish masculinity. Tony said that if he talked to co-workers about his loving bond with his girlfriend, they would have seen him as "pussy whipped." Not only did he want to flirt with women and cross sexual boundaries, he also felt the need to do so in order to be seen as masculine—a real man. As he began his recovery from sexual addiction, he was very uncomfortable avoiding peer pressure to act out. Not only did he have to fight against his own desire to sexualize relationships, but also he had to fight against his fear of the consequences if he did so.

The vast amount of shame that has been overlaid onto sex from birth prevents all of us from having sex while being entirely conscious of where we are, who we are with, and what we are doing. Without awareness of the process of removing shame, we as a culture have been left with the task of figuring out how to have sex. (I described the shame compartment and the various ways we have devised to get into it in Chapter 7.)

If we cannot have sex without shame, then we have had to figure out how to continue being sexual by setting the shame aside. If we must prevent feeling shame, then we cannot at the same time be present with our partner and ourselves during sex. *By definition, then, we must engage in an addictive use of sex to override the shame, to alter the thoughts and feelings that would emerge if we had sex while conscious and present.* It is the cultural shaming of sexuality that requires all of us to discover how we can be sexual without giving in to the shame. Many people are not able to and give up sex most of the time. But most of us have figured out how to use the various culturally approved methods of overriding culturally induced shame. These include lust, pornography, romance, the experience of a sex drive, flirting, sexual fantasy, and falling "madly in love." The addictive use of sexual energy is also served by using sex to prove that one is loved, to feel like a real man or real woman, to satisfy the requirement to be in a relationship, to try to conceive children, to feel safe, and to feel in control. These are all components of our culture's definition of appropriate sex, and they prevent us from seeing that our culture supports us in using sex addictively instead of supporting a real, life-enhancing, spiritually based, intimate, present, and loving use of sexual energy.

In order for each one of us to heal our sexuality, we have to create new mirrors for healthy sex and see that the old mirrors are, in fact, distorted from centuries of trying to deal with sexual shame. If all we can do is "cope" and "adjust," then the solutions devised by traditional sex therapists are as good as we can do. But if we want to truly heal our individual sexuality and that of our culture, we have to see what is wrong with the picture that is presented to us by our families, friends, the media, and traditional sex therapists. If we do this, then we have the chance to discover the true nature of this energy.

It Can Be Helpful to Call It Addiction

Many people arrive in my office knowing something is wrong, but they don't have a name for it. Many feel relief when they can see that their symptoms are common in our culture and can be addressed.

Tom came to my Healthy Sexual Energy class resistant to the idea that he was a sex addict. He had recovered well from drugs and alcohol but wasn't comfortable with his sexual relationship with his partner. He left angry at the end of the weekend, because he was beginning to see that he was addicted to sexual energy, and it was preventing him from having a loving sexual relationship. Tom's "bottom-line" behavior was looking at women he found sexually attractive and imagining having sex with them when he masturbated or had sex with his partner. This is not outside our culture's norm, and it is recommended by traditional sex therapists for people who want to spice up their sexual appetite. He would not be diagnosed as a sex addict by any specialist in sex addiction. He was able to work full time, go to school, and maintain a social life. His sexual choices did not interfere with time commitments or attention needed elsewhere. His only symptom was that he and his partner had passed the period of initial bonding, and both were losing interest in sex. Now in their forties, neither wanted to repeat old patterns of finding new lovers with whom the sexual interest would be stronger.

A year passed before he could enter therapy, which included a men's group, and begin to explore his sexuality. After a few weeks, he came to the group feeling lighter and explained that he realized that he was a sex addict, and that he could use the same methods that had worked with alcohol and drugs to approach this too. In addition, he could see from talking with the men that all of them had been set up for sex addiction by the shaming of our culture, by sexual secrecy, and by their mothers, whose lack of sexual boundaries did not permit them to see what they were doing with their sons. (*From Generation to Generation: Understanding Sexual Attraction to Children* offers information about mothers' lack of understanding of sexual boundaries with their children, the shame that accompanies it, and the difficulty perceiving that they are doing something harmful.)

The first step of the twelve-step programs, admitting powerlessness, helps remove guilt and shame from sexual behavior, thus making it easier to look at. Once Tom could take this step, he was able to look at his acting out when it happened and begin the process of examining the cycle that brought it about. He could learn that he felt like a failure right before switching into sexual scanning and fantasy. Then the cycle became obvious to him. When he scanned, he gave his power away to the women he looked at, feeling like their object and victim. He then wanted to masturbate to make himself feel better. But the masturbation added more shame, increasing the need to be sexual to relieve the bad feeling. In addition, he always knew that he was out of personal integrity when he used a woman for this purpose, and this increased bad feelings he wanted to medicate with sexual arousal.

As Tom's guilt and shame dropped, he was able to tell the group about the times he acted out in the old ways, and of his exploration of a more self-affirming kind of sex, even when being sexual with himself.

A man who came to a talk I gave offered a similar example. He told about his job in construction, which sometimes required cleaning very filthy, smelly places. One day, well into his sex-addiction recovery, he realized that he had gone into sexual fantasy in order to avoid the unpleasantness of the task. He could effectively remove himself from the present and have no feelings generated by what he was doing. As he told about this, I guessed that not many people in the room understood the significance of what he was saying. He went on to explain how fantasy put him further into his addiction, increasing the chances that he might act out more seriously, and how it had taken him out of integrity to pretend he was someplace other than where he was. He passionately knew the importance of staying in the present as much as possible to recover fully from any addiction.

In my own life, I discovered that my sexual-fantasy addiction prevented me from feeling shame in quite ordinary, everyday places. I had neglected to give money with the check to the clerk at a restaurant and didn't understand why he stood there looking at me expectantly. When I realized what had happened, as I reached into my purse, I felt the warm, loving arms of a man wrapped around me. The shame was pushed aside, replaced by feelings of being loved. Yet there was no man, and at that time, I had no man in my life. By becoming conscious of what I had done, I was able to see all the ways I used brief fantasy to prevent unpleasant feelings. If I were in a relationship, I used the man I was with. If I wasn't, the man would be faceless, but big and strong and loving.

I told this example to a number of people, and few understood its significance. It seemed small compared to getting drunk every night and missing work the next day. More recently, as I am around people who are seeking full recovery, I am receiving better mirrors for the seriousness of my fantasy addiction. People in general have a more difficult time understanding that this small event is part of a culturewide addictive use of sexual energy, even though it doesn't look as serious as my days of sitting through college classes unable to hear anything the teacher was saying because I was replaying my last sexual encounter in my head, unable to choose to stop.

The concept of the addictive use of sexual energy is most useful when viewed as a continuum that goes from no addiction to complete addiction. What follows is one view of how that continuum might look.

Continuum of Sexual Addictiveness

1. *There is a complete lack of addictiveness.* Our culture makes this possibility extremely slim. Sexual activity emerges out of your relationship as an expansion of intimacy that is already occurring. Masturbation is self-loving, focused on knowing yourself.

2. *Activities are completely acceptable by our society.* Basic quality of life is not disrupted. Thoughts and activities are reused to distract you from some general feeling of absence or

emptiness in life, often called boredom. Sex or romance seems appealing to meet needs not being met in other ways. Masturbation is often "something to do." A person at this level is not addicted to sexual energy but is using it addictively.

3. *Sex seems to be the most important facet of life.* You use a large percentage of your time to think about and plan for sexual encounters or masturbation. You know what a sexual-trance state is like and enjoy it, because it brings pleasure when life holds little elsewhere. You take occasional risks, such as having an affair or buying a prostitute, and then feel remorse and fear when you return to clear thinking. You find it distressing, even frightening, if your partner wants sex less than you do. The purpose of masturbation is to administer the sex drug. The addiction is underway.

4. *You feel driven and must be sexual, with feelings of urgency and pressure.* You are consumed by the need to do it again and again, and the sexual-trance state becomes a greater part of your life. Thoughts and intense sexual feelings focus on the search, the person, or the place that will make everything all right. For periods of time, life is unmanageable, but you have sufficient ability to concentrate on nonsexual things to be able to pull it back together once again. A person at this level is truly addicted.

5. *Sexual activities have resulted in severe consequences, such as loss of family, loss of job, or arrest.* Great amounts of time are lost to the pursuit of sexual activity. Money is spent with no regard for the consequences. Life is totally unmanageable.

§ ADVERTISING USES SEXUAL ENERGY §

One look at advertising will tell us that the vast majority of us will respond to sexual stimuli by changing our moods and thus our attitude toward the product. (I explain how advertising matches our cross-wiring—nudity, "sexy" people, and soft incest scenes—in Chapter 12, Advertisers Encourage and Exploit Unhealthy Cultural Attitudes.) In addition to our cross-wiring to respond to certain kinds of stimuli, we as a culture are drawn to the sexual as a way to divert ourselves from being in the present. *Advertisers didn't create this response. They have learned how to use it to get us to feel differently—the definition of addiction.* And then, as our feelings change, they want us to look longer than we might without the sexual stimuli, and as we look, associate a positive feeling with the product.

§THE VITAL ROLE OF SEX-ADDICTION RECOVERY§

Recovering sex addicts have discovered how damaging it is to be sexual in any but healthy ways. They have a large price to pay, because even simple things such as flirting with someone at a party removes them from themselves, from their partners, and may trigger a major form of acting out. Sex addicts must learn about the many ways we are triggered in order to heal. But the rest of the culture isn't, and so most people go blindly on exchanging sexual energy, objectifying and being objectified, without seeing that it is part of a cultural symptom. We cannot heal our culture until many of us discover all the ways we use sexual energy that do not serve its true nature, and by example, create mirrors for the rest to follow. This is why sexual-addiction recovery is so vital to the sexual healing of our culture.

§EXAMPLES OF "INNOCENT" ADDICTIVE USE OF SEXUAL ENERGY§

Sexual Innuendo

Sexual innuendo is a common form of lighthearted banter that plays on double meanings and stimulates a seeming aliveness. I find that when I have been around a person for some time who does this, I begin to do it myself. A part of my intellectual creativity becomes engaged, and I feel stimulated by how clever my mind can be. In addition, the charge from the subject of sex increases the stimulation even more. But the effect is negative. My awareness leaves my body, I disrespect myself, and my abuser patterns emerge. When this happens, I use the information for further healing. But after years of sexual healing, I find that when I engage in this kind of conversation, I don't like the feeling of losing myself, and I quickly want to stop.

In years past, when I was heavily into my sex addiction, I looked forward to evenings with people who would engage in this kind of banter. I always wanted an alcoholic drink first, which removed my inhibitions. If someone had told me this behavior was part of sex addiction, I would have been stunned. I might have pointed out that I didn't want to have sex with anyone. One of my favorite compadres was a gay man, proving that this wasn't about having sex. But the charge was sexual.

Sexual Stimuli

Sexual stimuli, such as posters of "sexy" people, that are kept on display are examples of the addictive use of sexual energy. The movement against sexual harassment brought to public attention that sexual stimuli are common in many work areas, and for the first time, labeled them as offensive. We now have a cultural disagreement. One faction says this is harmful, and another says this is just the way men are.

Anytime people look at a partially nude body while engaged in another activity, sexual energy is used to divert energy from the reality of their present lives. This is quite different from turning to another stimulus, such as looking at trees and flowers outside a window, an experience that can expand one, providing energy to pour into the task. When taking in stimuli in an addictive way, we become stimulated, but not in a way that enhances our whole life.

Sexual Highs

Another "innocent" use of sexual energy is when two or more men create a sexual high by focusing on women around them. Richard told his men's group about how he and a buddy pointed out "sexy" women to each other, asking questions such as, "Would you 'do' her?", working themselves into a fevered pitch with the conversation. He was less than comfortable when I told him this is a way men get to be sexual with each other without actually having sex. Our culture is homophobic, preventing most men from exploring the possibility of having sex with each other. When men can't explore that option, they remain curious and must suppress the curiosity and figure out how to express it indirectly. The sexual activity is primarily going on between men, and women are excuses to talk sexually and become aroused. This conversation is carried on in the context of addiction to women, because if the men were to talk seriously about being sexual, they might find themselves becoming sexual with each other. The "men are like that" belief provides safety.

Flirting

Flirting is so culturally acceptable that the person who is jealous of their partner is usually seen as the one with a problem. (See Chapter 5, Healthy Jealousy, for more information.) Our culture has integrated boundaryless sexuality into its sexual expression, which has rendered us unable to see that it is an addictive use of sexual energy. Because flirting isn't part of healthy sexuality (unless it is expressed by people who are available, and directed toward others who are available), it must be addictive, because it brings on an altered state of consciousness. People light up when they flirt. False boundary dropping takes place. Moods elevate. If it is done in the service of a healthy search for a partner, or to rebond partners, then it can be fully life enhancing instead of functioning to alter one's mood.

Romance

Romance is built into our culture, and is confused with the initial, intense period of sexual bonding that allows two people to quickly become a family.

§ ARE YOU USING SEXUAL ENERGY ADDICTIVELY? §

Yes. Because you were raised in this culture, you can assume you are in some way using sexual energy to change your feelings or to communicate with other people in a manner to heighten the exchange. The only exceptions are people who have engaged in extensive sexual healing and released great amounts of shame.

For centuries, people have tried to use religion to absolve themselves of shame. Others have worked to clean up sexuality through laws and public outcry. But these methods don't address the need to relinquish sexual shame, and most people don't realize that we will automatically find sexual health if we do so. Instead, religions often add further shame when members are unable to abstain from their cross-wired activities. Those who are able to follow the religious sanctions can feel successful and thus not feel their shame. But although they have been successful in not acting on cross-wiring, healing of sexuality has not occurred. Although this can help people feel better about themselves, it doesn't *remove* the shame attached to sexuality.

If you have tried to suppress all evidence of your sexuality, you haven't succeeded. Even if you don't feel sexual at all, you cannot have clear sexual boundaries. Instead, it is coming out in ways that you don't recognize. In my pubescent years, two sisters in their sixties, who were friends of the family and never married, admired my summer tan. I was flattered and loved the attention, not realizing until years later that these seemingly sexless women were using sexual energy and I was the sex object. If a boy my age had done the same, I could have seen it more clearly, but our culture defines old women as sexless, particularly if they have never married. These women might have been lesbians, or they might have inhibited all overt expression of sexuality. In either case, they did display sexual energy in a manner that felt safe to them.

My client Kenneth told about how his "acting out" took the form of conversations about food with women—strangers—in checkout lines. He noticed what was in their baskets and spoke with well-developed charm about what they were going to fix. The conversation often became filled with details about sauces and delicate seasonings, with moans of pleasure and sexualized facial expressions. He knew the women would leave the store feeling more lively and never consciously know they had just had a sexual encounter. Many of these exchanges resulted in women wanting to be sexual with him, believing it was their idea. In his recovery, he knew he wouldn't have sex with them, but he still enjoyed the addictive "hit." This was a more difficult behavior to add to his list of what to let go of to achieve "sobriety."

In addition to being a gourmet cook, Kenneth also knew a great deal about expensive clothes, which he wore for effect, even when he couldn't afford it. He could engage women by how he looked and then discuss the designers of the garments they wore. He did this while looking closely at their attire, admiring, and sometimes touching fabric. As his charming, charismatic, sexualized attention poured out, he was able to cross physical boundaries that women would not permit most other people in the mall.

Early in his recovery, Kenneth couldn't compare this behavior with his search for prostitutes and for a woman who wanted to admire his penis. But as his education grew, he came to see that flirting over discussions of food and clothes was accomplishing the same thing as did the socially unacceptable forms of sexual acting out.

People around Kenneth and the women he conversed with wouldn't have seen anything wrong with what was happening. In fact, I'm sure many were envious and would have liked to join in. Instead of seeing sex addicts and their drugs, they saw a pair of beautiful people, perfectly dressed, on top of the world, and having a perfectly lovely exchange.

§ WOMEN EXCHANGE SEXUAL ENERGY §

Heterosexual women who use sexual energy to gather attention from others will frequently do so with other women too. It is called charm and charisma, as it was with Kenneth. When I am wondering if my perception is accurate, I ask myself how I would feel if my husband were either giving or receiving attention like that. If I would be jealous, I can make the switch to seeing that the interaction is laced with sexual energy. I would also expect their partners to feel left out and appropriately jealous. Often such women are coupled with men who also put out charismatic charm, and they can all join together to share it. Kenneth described a situation in which he and his partner met a charming man, and the three of them exchanged sexual energy. The man's wife didn't join in and was considered uninteresting and dull. Kenneth and his partner got a hit without instilling jealousy in each other. One way to begin your education is to notice when people—or yourself—are exchanging looks that seem appropriate to lovers.

§ MOTHERS WITH CHILDREN §

The exchange of sexual energy between mothers and children is the most forbidden area to explore in our culture. Yet it is commonplace for mothers to direct sexual energy when they are unable to engage fully in a sexual relationship or send out sexual energy toward available people when not in a relationship. As with Kenneth's examples, our culture is so accustomed to mothers' flirting with their children that we don't perceive it as sexual. We usually see it as loving and affectionate, a sign that a mother really cares about her child. The mother isn't aware that she is using sexual energy either and so doesn't understand when her child then approaches her sexually. The child receives the sexual energy, perceives it as fitting into this broad category of feeling, and so engages with her as if she were the one who started it. But the mother feels like the child's victim when the child persists.

Lauren was unaware that she directed sexual energy toward her child. She and the child's father separated in her infancy, and Lauren moved in with her ex-husband, now a friend. Lauren watched her ex-husband have an active sex life, while Lauren was having none. In fact, she felt quite sexless. Prior to the birth of her child, she had been highly focused on her sexual attractiveness, attending to her clothes, makeup, and hair. But when the child was born, she turned away from her pursuit of sexual attention. Unknowingly, she directed her sexuality toward her daughter, confusing it with the intense energy involved in bonding between mother and infant.

When the child was two, she would regularly go to her mother, put both hands down her mother's shirt, and fondle her breasts. When people commented, Lauren calmly explained that she had always done this, and it was because of the importance of breasts when she had been breast-fed. Lauren didn't think it was right to stop her, because it seemed to provide reassurance. In fact, the child was using a known method of getting her mother to attend to her. This could be the beginning of addiction to sexual energy that could last into her adult life. She might seek sexual attention from men, as her mother had, as a way to reexperience the reassurance she sought from her mother.

As I write this, I know that you may be confused about your own sexual energy and wonder also about those around you. The answers may not come easily. It takes substantial sexual healing to know if and when we are sending out sexual energy, because our culture has told us that so much that is sexual isn't (and that much of what isn't sexual is). Even if you are sending sexual energy toward your child, you can't just stop by deciding to do so. A lengthy process is required, including meeting with other women or men to share stories. Raising consciousness is the vital first step—seeing how others are exchanging sexual energy and remembering how your parents were with you, for example. I want to caution you not to avoid your child from fear that you may be violating him or her. Pulling back from physical contact is harmful to the child too, teaching that his or her body is to be avoided. If you can, accept yourself as you are, knowing you have been harmed by this culture and that there is no way you can provide your children with a perfect sexual childhood. Please read Chapter 3, Monogamously Bonding Creatures in a Healthy Culture (or listen to it on an audiotape, entitled *Healthy Sex: Real Life Stories of Bonding, Monogamous, Joyful, Shame-Free, Rule-Free Sex*). It can help you see how different the ideal is from how you grew up, and from the culture in which you are trying to raise children.

§ WOMEN MAKE THEMSELVES UP TO BE "SEXY" §

Our culture reveres beautiful, sexy women, as long as they don't look like prostitutes. As we have created men to search lustfully for beautiful women, we have created women to be the counterparts—the one who is a worthy lust object. It is confusing to women to have our value defined by our sexiness and, at the same time, to have that sexiness used for impersonal lusting or as the reason a man wants to be in a relationship, irrespective of our other qualities. Living in a sexually addictive culture has made it impossible for a couple to bond with each other and exclude sexual energy going elsewhere, unless they have been in substantial sexual recovery. We are cursed by our culture's beliefs.

I have often heard women say that when they age, they become invisible. The truth is, they are no longer lusted after. They are no longer culturally defined sex objects. Even when they were, they were not seen. They have lost nothing except false attention to something that is not inherently about them.

But our culture's valuing of certain qualities that have been defined as sexual makes them feel that they have lost something when they no longer elicit lust. This cultural dynamic will continue until enough of us have refused to be involved, even if it means we cannot be in relationships. Some recovering male sex addicts are finding that as they become the kind of men they have heard women want—sensitive, nonlusting, loving, and not responsive to external sexual stimuli—many women are no longer interested. Women want to be loved and cherished, but the strong cultural association between sexual attractiveness and worth can prevent them from being with such a man.

§ ADDICTION TO ROMANCE §

Women in our country have always been allowed to use sexual energy romantically. In the past two decades, women are allowed to invite sexual activity more directly, but romance remains the primary sexual expression that allows women to move into the shame compartment and reduce sexual shame.

In my own history of addiction to sexual energy, romance was the primary form of my fantasies. As I created ongoing stories of my relationships with men, rarely did sexual activity occur. The focus of my arousal was on the man's attention to me and then violating me. If I had imagined having sex, my shame would have emerged, and the purpose of the fantasy—to remove feelings of emptiness and loneliness—would have been negated.

In current years, a woman can fantasize actual sexual interaction without bringing on shame if the man they are with focuses on being in love, admires her beauty, and expresses interest in sex as a desire to couple with her. Or she can imagine feeling hurt if he has sex in ways that aren't based on this kind of love.

Many women use pornography and fantasize sex for the sake of sex, but the point I want to make is that the culturally sanctioned use of sexual energy is within the context of a romantic relationship. If a woman uses sexuality in ways that are sanctioned for men, she will have to use the same methods for avoiding feelings of shame that men are allowed to use. One effect of feminism is that women feel more entitled to approach sex in ways that men have. This change hasn't allowed women to have a healthier use of sexuality. Rather, it allows more choices of ways to get into the shame compartment and different ways to express sexuality.

Differentiating romance as an addictive tool from real feelings of affection and love is not easy. Romance is a distortion of a very real, intense, loving, sexualized exchange that is part of a natural, human process—bonding into a couple. During that early period in a relationship, it is healthy for two people to contact each other frequently, to want to touch each other often, including in public, to express feelings about the developing love bond, and to make clear that this other person is most important. This initial intensity will pass as the relationship takes on more the quality of normal life, and sexual energy will be used more to reaffirm the connection.

Addictive romance is the use of these activities in ways that don't serve the coupling bond, and instead, distract from unpleasant feelings. Instead of sex healthily emerging out of intimate, loving, shame-free feelings, it comes from a need to avoid unpleasant feelings, such as shame, emptiness, and loneliness. One of the most important feelings is sexual shame, generated by our culture's shaming of sexuality. If a woman doesn't continue receiving romancing from her partner, she may find it more difficult to override the shame and become sexual. She is no longer able to use either the initial bonding or the romanticization of the relationship to enter the shame compartment. People who are addicted to romance often like long-distance relationships, because it is easier to maintain the romance and yearning that accompanies early bonding. As they are perpetually torn apart, they naturally focus on sex to rebond them. Such relationships often fall apart or have sexual difficulties when the couple reunites.

Addiction to romance can be seen as a form of sexual energy addiction. Sex itself isn't necessarily part of the addictive acting out, but the feeling of sexual-bonding energy and the desire to be together sexually serve to make the rest of life tolerable or irrelevant.

Our culture supports this kind of addiction by glorifying romance. Valentine's Day is a day of prescribed romance, and men are evaluated and compared on the basis of their ability to sweep a woman off her feet. If he doesn't, she is entitled by those around her to feel hurt and let down. No one suggests that perhaps the expectation is harmful, and that roses and restaurants have nothing to do with love.

§ Learning about Socially Sanctioned Sexualization §

There are countless forms of sexual expression that we don't see, or we accept as normal. I invite you to begin your own questioning, perhaps starting with how you express sexual energy. You could also look at those times you have been uncomfortable but haven't been able to identify the cause as an exchange of sexual energy. I spent years wanting to be sexually attractive and buying clothes that made me look that way, only to find I was too uncomfortable to wear them. Only now can I see that the discomfort was from being a sex object of people who were looking for a fix. I wanted both to be objectified—to meet our culture's definition of female worth—and not to serve as female body parts.

Kenneth's group of three couples met with me bimonthly for months before they were able to see that they put out sexual energy with each other and others in order to feel more strongly bonded and important to each other. When I first described a woman putting out sexual energy, the group was shocked. They wanted to tell me that she and the others always did this, and it wasn't sexual. But very quickly they could see that it was, and they began looking at all of their sexualizing. Their conscious-ness had been raised by one example, and they were able to then examine for themselves what they were doing.

§ LEGISLATION IS NOT THE ANSWER §

Although laws are necessary to protect us from violent acts against children and adults, legislation that tries to define obscenity and control sexual acts between consenting adults will not bring about cultural change. Instead, we have had argu-ments for decades about what is acceptable sexual behavior and what isn't. These arguments are useless, because change in sexual desires and behaviors doesn't come from laws. In addi-tion, laws further shame sexual behavior, which will have an effect the opposite of that which is desired.

As we talk about sexuality, remove shame, and discover the healthy kind, interest in sexual activities that are not healthy will drop automatically. It is then that we will see decreases in the purchase of sexual services. As each person discovers how it feels to engage intimately with sexual energy, there will be no need to purchase cross-wired stimulation.

§ CHILDREN CAN'T TALK OPENLY ABOUT SEX §

As I wrote this chapter, I fought my inner voices that were saying I was making it all up. Our culture can't be so blind and cut off from sexuality as I have been making it out to be. Certainly, with all the sexuality on television, children under-stand sex, accept it, and are more healthy than we were when we were their age. But I got to see again the truth of what I was writing as I finished this chapter on a Lake Washington dock. A boy about eleven curiously watched me typing on my laptop computer. He was part of a normal-looking family of five, with affectionate parents and an adored baby. Finally he approached and asked me if I was an author. When I said "yes," he eagerly wanted to know the names of my books. I hesitated momentarily, guessing that he didn't want to know they were about sex. Sure enough, he stepped back as I said the names, his energy pulled in, and his interest dissolved. By the time I got to the third title, I was talking only to myself. He moved quickly away. A victim of our culture that shames sex, he can't talk about it openly—particularly with an adult woman. He had no way to get in the shame compartment in my presence. He couldn't joke or whisper. Minutes later I saw him giggling with his brothers, apparently telling them about me, now able to use methods to avoid feeling shame.

10

THE MATING DANCE GONE AWRY

§

Sexual Harassment and Objectification

In an ideal world, two unattached people send sexual energy toward each other, exploring a potential love relationship. This is healthy. But when the pleasure of sending and receiving sexual energy becomes cross-wired to lust, control, power, searching for love, self-esteem, and myriad other nonsexual facets of life, then we have sexual relating that isn't healthy—one form of which has become known as sexual harassment.

This subject has gained in popularity since the advent of the women's movement and particularly after the accusations of Anita Hill prior to the confirmation of Clarence Thomas to the Supreme Court in October 1991. The media generally polarize the issue by seeing either the man as guilty and shameful, or the woman as responsible for enticing him, lying to harm him, or not setting clear limits. Men feel shamed when accused of being inappropriately sexual.

The perception of women as victims or shameful accusers prevents us from seeing the whole picture. We can instead take a look at the behavior of both men and women and see how it fits into the cultural sickness that prevents us from respecting each other's sexuality. This sickness is better labeled "gender objectification," with sexual harassment falling at one end of a continuum.

§ SEXUAL HARASSMENT IN THE WORKPLACE §

Sexual harassment is a form of objectification, with an aggressive or desperate component expressed toward another person. Cases that arrive in court are made up of people whose lives are made difficult after refusing to have dates or sex with a boss; people who are tormented with sexual comments; and people who are subjected to sexual jokes, pictures, and other communications from the shame compartment.

Susan Webb is a Seattle-based expert on the subject and an educator for businesses of all sizes. She publishes a newsletter that recounts stories of prosecutions and other valuable information. An article by Webb took a look at research on bullies.[1] She says that bullies in childhood remain aggressive in adult life and suggests that those who harass others sexually may have been bullies as children.

Those who harass differ only in degree from those who objectify in ways that are culturally acceptable. As the women and men in my groups spoke about ways they objectify and are objectified, the stories were similar to those of people who are prosecuted. The law only limits the extreme form of culturally programmed behavior, with little understanding of the broader phenomenon that underlies it. As with other sexual difficulties addressed in this book, sexual harassment will only disappear as our culture changes its views of sexuality.

A contradiction appears throughout Webb's reports on surveys asking employees about what goes on. Men are seen as the harassers and women as the harassed, even though research consistently indicates that for every three women who on a questionnaire indicate they were harassed, one man will also report that he was asked for sexual favors or otherwise affronted sexually. Our culture supports lack of reporting by men. If a man is sexually suggestive with a woman, she can find this unpleasant and object to it. But if a woman is suggestive with a man, he must view it as flattering if he is to be seen as a "real man." He cannot object.

Eddie Murphy's movie, *Boomerang*, portrays the situation in reverse, with his character playing the female role, and his female boss playing the male role. His character portrays the stereotypical behaviors of women who are seen as the sexual objects of men, including waiting by the phone for her to call, waiting for the next date, being angry when she doesn't show up for an expensive date because she took a later plane from a business meeting, and falling apart when she dumps him after he falls in love with her. The boss is given the traits associated with men. She couldn't care less about a delicate seasoning he prepared for the salmon, wants to eat the gourmet meal in front of the Lakers' game, controls his sexual arousal and doesn't respect his desire to postpone his orgasm, is always on top during sex, and comments on how sex was good for relieving her tension. She says she will call him when she has time to get together again, and she has her secretary make their dates. When she dumps him, his self-esteem drops and drops again when he goes to the office to find all the women smiling knowingly at him. His depression deepens until he falls in love with another woman. When he comes out of it, his boss again wants to have sex with him, telling him she likes it that he is back to his old self. The story is classic. Only the roles are reversed. The points are hard to miss, especially when the person who is harassed is played by Eddie Murphy, noted for sexual confidence.

§ MEN AND WOMEN HARASS AND ARE HARASSED §

I invited members of both the men's and the women's groups, introduced in Chapter 4, to discuss their feelings and experiences on the subject of sexual objectification that leads to harassment. Both groups spent a year discharging shame on the topic of sexuality by talking in detail about sex and sexual relationships. As shame dropped over the course of the meetings, each person became able to see his or her own sexual patterns and was better able to see the issues of the other sex. Each group met for four hours and then came together for another three hours.

§ The Men's Group §

Allen launched into his observations as soon as the group convened. In his mid forties, Allen is a successful businessman with his own company and a large circle of friends. He entered therapy because he had not been able to enter into a long-term relationship leading to marriage. Over the past year, he made a radical shift from evaluating women based on leg shape and the amount of sexual energy they exuded, to seeing the whole person. He was now in a new relationship, one based on honesty and in which the unfolding of sexual energy and commitment were permitted. For the first time, Allen was able to discover commitment from the inside-out, in contrast to his attempts to "make a commitment" and stick with it. This prior approach served only to force him to withhold feelings and quickly grow to resent his partner.

Allen talked about the "male bonding" function of "going out to pick up chicks," as his high school friends had called it. The men could be together as buddies and at the same time invoke the excitement of the bonding instinct. When I asked this man, now so aware of women's feelings, how men could drive on a freeway in an open Jeep, calling out to a woman in the next car, who obviously did not invite or want their attention (a scene I had observed days before), he told me they didn't have any idea what was happening with the woman. Their behavior had been so automated, and the connections between the teenage men and women so absent, that the women were truly no more than objects to which they were supposed to relate in predictable ways. The culture had so entirely determined their behavior that they didn't know what was really happening.

Allen told of walking with his date and her sister, who had large breasts. A man driving past said, "Nice tits." When Allen saw the woman's reaction to this uninvited comment, he, for the first time, saw that this was painful to her. It was many more years until he, in the men's group, could see that his choice of women based on body shape was also part of an unreal perception. He lamented the lack of dialogue between men and women that could have allowed him to understand years earlier. He found the workshops, where the men's and women's groups came together, incredibly informative, providing information and understanding he needed when he was a teen.

Allen elaborated on the difficulty men have understanding the pain women experience when they are sexually objectified. He pointed out that men are taught through the existence of *Playboy*, jokes, and innuendo that women are present for the purpose of helping men get off sexually. Our culture sets men up to feel like a "bubbling caldron of sexuality" by repressing direct expression and even direct conversation. "Seeing a beautiful woman made me feel good. She stepped out of the magazine. There she is. They really are walking around looking like that." The *Playboy* centerfold becomes a way to "bleed off this energy by masturbating, providing an escape valve." The women in the magazine give permission to be used for sexual release, and young men adopt the view of women as there for this function in their sex lives.

Allen went on to explain that when the real thing appears on the street or behind a desk, it seems to be an extension of the *Playboy* model—there for his use. The women's feelings are not seen, because they have never been part of a man's sex education, and so he can easily use her without knowing that what he is doing is not healthy for her or himself. Allen said, "There is a mythical link between the man and the bunny. You don't expect interaction with her; it's just a fantasy relationship. She isn't anything. Seeing a real woman just takes it one step further. You project the image onto her that she likes that and is complimented by it, as the bunny seems to be."

As he continued to talk, Allen recounted an evening from the week before when he was ending a business discussion with a man at the door to his office. As Allen turned to reenter the building, the man asked him to wait with him a minute. Allen noticed a woman walking toward them and realized that the man wanted Allen to stand there with him as an excuse to watch her pass. After his year in the men's group, Allen saw the scene through two perspectives. He automatically joined the man in an almost lifelong response to women who have made themselves up to be "sexy," and at the same time, saw the position the woman was in.

The woman was aware that men were watching her, and that they would stare more openly once she had passed and could no longer see them. Allen decided to do nothing different and just observe. As he did so, he imagined changing the scenario in a couple of ways. One was to continue standing with the man, but look at *him* and not the woman, not joining in the usual camaraderie expected of him. He believed the man would be uncomfortable and feel some alienation from Allen. If he were to go a step further and tell the man he was objectifying the woman, which is a form of harassment, the man would look at him as if he were crazy. He might also be angry and perhaps change his relationship with Allen's company. As he pondered the circumstances, Allen could see the plight women are in as they wish to draw limits around sexualization of relating, but are afraid of the consequences in the workplace. Allen experienced similar concerns as he considered setting limits about his involvement with others who want to objectify women.

Kenneth, whose sexual-addiction recovery was introduced in Chapter 4, brought up the fact that he doesn't know how to be with women without being sexual. Only since his sexual recovery began has he opened himself to exploring relationships that are not based on sexual exchange. Like Allen, he had no opportunity during his adolescence to explore sexual feelings openly, and girls and boys were not able to talk about what they were experiencing. In our culture, the division between men and women can be crossed by people who enter sexual relationships. As a result, men and women who aren't in relationships know primarily about sexualized exchange as a way to relate. Few people have the benefit of growing up in a community of peers, where both sexes really get to know each other. Even for those who do, the area of sexual discussion is usually off-limits, and so remains a mystery.

Kenneth went on to say that now that he has agreed to stop objectifying women, he is even more aware that they seem like strange creatures. As he gets to know each one, as in the mixed therapy group he attended for two years, she becomes a person. But even this intimate relating, along with other friendships, hasn't erased the perception of women as belonging in a category of humanity that is beyond comprehension. Men seem to be "people," and women seem to be "something else."

Kenneth went on to explore the nature of his feelings about bonding. He said that he doesn't feel secure in any relationship unless it is sexual, because the bond can be so easily broken. With both men and women, he doesn't believe he is sufficiently valuable to others that they would want to remain his friend. In contrast, when sexual bonding anchors people together, they have great difficulty separating. Although the relationship may not be good, the bond is difficult to break. Kenneth was aware that this encouraged him to use sexual energy with women, even if neither he nor they were available for relationships. The result was a number of friendships with women, which made his ex-wife jealous when they were married. She intuitively knew that the sexual bond was a misdirection of his sexual energy away from her bond with him. Both, however, thought that his flirting was harmless and she had a problem with jealousy. But his need to be sexually bonded with women also led him to put out sexual energy when it was not welcomed. And so, prior to his sexual recovery, he approached women in ways that brought up their victim patterns. By being the "victimizer," he engaged women who would immediately respond with their own history of being victimized and not be able to stop him. If they had been able to press charges, he would have been guilty of sexual harassment.

Andrew pondered what he was hearing from the men in the group and then offered his experience about being sexually harassed by men. Andrew is a sex addict whose sex object is men.

As he spoke about sexual objectification, he expressed his belief that if he is open with others and they want to be sexual, he has no choice (much as the women approached by Kenneth cannot say no). If he is to receive affection, then he has no choice but to be sexual, if that is what is wanted. Although he believed his perceptions were colored by the homosexual nature of his sexual activities, the rest of the group could see that his were identical to theirs. *Men are required to be sexual if a woman wants that, and women feel pressure to cooperate if a man wants sex.* Andrew's way of responding to this cultural myth is not to have relationships and to control the interactions he had with men. He saw them once, when he had decided ahead of time that he wanted to be sexual. In this way, Andrew prevented himself from feeling abused.

As Andrew could see how his choices had served him, it also became clear how Kenneth's understanding of the requirement to be sexual fit in here too. Kenneth felt entitled to use sexual energy, whereas Andrew felt obligated to provide it for those who felt entitled. The cumbersome requirements to bond with sexual energy make it unappealing to many, as it was for Andrew, whereas others avoid loneliness by coercing partners to bond.

These men are expressing the confusion that leads to sexual harassment. *The real nature of sexuality, with boundaries and choice free of obligation, is difficult, if not impossible, for those in our culture to access.* The confusion about what men and women deserve from each other and the lack of understanding of the inside-out unfolding of sexual energy sets up both genders to violate each other's boundaries.

Shame, Authority, and Harassment

None of the men in the men's group had been in a position of power with women employees and harassed them with sexual demands or comments, so they could not shed light on the experience. However, each could understand how a man might feel victimized by the mere presence of a woman who was considered higher on the attractiveness scale than himself, and who would not validate his manhood. If such a woman were to come under his authority, it was understandable that he would want to use that authority to gain sexual favors and bring the woman "down to his level," or bring himself up to hers. He can reduce her "value" by having her sexually, or he can enhance his perception of his worth by having an attractive woman be sexual with him. The cultural competition for looks and other forms of external status sets him up to be angry at women who hold some of the keys to feeling acceptable.

When women are able to communicate from a place of equal power and self-respect that they are not interested in sexual relating of any nature, then most men will not pursue. Those men who coerce their employees to have sex, when the person has tried to say no, are usually responding to the person's childhood and cultural patterns that prevent them from maintaining boundaries.

If he is propelled by power and control, and she is the object of these unhealthy needs, then he will be fueled by her distress. Experiences from his own childhood in which he was the victim of a controlling, power-driven person are translated into the present, where now he can be in control. His unhealthy patterns light up when he moves into a position of authority over people. He can control by their dependency on a paycheck and their cultural training to respond from a one-down place with men who act like that. Here are the pawns that allow him to tell the story of his own childhood and, at the same time, feel the power that lets him know he is no longer vulnerable to being a pawn.

The woman who is the object of his sexualized power is put in a remarkable position. She is handed power. The powerful person has singled her out for intense interest. He wants her. For a woman who is struggling to earn a living and feel like a full-sized person, turning down this attention is difficult. Yet if she accepts a little, she sets up a situation that becomes impossible to manage. Her response to initial flirting indicates to him that he is taking possession of her. If she attempts to set a boundary down the line, he will be more eager to violate it in order to win. A woman can only be safe from men who want to overpower her by being clear in the very beginning, with both words and body language, that she is not responsive to sexual communication. She must feel like his equal as a person, have clear boundaries about her physical person and her sexuality, and not turn away when he begins the suggestive process. When establishing her limits, she cannot be defensive or otherwise give up her power. In our culture, this is almost impossible.

Women who work for men, or are otherwise subordinate, have a cultural and personal history that promotes acceptance of ownership by men in authority. First their fathers, followed by teachers, clergy, and other male relatives, owned their bodies. Almost no young women grew up with sufficient self-respect to feel entitled to have a work relationship free from harassment. All of us expect it and gear up to go along with what is necessary to keep the job. This might be attempting to humor him, placate him, or otherwise keep him happy so he doesn't cause trouble or cost her the job.

When a man hands a woman power by showing sexual interest in her, if she is not interested, she may use it subtly—or not so subtly—to shame him. I observed such a scene when on vacation at a resort in Mexico. Two young women were tanning in the later afternoon when approached by two men in their twenties who had just arrived at the resort, and who had become drunk during their trip. Now it was time to find female companionship. It was clear that the women had no interest in relating with these two, who were being quite obnoxious and pushy. Yet they talked to them with smiles and derisive laughter. Their words said they had no interest, but their nonverbal communication said they liked the power they had to refuse. One man backed off quickly as he saw the nature of the developing conversation, but the other became increasingly hostile. He paced back and forth in front of their lounge chairs, asking questions one would expect if they were meeting in a bar, but his tone of voice conveyed more. With a chip on his shoulder, he challenged them to indicate interest by answering his questions. They both said "no" when he asked them for dates, but their manner said they wanted him to continue asking, so they could shame him by saying no. He responded to the nonverbal communication that conflicted with the words.

I was concerned for the safety of the women, and so I remained in the area beyond the time I had planned. But I was angry with them for not seeing how very serious he was, in spite of being drunk, and that they were increasing the possibility that he might assault one of them. They shamed him by laughing at him, and as he became more abusive in response, they were given even more reason to shame him. These women didn't understand that aggression is a product of shame, an attempt to feel big and in control. Although this aggression may be expressed at people who have not caused the shame, it is more likely to occur toward someone who is shaming.

This man's inebriated condition intensified feelings that exist for him at all times. He sets himself up to be shamed by women, a situation familiar to him, and then he hates them for it. At the same time, he gave the women an opportunity to express their long-standing hostility at such men.

If this man were in a position of superiority over women in the workplace, his anger might be expressed sexually. Any woman who cannot set clear limits will become his victim, because she will be seen as like the women at the resort. He will feel assaulted by her covert invitation and will not see that he also has created the environment of hidden hostility.

In the work environment, the woman who is given sexual attention and, therefore, supposed power can act more like the man's equal, demanding more and appearing to deserve more than others at her level. If she shames him, as the women at the beach shamed the men, he will unconsciously be reminded of his childhood and increase the intensity of his desire to dominate her. He may actually tell her, and believe, that she has indicated she will be sexual with him, when she has done nothing of the sort. As they act out their personal and cultural history, mutually abusing one another, each feels victimized and controlled while trying to control the other. The hidden power struggle can erupt in his firing her, her suing him, or other attempts to "win."

Alternatives to Sexual Relationships

As the men talked, the focus returned again and again to the belief that relationships with women must always include sexual energy. They mourned having no models of healthy camaraderie and playful, affectionate exchange that does not include sexualization.

Jeff, a recovering sex addict who was recently divorced and exploring new relationships, pointed out that sexual relationships are more secure. He told of a recent friendship that he had hoped would develop into a committed coupling. However, when they agreed that they would wait and see what happened before adding sex, the relationship began to fade and soon ended. He believes it would not have done that had they had sex.

Robert talked about how the very definition of male–female relationships is a man in pursuit of a woman. He can't envision a relationship with a woman he doesn't have to pursue. This required pursuit becomes entwined with sexual energy for him. If a model for an egalitarian relationship doesn't exist, or doesn't seem to work, a man has little choice but to fall into the conventional script that calls for sexualized relating. Robert exudes sexual energy, because he is not yet able to believe that his friends and colleagues will like and respect him if he doesn't add an element of sexualized friendliness.

The men went on to talk about how they grew up thinking that getting female attention was the most valued thing in the world. They yearned for it and searched constantly. If a woman wants to be sexual, it is the greatest compliment. If the woman is attractive by cultural standards, then other men will see him as successful, as winning the competition.

They also expressed anger about women dressing and making up in ways that attract them and then not "following through." The men wanted it acknowledged that women play a role in the misguided mating dance. They send out messages that they are available when they aren't. Although women are not consciously aware that the push to look a certain way with dress, makeup, hair, and jewelry—supported by advertisers and the media—is conveying sexual availability, the men want it on the record that this is what they see. As the stories and feelings poured out, the men turned back to what happens with them when they see women as objects.

Kenneth pointed out that when he is in a sexual trance, he sees women as objects or body parts. When he is focused on breasts, legs, or butt, he cannot see the whole woman. He said that there are two separate processes that can go on. One is the limited, constrained but intense experience of objectification, and the other is an interest in an alive person. Then he doesn't see body parts.

Kenneth achieved much of his self-esteem by dressing in very expensive clothes, presenting an illusion of a wealthy man of the world. His manner matched his attire as he projected an interested, fascinating person who seemed capable of going anywhere and doing anything. In truth, he was a spending addict, living on an average income, constantly terrified about where his next paycheck would come from. His manner and clothing achieved the desired effect, and women flirted with him. But after he entered therapy, and his self-esteem increased from the inside out, he began to dislike the attention he received. He could see that the women weren't looking at him as he really was—a construction worker. Instead, they saw an image of financial security and an opulent lifestyle. He was then terrified to reveal to them that he wasn't what he seemed, because they would remove their flirtatious attention, which had seemed so valuable.

As Kenneth was telling this story, he expressed distress about being objectified by women as he described how it felt to have a woman "look him down." He said that it was only his clothes and pocketbook that were being evaluated, which felt bad, and so he could imagine what it would feel like if his body parts were included in the evaluation.

Kenneth talked about how it feels if a woman appreciates something he is wearing, not as an indication of his cultural worth, but as an expression of pleasure in seeing the clothing. A friend told him his shirt was fun to look at. He was able to join in her pleasure and feel close to her in a way that didn't indicate sexual attraction.

Robert had been thinking seriously while he listened to the other men. He began to talk, with some shame, about how he used flattery to get women to like him. He knew he shouldn't say, "You look great, Baby," because this doesn't get inside a woman's defenses. Instead, he has commented on qualities about which he can see she doesn't feel confident. He does this indirectly, as part of a conversation about something else, so it slips in, and she doesn't have to respond directly.

As Robert reflected on his past womanizing, prior to his eleven-year marriage, and how he got women to agree to have sex with him, he could see how his feelings about himself were measured by the woman on his arm. He said the degree to which his values were based on the *Playboy* model (car, money, status, clothing) was the extent to which he would objectify women. He could believe he earned the trophy on his arm and feel good about himself for it. If he were unable to achieve the income, car, and status, then he felt badly about who he was, and the objectification became really intense. The trophy would indicate his worth, so he didn't have to feel like a failure. Robert noted that using women for this purpose entirely prevented him from seeing the woman. At the same time, he said, it was hard to believe that it wasn't a good thing, because it felt so good.

An interesting twist in Robert's life is that he married a woman who objectified him and wanted him as her trophy. She pursued him with flattery and desire, and he couldn't resist marrying her, even though he was aware that he didn't love her. But she was marrying the illusion that he marketed—the successful, well-dressed, hot lover. But it didn't work. He slowly died under the pressure to make money to pay for the expensive house and cars, and to keep her sexually satisfied.

He knew her insatiable lust was supposed to be a man's dream, but soon he became impotent, rarely able to have intercourse. By the time he reached my office, he hated her, planned to divorce, and was terrified of "failing" sexually.

Jeff spoke again, remembering the time he went to work in a bank with a woman boss. She flirted with him, and out of shyness as well as difficulty believing his boss was really sending out sexual invitations, he didn't respond. When he didn't join her, she became very cool to him, and the rest of the time he was under her supervision, he was uncomfortable. Jeff wanted it made clear that women sexually harass men too, and that the consequences of threatened job security and decreased pleasure accompany it. He believes that as the work world changes, so that larger numbers of women are in positions of authority over men, sexual harassment of men will increase.

The men talked about what it is like to have a woman come on to them at work. They agreed that it is never clear what she intends. Some women want to have sex, others a relationship, but the most common wish is to get a man interested and take it no further. The men called it "catch and release," but sometimes the hook is left in.

A man knows that if he comes on to a woman, he is ready to have sex with her. It is confusing when a woman's communication is not clear and sets the man up to make a mistake. If he responds with interest in having sex, the woman can say he is harassing her, or all he is interested in is sex. But if he doesn't respond, then she may be offended and take it out on him.

As they discussed these possibilities, the men were aware that the ability to talk about all this as it happens is a way to circumvent the confusion and pain that is now an integral part of their relating with women. They also increased their awareness of the value of abandoning the objectification of women in order not to be objectified any longer themselves. Even these men who had been together for a year, talking about sexuality and relationships, found their understanding of what they really wanted expanded. *They had to see that what they do to women, and what is done to them, are the same. Once they could, then they knew intuitively that it was not healthy relating.*

Andrew, who has been sexual with men, is uncomfortable when a co-worker always looks at his eyes, then his crotch, then his eyes, and asks if he is dating anyone. Mark said that he has also had women look at his crotch. The men reframed this as being "looked down," a distressing experience for either sex, whether the implications are sexual or not. The recipient typically feels controlled, in a subordinate position, and reduced in energy. Mark said that the situation at work feels particularly like sexual harassment. He pointed out that it is especially difficult to confront this behavior with the co-worker or the company because of its same-sex nature. He is considering telling the man he doesn't like it, and he anticipates denial and other shaming responses.

Kenneth remembered a way in which women objectify men that is built into our culture. Women often choose their partner's clothing, dressing him to play the appropriate part. When Kenneth is dressed in his expensive clothes, men ask him if his lover dresses him! On the contrary, Kenneth has dressed, made up, and done the hair of women he was in relationships with, creating the illusionary goddess that other men would grant him esteem for possessing.

Membership among the "beautiful people" is threatened by competition, Kenneth pointed out. As his esteem in the eyes of peers rose, their desire to have what he had also rose. In addition, Kenneth searched for women who competed with his partner to see if another man was winning. His most "beautiful" partner was constantly jealous when they went out together, because the women he looked at respond with interest. Their relationship was so fraught with anger and vengeful attacks that it soon perished.

The group interview ended with a discussion of objectification of men in more than sexual ways. Robert talked about going to political functions that are dominated by people with money. He watched them size him up, learning how much money and other commodities he had that could be useful to the cause. When it became clear that he had nothing but his time and interest to contribute, he said they looked right through him. He observed that his need to have the perfect woman on his arm to be seen felt similar to wearing the right clothes and driving the right car, so these people would evaluate him favorably. Although his childhood prepared him for this game, he knows that our culture set him up to evaluate his self-worth based on these responses.

§ THE WOMEN'S GROUP §

The women's sexuality group began their four-hour interview by telling stories of what men had done to them and situations in which sexual harassment was common. Only later, after venting their frustrations, did they look at the broader social context in which it all exists.

Rose and Deb both work for a huge aerospace company, but in different sections. Deb, in long term recovery from romance addiction, works in the area dealing with military contracts, heavily staffed by retired military men. Her observation of the level of sexual harassment incorporated into the military subculture is far higher than Rose experiences in the civilian side. Even here, Rose has been appalled by what goes on.

Rose (whose story was told in detail in Chapter 8) gave an example of blatant sexual harassment. A man she worked with asked her to put her hand into a paper bag he was holding. When she did, he said, "I always did want to get you in the sack." This kind of behavior is typical of this man, and he has never been reprimanded for it. When I asked what kind of education had been provided so that employees would know when they were breaking the law, Deb angrily told about her efforts to put a program in place. Her contacts with the personnel department were met with lack of cooperation.

Kathryn, who is Kenneth's ex-wife, and who has been in avid sexual recovery for three years, talked about being an arm wrap for men. She had been very good at it, with the help of clothes, makeup, and breast implants. In addition, she has features that, when made up, are so striking that people stare. Kathryn said that she doesn't know if men are really interested in her or only her role as their trophy. She finds it confusing when men continue to act as if she is there for their use when she no longer prepares herself to be a trophy. She wonders if she is sending out signals she doesn't recognize, and men are responding.

Sarah (whose story was also told in detail in Chapter 8) expressed her anger about her job situation. She is a plumber, working on large jobs, mostly with men. As one of few women in a trade in which women were nonexistent until the last two decades, she confronts men who have old-fashioned ideas about the place of women in their lives.

When Sarah first began work in plumbing ten years ago, she did everything she could to be accepted. She thought that meant being pretty, harmless, and cooperative. When men flirted with her, she received it. She never complained if the flirting moved to the level of harassment. She paid attention to her makeup and clothing to emphasize her femininity and developed a style of responding to sexual jokes and flirtation. In the beginning, she really enjoyed her position as one of few women and the object of so much male attention, and she was willing to put up with anything.

As years passed, the numbers of men Sarah slept with mounted, and her discomfort over the nature of the sexual attention increased. During this time, Sarah stopped drinking, went into recovery, and changed her lifestyle to improve her health. These dramatic changes allowed her to see more clearly the nature of the male attention, and she began to regard it as harmful. Gradually she pulled back from it, isolating herself from the men and refusing to respond to their overtures. She found this difficult to do, in part because she had established an expectation for certain kinds of behavior, and because the construction sub-culture had no model for how to be with women as peers.

Sarah cut back on her use of makeup and learned how to stop putting out sexual energy. But she had to abandon any sense of community with her fellow workers in order to stop being objectified and harassed. If she was friendly, it was treated as a license for sexual comments and joke telling. So she read, or otherwise spent time by herself, during the lunch break and minimized social time spent with others. The subcultural attitudes toward women are so well-defined that she has been unable to create a context in which she can relate in a friendly, open way with the men.

Sarah talked about another woman who works in her current construction project, who plays on her role as sex object to get male attention and be part of the community. Sarah found herself angry with this woman for doing what she had done in the past. Sarah found herself jealous and critical at the same time. Part of her still wanted the intense attention that allowed her to be the center of everything and the focus of attention for so many people. The other part of her was angry that she was required to be a sex object to receive attention and interest. She hated that she had to isolate herself in order to avoid being objectified and harassed.

She talked about the things that happen on the job. Most of the men, she believes, don't try to offend her. Some don't know the difference between offense and friendliness, and still others try to offend. She characterizes the dominant attitude as "That sure is a cute little gal out there, sure would like to fuck her." One man from her past was assigned to her current job. He called her Black Boots Betty. Years ago, she had laughed along with him, knowing she was being singled out as special. But now it felt clearly sexual, indicating that he knew she has had casual sex with other men on the job.

Sometimes when Sarah runs into someone she knew years ago, she falls into the same smiling, flirtatious manner she had in the past. She said it feels automatic, as she watches herself from afar, seeing the woman who was programmed to be an automatic sex object for anyone who might want her in that role. Sarah has a long history of believing she must be available for men's needs to the exclusion of her own, as portrayed in Chapter 8. The cross-wiring is fading as Sarah feels better about herself for not using men's cross-wiring to enhance her self-esteem. But it isn't gone yet. In addition to the influences from her childhood, our culture sets her up to choose between sexual harassment and isolation from her peers if she is to work in a man's field. She is among the pioneers who will eventually change the subculture, so that it is more respectful of women. In the meantime, she suffers a very real loss. Women who aren't willing to be isolated will perpetuate the old, damaging, stereotypical relationship between men and women who work with them.

When Women Are Angry with Women

As we continued to talk about sexual objectification and harassment, feelings came up toward each other. We would divert briefly each time to work it through. In the year that these women had been together, they had discovered the need to have their feelings, express them, and move to a new place. And so, in this new context, which was not therapy and so was not defined as a place where feelings are to be dealt with, they still automatically brought up their anger.

After the third time this happened, Deb got annoyed. She said she had come for an intellectual discussion and thought she could leave her feelings out of it for a time, and here we were doing what we do in group therapy. She said that she is seen by men as a bitch and a backbiter for having feelings, and it is dangerous. Rose spoke up, saying that if we leave our feelings out, then we will focus our anger on the men, blaming them for sexual objectification and everything else. She stressed that we must take a look at the whole picture of how we contribute and see what we can do to change the situation instead of just blaming others. As we take back our power and refuse to be victims, blaming is no longer the only way to feel strong.

Then everyone joined in, talking about relationships between women. We realized that the difficulty of doing exactly what we were doing—being angry with each other and working it through to the other side—created some of our role in being objectified! If a woman cannot be angry with another woman and know the other woman won't leave the relationship, then she is likely to use the security of a sexually bonded relationship to avoid abandonment. If she bonds sexually with a man, he won't leave unless it gets really bad. We can express patterned, and real, anger at our male partner. We are secure. But women friends leave, or we leave, if anger seems too overwhelming to handle. We saw that if we can sit together in a room with a task to do, and take time out when someone has feelings that need to be expressed, and the others will listen with respect and patience, then we can have clean relating with women that isn't threatened. When we can do that, we don't need relationships with men. We can enjoy them, begin them, and make them the center of our lives, but we don't need them to take care of needs that can be met with numbers of other women.

The room lit up with energy as we saw that what we were doing in our meeting was the most important thing we could do in order to change our role in our own objectification, and in ways we objectify men. When we can see them as interesting people and potential partners or friends, then we won't respond to their objectification of us. We won't need to work at being sexually appealing in order to achieve safety and create community. When we no longer respond to men's objectification, they will stop doing it. And when we stop objectifying men, based on their ability to provide us with family and community, they will feel respected and invited into real relationships.

Kathryn said that she chose sex addicts because the sexual bond was even more intense than with men who were more casual about sex. No matter how awful she feared she was, she knew he wouldn't leave.

Susan, age forty, a woman who wanted no sex with her husband, described how she got gas on the way to our meeting, and as she prepared to pay, she found herself looking into the face of a man who was looking at her sexually, proceeding to look up and down her body while talking on the phone. He told the person at the other end of the phone that he was talking to Susan, in a seductive voice that let her know he was looking at her as if she were without clothes. She was shocked to find that she wanted to put her breasts up more, flirt, and be coy. She said she felt shallow, not like herself, and as if she were asking him to put his hands on her body. She also felt controlling, dishonest, and powerful, all at the same time. "In a sleazy way, I feel like a slut, and I have power." She felt that if she had acted, she would have annihilated herself by doing it, and yet there was the thoroughly conditioned temptation. *When a man is sexual with a woman who is not his partner or potential partner, it is as if he has handed the woman power over him. At the same time, a man feels power when he gets her to respond.*

Susan talked about what it is like to have to wait for a man to initiate relationships and sex. Women must hold back their natural interest to obey this rule, and men are cast into a position that more easily lends itself to harassment. Because they must initiate, men's anger can get out of hand. Women, who must only respond, are encouraged to feel helpless.

The meeting ended with a story from Barbara about seeing two husbands of her friends put out sexual energy toward her. In the past, Barbara wouldn't have noticed, because she was drawn to triangle relationships and involved with men who were lying to her about having sex with others. Now, after therapy, she is no longer willing to be in triangles or even to be around what she calls "airleaks" of sexual energy. Barbara doesn't want to be tempted into that kind of relating, and she also wishes to be around clean sexual energy. After recently ending a long relationship, she is preparing to choose a man who, for the first time, isn't putting his sexual energy out to others.

§ THE WOMEN AND MEN MEET §

Members of the women's and men's groups often spoke of their interest in hearing what the other gender had to say about sex. They had met on two occasions some months ago for conversation that elicited their fears of each other, as well as curiosity, satisfaction, anger, and relief. I invited them to meet again for the specific purpose of discussing sexual objectification and harassment. As before, the amount of fear in the room was far higher than when one gender meets alone. My office was damp and warm in spite of air-conditioning designed to keep the temperature under seventy degrees.

As conversation unfolded about people who dance sexually and strip for a living, Allen told about a man he knew who was managing his wife's "career" as a table dancer. They had a five-year plan, which began with having her breasts greatly increased in size and other plastic surgery to mold her body into a caricature of the large-breasted, thin-waisted person a man is supposed to lust after. They knew she could make hundreds of thousands of dollars a year by becoming one of the top bodies in the business. They planned to invest the money, and at the end of five years, she would have her breasts restored to their original size. Allen wondered whether this is unhealthy or just use of an opportunity in a positive way.

The women reacted in unison. All believed this was damaging for the woman, and that she could not be leading a healthy life, sexually or otherwise, by playing to men's sex addiction. One woman said that it parallels being a drug dealer and feeding heroin or cocaine addicts their drug, only it is worse, because not only is she drugging them, but also she must use her body and lie to create the drug. The men affirmed that almost all of the patrons of these places are sex addicts. Small numbers go in groups for a "night out with the guys."

Allen took the floor again, in his usual style of introducing topics not addressed in "mixed company." He told about his new lover's intense reaction when he referred to her vulva, or female genitals, as "pussy." She felt it was degrading and asked him not to do it again. Allen was confused, because he had not heard a woman have that reaction, and he also didn't know what word to use instead. His lover didn't have a new term, and so he wanted to know the thoughts of the women in the group. They unanimously and firmly told him that they agreed with his lover. Yet they had no alternatives either.

Women and men put out their thoughts about this subject. They pointed out that there are no positive words for female genitalia. "Pussy" is the least offensive and the most used. They agreed that "cunt" is the most negative word that can be applied to a woman, and yet most words that mean penis are not taken as derogatory. One man heard another call a third a "dildo," which was taken offensively, because it means imitation penis.

When Allen asked about anatomical language, the women said that "vagina" sounded too clinical, and "vulva" was too new to feel correct. I suggested that correct words feel uncomfortable, because they don't belong in the shame compartment. In the same way that shame came up when the "clean" picture of penises was seen, as described in Chapter 7, correct sexual language can take people out of the shame compartment, forcing them to feel their shame.

When the possibility of using pet names was brought up, several people said that this didn't feel right either. They agree that it avoided the issue instead of truly finding a solution that is consistent with healthy sexual energy. As they talked, Allen realized that slang words added to the possibility of sexually stimulating his partner, and so were attempts to pull her into the shame compartment. This didn't work for him anymore, and so he felt ready to use the correct words and have the feelings that might come with it. He believed that a loving use of sexual energy would feel more consistent with use of the real words for body parts.

Robert responded by talking again of feeling like a piece of meat with some professional women he has encountered. Susan angrily told him that he had nothing to complain about: Men hold the power in our society, and they have the best of everything. Robert pointed out that he had been just as objectified for money, a house, and sex in his ending marriage, and Kenneth contributed his own experiences of being used for image and attractiveness. Susan could finally hear that men may hold economic power and the dominant position of the sexes, but they *feel* just as powerless and vulnerable. The men wanted her to know they were not trying to deny the implications of economic hardship that women more often experience. At the same time, the position of economic superiority does not automatically make men happy. It can become a means to the end of luring a valuable woman and keeping her—a no more attractive position to be in than the woman who chooses a man based on his ability to provide for her. Everyone loses in this system.

Kathryn changed the subject, finally able to voice her perceptions of the beginning of the meeting. She told Allen that she was both angry with him and attracted to him. She described how he walked into the room and took over, his power dominating things. The energy in the rest of the room dropped, she felt, as he was given the position of the dominate male. Her conditioned reaction was to be attracted to him, focus on him, and become his female counterpart. This was an old role she used to play during her "Barbie doll" days, using her skills to attract men and win over women competitors. Now her desire to do it again made her angry with the system that promoted it, and with Allen, who she felt was still playing the male part. She went on to describe Allen as a peacock and the women as hens. If she passed on the opportunity to be the hen to the number one peacock, then she would lose her standing among the hens. Kathryn said that hens leave if she focuses on them, but they will stay if she takes first place, because they hope some of it will rub off on them.

Deb said she was angry about the competition among women, because she can't win, she's not good enough. She felt that competition isolated her from her friends. Rose remembered how difficult it was when she was in the Navy to evaluate the societal worth of the other women, because they all looked the same. She had no basis to decide with whom to relate.

Susan pointed out how different the women were when meeting with the men. She said that Deb was more absent and pulled back, Kathryn was more forward and spoke more, and Rose was charming and funny. Sarah was angrier and less available to the women.

As the men took their turn talking about how they were different when women were present, their confusion of how to be when moving from the old, culturally defined way to be a man to the new place of acceptance and equality was apparent. Allen said he liked to be seen as powerful but, at the same time, wanted to be really seen as the man he is, free of illusion of power. Kenneth said he wanted Allen's power and didn't want it. Jeff valued his developing self-respect and autonomy, and also had feelings of wanting attention at any price.

§ HEALING AT A CULTURAL LEVEL §

Sexual harassment and objectification are not something bad men do to innocent women. They are products of our culture, a culture that is passed on to the next generation by both sexes. It is harmful to be the object of harassment, and it is harmful to be the objectifier. Although public attention to the subject is a new and powerful acknowledgment of the need for change, the focus for that change must be on the culture as a whole. Instead of holding objectifiers to blame, each of us can take a look at our role in the phenomenon. Each of us can know that our individual sexual healing is necessary in order for all kinds of harmful sexualizing to stop.

11

HOMOSEXUALITY OPPRESSION

§

The Shaming of All of Us

"Homosexuality" means that people of the same gender are attracted to each other with sexual energy, engage in sex, and may bond into a new family. This is all it really means. But cultures through time have ascribed many more attributes to same-gender choice, rendering it complicated and confusing. Our culture, as well as many others in the past and present, have poured shame onto people who are attracted to the same gender, multiplying the effects of sexual shaming received by all of us.

§ HOMOSEXUAL SEX IS CULTURALLY SHAMED §

If homosexuality were accepted, then those who choose to have sex with the same gender would be just that—people who have sex with the same gender. There would be no need for a separate subculture of people who are required to band together, because they share a sexual orientation. But this culture shames homosexual sex above almost any other kind of sexual expression, and so it has become necessary to create a subculture for support and to fit in. If a gay man wants to openly hug his mate in public, or a lesbian woman wants to hold hands with her partner, they will receive intense shaming responses unless they are in the rare environment where homosexuality is accepted as normal. Heterosexuals grow up with intense shaming that damages their self-esteem and sexual expression. Much more happens to people who find themselves attracted to the same sex.

Whereas some people know when they are young children that they are attracted to the same gender, others learn with the blast of hormones at puberty. Still others believe they can be heterosexual in spite of same-sex attraction, until they first fall in love and learn they can't. Even without being told directly, everyone knows this feeling is unacceptable and must be hidden. In contrast, heterosexual people know they aren't to talk directly about sexual feelings but are permitted to be attracted to the opposite sex.

No marriage license is offered to sanctify the sexual choice of homosexuals, as it is with heterosexual people. Ceremonies offered in some churches try to compensate, but they do not provide the same validity for the creation of a new family as heterosexual licenses and marriages. Homosexual people are seen as "living together," even if they do so for decades.

Gary and his partner Bart have been living together for six years. They are open about their relationship and have not wished to keep it a secret from their neighbors, all of whom are heterosexual. They have received outward acceptance of their relationship. But at one point, they decided to separate for a time while still living together. Gary mentioned to neighbors that he was now sleeping in the downstairs bedroom, and he could see that they were unable to express the natural reactions they might have if the couple were heterosexual. They didn't ask what the problem was, or if they were getting a divorce, or express their feelings over the coming split of a couple they valued as neighbors. Questions that are appropriate to heterosexual couples were not permitted by our culture.

These neighbors all knew that Gary and Bart had a sexual relationship, but they were required not to know it at the same time. Or at least, they were required not to let on to Gary and Bart that they knew. Because of this prohibition, they couldn't have the normal reaction that is allowed for heterosexual couples. One element in common with heterosexuality is the prohibition against asking if the issues are sexual ones, and if sleeping in separate bedrooms means they are no longer having sex. Sexual relating is off-limits for discussion with all people. In addition, sexual bonding and marrying is off-limits for discussion with homosexual people. The silence of the heterosexual is intended to prevent gay persons from feeling shame about their socially unacceptable behaviors. It has the opposite effect— silence adds further shame. Gary feels no shame about his choice of a male spouse, yet his choice is shamed by the silence of even well-intentioned neighbors.

All people who find themselves drawn to the same gender when looking for a mate must go through a frightening, shame-filled process of telling relatives and community. Each must discover what it feels like to be attracted to someone of the same sex and then bond into a couple. Many homosexual people choose not to be in couple relationships to avoid the external and internal shaming that results. (I have written in Chapter 7, "How Sexual Shame Inhibits Us and How We Avoid It," about the choice not to be in a relationship to avoid shame, which is particularly intense for homosexual people.)

§ Is Homosexuality Genetic? §

We are presented with information about possible genetic or physiological differences between homosexuals and heterosexuals, as if proving that "they can't help it" makes a difference. Such scientific information may be helpful in convincing those who think homosexuality is morally wrong that they must change their views, but it also does a disservice. The fact is that making love with someone of the same gender is not morally wrong. It doesn't matter if the "cause" of homosexuality is genetic, due to brain differences, or if it is caused by sexual or relationship abuses from childhood, or a conscious decision to partner with someone of the same gender. The error lies in the cultural shaming and lack of acceptance. As cultures come to change their perception of homosexuality, accepting it as no more than one way people choose mates, then the cause of the choice becomes irrelevant.

To accept homosexuality will require all of us to examine the factors that lead to condemnation of a group of people. These might include fear of being or becoming gay, or of a group of people who are different from us, and difficulty in giving up training from others in our community who focus shame and anger onto a particular group of people.

My men's therapy group discussed their fears of becoming gay and their resulting fear of becoming too close to a gay member of the group. Andrew came out to the group a few months after joining and received tacit support. It was many more months before the other men could express their discomfort. Two of them, both with strong masculine characteristics, had become friends with Andrew outside of the group. Although they don't judge him for being gay, they have come to realize that they fear feeling sexual when they hug or touch, and that they will feel compelled to see themselves as gay if this happens. Both men confuse touch with sex and are likely to feel sexual if they are physically close to Andrew. Cultural condemnation sets them up to shy away from their friend in order to avoid a feeling that will make them condemn themselves.

Men are afraid of touching heterosexual men too, of course, for the same reason. Men can be freed of this inhibition by cultural change in perception of homosexuality. This change is under way in the United States, as reflected by the growing acceptance of gays on television and in movies.

§ REDUCING THE FEELING OF SEXUAL SHAME §

The homosexual community has tried to avoid shaming from our culture by working to stop feeling shame for their sexual activities and feelings. The cross-wired behaviors of casual sex, lust, focus on the "right" bodies, the sexual imitation of women, and more, serve the function of overriding the shame from wanting to be sexual with the same sex. (They have other functions too, such as telling stories of childhood sexual abuses, but that is not the focus here.) People who engage in certain kinds of sexual activities have always wanted to be around others who did too, in order to feel less alone and less "perverted." Traditional sex therapy has supported this approach by assisting in the creation of groups, so that people with the same cross-wiring can meet and share their experience. For example, regular gatherings of cross-dressers of both sexual orientations are scheduled in Seattle.

Although meeting with others who have the same sexual issues can help people feel more comfortable with their activities, it doesn't address the fact that homosexual sex is shamed by our culture, and the cross-wired behaviors would not be the chosen sexual expression if shame were removed from same-gender sexual activity.

Gary was able to tell me how bathhouses function as more than a place for men to freely have casual sex. Bathhouses are halls with showers, sometimes a swimming pool, Jacuzzis, saunas, and separate rooms with small beds. Pornography is played on video screens, and the music is loud. Men have sex in public, as well as in the private rooms.

But in addition to the sexual nature of the environment, other functions are served. One is making public the nature of sex between men. Instead of hiding behind closed doors, which intensifies the shame for wanting homosexual sex, this environment declares sex as acceptable, thus reducing the experience of shame. Although sex clubs serve this function for heterosexual people too, it is perhaps more necessary for gay men to reduce the feeling of shame. An environment is provided in which men who act on culturally shamed desires can be together in community with others who are also culturally condemned.

Of course, the shame isn't removed from sexuality in bathhouses and other congregating places. It is actually anchored even more firmly. The route to real shame removal is the gathering of these same men in an environment where sex isn't acted out, and the shame is allowed to be felt. Releasing the shame then becomes possible. Gary viewed bathhouses as part of his routine sexual and community functioning, until he understood the nature of sexual healing. Not only did he have to move away from addictive sex in bathhouses, but he also had to stop using the acceptance of public, impersonal sex as a way to avoid feeling shame. Gary told me that after he read an initial draft of this chapter, he felt the shame that he had avoided in the subcultural acceptance of being sexual with other men.

§ Our Culture Doesn't Like what It Creates §

Although our culture shames homosexual people for their manner of sexual interaction, in addition to the choice of same-gender partners, it is, ironically, our very culture that prevents most homosexual people from discovering their healthy sexual expression.

Heterosexual people want gay people to behave differently, but don't see that these very attitudes prevent them from doing so. Dramatically portraying the opposite sex in manner and clothing isn't inherent in mating with the same gender. (It is also not inherent to heterosexuals. We have defined "woman" and "man" as including clothing, use of accessories, ways of speaking and acting, etc. We are naturally far more like each other than our acculturation allows us to experience.) Gay men acting like women and gay women acting like men is a way to make sense out of a desire that isn't reflected in our culture—to belong to a gender that mates with the same gender. Gender confusion, in a culture that doesn't accept homosexuality, is a natural product of wanting to mate with someone of the same sex. Our culture has no acceptable category for men to be with men or women to be with women. "Man" means having sex and mating with women, and "woman" means having sex and mating with men. Much of the right to call oneself a man or a woman is based on these preferences. Where does that leave a person with the opposite desires?

§ MATING WITH ONE GENDER WHILE HAVING SEX WITH THE OTHER §

Another source of confusion is when a person is attracted to one gender with sexual-mating energy and to another for sexual activity. Neil had relationships with women that were fraught with sexual difficulties. At the same time, he went to adult bookstores for impersonal sex with men through holes in booths. Neither situation met his real needs. Once he was able to remember that his father had been sexual with him when he was a young boy, and could begin the work of removing the effects, he lost interest in casual sex with penises. He then married a woman and was able to work with her to create a loving, sexual relationship. But his earlier interest left him confused and not sure of his gender identity or his sexual orientation.

For several years Neil identified himself as gay and entered a relationship with a man. During this time, people assumed he was gay, even without knowing with whom he had sex. But once he was able to work through some of the effects of sexual abuse and lose interest in impersonal sex, he became more androgynous, assimilating the qualities of both sexes, no longer appearing "effeminate." He was no longer confused about being a man, even though he knew he was bisexual. If his marriage ended, he could choose a mate from either sex. His choice of mate was not related to his maleness. He could choose based on the qualities of the person. Neil's history of sex with men allowed him to challenge our culture's views of same-gender sex and know that he was truly a man, regardless of the gender of the person he had sex with and married.

§ CULTURAL SHAMING OF HOMOSEXUALITY BREEDS SHAMEFUL SECRETS §

Gary offered me many examples of the secret life that our culture requires of homosexual people. Anytime a person has to lead a secret life in order to avoid shaming from others, more shame is attached to the person.

Most secrets won't elicit shaming when told. Psychotherapy clients find that once they reveal themselves, they can release shame, because others don't respond as they had feared. But with homosexuality, it is predictable that some people will respond exactly as feared. The choice becomes telling and being shamed, or keeping the secret and self-shaming.

Gary and Bart had been together for six years. Bart hasn't told his parents that he is gay, even though they know he and Gary moved to Seattle together. Bart's parents treat Gary as if he were a son-in-law, giving him gifts for birthdays and Christmas, and telling him how glad they are that he is in Bart's life. This suggests that they know the truth but feel compelled not to name it, because Bart hasn't.

Now that Bart and Gary are splitting up—actually divorcing—they can't deal with it in the same way a heterosexual couple would, or the way they could have if the secret hadn't been kept. If Gary continues to keep the secret, he can't go to his parents-in-law and grieve for the loss of his relationship with them. And they can't do so either. Everyone has to hide feelings to support the deception.

Gary has felt constrained by Bart's choice, believing that he had to go along with Bart's decision. He was also angry about heterosexual people not putting into words their knowledge of a relative or friend's homosexuality, wanting the heterosexual world to join the truth telling instead of leaving that to the gay person. I pointed out that he was engaging in the same kind of secret keeping by not telling Bart's parents that they were lovers. He has the right to reveal his own story, just as he wants heterosexuals to reveal their knowing about homosexual friends and relatives. He was startled by this thought. The subject of secrets is confusing, making it difficult to differentiate between harmfully withheld information and reasonable boundaries around information. In this case, it appears that Gary is joining Bart in withholding information that is already known and to which the parents wouldn't react badly. (Other times, however, not revealing such information may be the best choice.)

Gary talked of another example of homosexual shame. When he and Bart were first together in the sexual bonding period of their relationship, Bart wanted to kiss when they were at stoplights or other semiprivate situations. They lived in a city that is not known for acceptance of homosexuality, so it could be assumed that some of the people who observed them would be critical and disgusted. Their choice was either to express affection and receive cultural shaming, or to experience shame by holding back the expression. (A third option available to some people is to convert the shame into sexual arousal in order to not feel it; such people might want to be sexual in public, where they might be seen.)

Gary's stories pointed out how the experience of sexual shame is perpetual for people who bond with another of the same gender. It makes sense that this group of people has had to take steps to create environments in which the feeling of shame is minimized.

Seattle has a gay and lesbian bar in a beautiful old house. Dance lessons are given, and an atmosphere of having fun is stronger than the common interest in alcohol and picking people up. These usual bar activities go on, of course, but the degree of sexual shame seems to be less than in bars where the door is hidden, and it is difficult to tell that a place of entertainment is behind it. The atmosphere of "sneaking in" has been lessened.

§ THE SHAMING OF HOMOSEXUALITY SHAMES ALL OF US §

As we become sexual people, it is natural to find ourselves attracted to lots of different kinds of people and even animals. If sexuality weren't shamed, we would narrow down the field to those with whom it made sense for us to couple. In this process, it is natural to feel attracted to people of the same gender as we discover if we want to couple with the same or opposite gender. But because our culture shames same-gender attraction, even those who want to select the opposite gender for mating are not allowed to explore this other part of the self without adding further shame to the pile. The result is that most people who engage in homosexual sex do not do so from a position of choice: If they had the choice they would take the less shamed, socially acceptable option.

In order to avoid added shame, many people condemn homosexual sex in an attempt to prevent themselves from engaging in it. Self-shaming is turned into shaming of a group of people who engage in the feared behaviors.

Additionally, if we aren't allowed to examine our own attraction to the same gender, we shame ourselves with the belief that to do so is wrong, even if we don't shame people who engage in homosexual sex. My women's group talked about attraction to the same sex and our shame from having such feelings. We talked about how we felt anger at "sexy" women in order to avoid feeling sexually attracted. Through this discussion and observation of how women's magazines use same-gender attraction to lure us into buying the magazine and the advertised products (the *Cosmopolitan* cover picture isn't for men, it's for women), we were able to see how we are required not to know about our attraction to women. We could then understand that we shame ourselves for it. All of us have chosen not to act on the attraction, but this lack of activity doesn't diminish the shame we carry. Women and men will continue to carry it until our culture changes.

§ CULTURAL SEXUAL HEALTH INCLUDES ACCEPTANCE OF HOMOSEXUALITY §

As long as same-gender sex is considered bad by a culture, the culture will not be able to obtain sexual health. As I explained earlier, each of us carries the same interest, even if we haven't acted on it, and even if we feel strongly heterosexual. As a result, the shaming of homosexual people shames the rest of us as well.

We cannot have sexual health for heterosexual people and exclude this other group. They are different only in that they have acted on the attraction and perhaps have a stronger same-gender attraction, as well as a lack of attraction to the opposite gender. As we can come to accept our own same-gender sexual attraction, then we will be able to accept others with this attraction. As a culture, we can remove shame from this component of humanness.

§ MARGARET LEARNED SHE WAS A LESBIAN §

I spoke at length with Margaret, who shared her story of discovering she was a lesbian. It is filled with the effects of our culture's shaming of homosexuality, as well as our definition of heterosexuality as normal.

Margaret is a hairdresser whose clientele consists almost entirely of gay and lesbian people. While she cuts, she asks her customers questions about their relationships and what it's like being homosexual. This process of several years has allowed her to see more clearly the nature of her own sexual orientation, as well as that of many others.

Margaret knew she was attracted to women from the time she was a child, but she didn't realize the meaning of this until her teens, when she didn't feel like one of the group of girls with whom she associated. They were falling for boys and, although the bonding looked appealing, she didn't identify with their choices.

During her early years, Margaret thought homosexuals were child molesters and evil perverts—a group with whom she didn't want to identify. At the same time, she was attracted to women. This confusion resulted in feeling like a freak, and she seriously wanted to kill herself. Only one other alternative seemed possible. Having grown up in a religious family, she could become a nun. She hoped that her lack of attraction to men meant that God was calling her to be a nun. But that choice didn't seem right, and Margaret didn't pursue it.

Reaching puberty was significant. Margaret had thought she was a boy, even though she didn't have a penis and was called a girl. But when her body changed into a young woman's, she realized that she wasn't a boy. She grieved and went through a period of depression.

When she was in her midteens, a gay man she worked with told a third person that he thought she was a lesbian, even before she was able to let herself know. When she was eighteen, she dated men, hoping to demonstrate her heterosexuality to peers. She kissed them, even though she had no sexual interest. During this time, Margaret suffered greatly from the cultural attitude toward homosexuality, which prevented her from being able to easily discover her sexual orientation and proceed with learning about her sexual self. She talked of going to a dance with her friends and watching them slow-dance lovingly with their boyfriends. She cried deeply as she realized she wasn't like them. Unable to stop her grief, she went home.

It took Margaret many years to fully realize the implications of her sexual orientation. In retrospect, she had all the necessary information available, but her shame and our culture's lack of a place for her feelings prevented her from fully seeing herself. She pointed out how our culture brainwashes us into believing we are heterosexual through movies, television, and our language. Nowhere is the experience of same-gender attraction spoken of as natural and as one option for how to live one's sexual life— until a person finds their way to the homosexual community.

At twenty, Margaret fell in love with a woman and could no longer maintain the foggy state of not quite knowing. Although this experience was powerful, she was, at the same time, set adrift from the world as it had been defined for her. Her parents were strongly religious, and her mother hated lesbians. Margaret had become what her family hated. She grieved for the loss of the life she had expected as a girl growing up in the United States—marrying a man, being taken care of, and blending in. Instead, she realized that she was on her own. There would be no protector, no caretaker. Margaret even broke up with her girlfriend several times, because it was hard to digest the change in how her life looked.

Coming out took many years. Margaret, along with so many homosexual people, thought she could keep it a secret. But her sister figured it out and told the rest of the family. When Margaret found out, she became very sick and thought she was going to die. As she expected, her mother reacted strongly. She disowned Margaret, telling her that anything further she had to say would not be valued.

A decade later, her mother still prays that the "homosexual spirit" will leave her, but she is somewhat accepting of Margaret's life. When Margaret visits with her girlfriend, they sleep together, but they have to come up with a "reason," such as the lack of beds. When she explains to her mother that she is on a spiritual path, her mother thinks this means she will stop being a lesbian. She explains that, instead, she is becoming a more spiritual lesbian.

After hearing Margaret's story, I realized the immense shaming homosexual people have to go through as they realize they don't have the choice of leading a socially prescribed life. This has to be one of the factors in the high suicide rate for homosexual teens. Death is one way out of the excruciatingly painful situation forced on them. To be unacceptable to our culture, and as yet having no accepting community, has to be one of the most dramatic sources of the decision to stop living. Ostracism from one's community *is* a form of death. People will do almost anything to avoid it. But the choice of an opposite-sex mate to fit in is not possible. So many of us feel as if we are ostracized, because we experience ourselves as shameful. Imagine adding real ostracism to those feelings.

§ NEIL CAME OUT §

Neil didn't initiate conversation about his sexual orientation with his family. His mother wrote him a letter, asking him if he was gay. He responded by saying that he was living with a man with whom he had sex, and she could call it whatever she wanted. Neil's father said nothing to Neil about his homosexuality during the entire six years Neil lived with a man and associated almost exclusively with gay people. His siblings were able to discuss it, which allowed Neil to retain some sense of family while engaged in a socially unacceptable relationship. They were able to be open about it, because one sister had been in relationships with women, and his brother had had casual sex with men, even though he was always in a relationship with a woman. This brother had also been sexual with all of the younger siblings when they were growing up, a fact that Neil brought to the attention of the parents during his sexual healing.

When he came out to his parents, Neil was living across the country from them, avoiding issues that are common for those who live closer. After several years, Neil's mother came to defend Neil's lifestyle to the extended family. But when Neil eventually fell in love with a woman and married, she was happy about the change. We can assume that one reason was her appreciation that Neil would no longer be subject to our culture's condemnation of him, and he could have a life with less difficulty. But Neil could see that it was more than this. Her life became more acceptable without a gay son. In addition, one element of their family system is women bonding together against the men. This is awkward or impossible when a son's mate is a man. Neil could rejoin the family in prescribed ways by marrying a woman; however, Neil had been involved in healing from childhood abuses, and never did rejoin, to his mother's chagrin.

§ Talking about Homosexual Sex §

As is clear from the rest of this book, not talking about sex continues the shaming of sexuality. As true as this is for heterosexual sex, it is far more intense for homosexual sex. It can be discussed in innuendo, jokes, and sexually charged conversation, but it is rare for two or more people to openly discuss the mechanics of sexual interaction between two people who both have penises, testicles, and anuses, or two people who both have vulvae and breasts. Our heterosexual culture defines sex as vaginal penetration by a penis. Anything else is considered "foreplay" or less than real, even if done by people without the necessary combination of body parts.

For homosexual and heterosexual people to change individual and cultural attitudes toward homosexual activity, we need to talk openly about sexual behaviors. The AIDS epidemic has contributed to this education by making the term "anal sex," commonplace. It is also obvious that men put their penises in each other's mouths, because that is an activity that is increasingly accepted in the heterosexual community. It is also easy to figure out that lesbian women employ hand and mouth stimulation of breasts and vulvae. But we can't really know what happens—the whole picture of a homosexual couple engaging in satisfying, complete, sexual lovemaking. It is hard to translate from heterosexual sex that is defined as vaginal penetration by a penis, and orgasm.

But, of course, most heterosexual couples don't have sex according to the stereotype either. We don't hear the stories of couples who stimulate each other to orgasm with their hands for most of their marriage, or those who have oral sex and forego intercourse. Even when we are presented with sex surveys that give us percentages of people engaged in certain activities in the United States, we don't know what it looks like for couples to begin sexual activity, go through some process, and decide they are finished. Pornography doesn't offer this information.

In the early 1960s, when I was first sexual, I didn't follow the prescribed view of sexual encounters that I had learned without ever being told. At first I couldn't bring myself to take off all my clothes. Later, oral sex was always involved. Stimulation through pornography assisted when I didn't want to have sex but felt I should. Because these activities were never talked about, I felt like an odd person, with the rest of those around me doing the "usual"—intercourse, missionary position. Even my psychoanalyst, trained to look at sexuality as important to therapy, didn't know what was going on with me sexually.

In order to bring sex into the arena of normal, everyday life, we will have to take the shame off it by talking openly in ways that aren't intended to bring on arousal for the sake of avoiding shame. Homosexual sex is more shame-loaded, not only for homosexual people, but also for heterosexual people. As we heal our culture from sexual distortion, we will, at some point, find ourselves talking more openly and with less shame.

12

ADVERTISERS AND UNHEALTHY CULTURAL ATTITUDES
§

The subject of sex in advertising seems obvious to everyone I speak with, yet most people continue to be exploited by their cross-wiring. If we are to go an additional step and refuse to respond to the media's barrage of sexual energy, we need to be able to see more clearly what really is happening and make decisions about how to respond.

§ TELEVISION PROGRAMS PEOPLE WILL WATCH §

Television assaults the greatest number of people with sexual stimuli. Commercials and shows alike use flesh, breasts, "sexy" movements, and flirting to grab our attention. Because television controls the length of our viewing time, it can use our sexual deprivation against us. A scene is flashed on the screen and before we have a chance to look and digest, it is taken away. For example, a popular underwear commercial flashes pictures of women in bras and panties, moving to the next shot before we can digest the one before. This leaves us wanting more, etching the scene into our memories. If we were able to look until we were satisfied, we could let go of the image more easily.

Television advertises itself and the products it sells effectively by using sexuality in order to compete for ratings. Long-lasting series, such as "Melrose Place," as well as daytime programs, show bodies, sexual activity, and passionately frustrated coupling to grab the attention of viewers. Repressed sexuality, and the coupling drive are used to hold our attention.

Calvin Klein demonstrated the general appeal of child pornography by producing commercials with young-looking actors (it turned out they were all of age) in sexual situations. It is unlikely that he would have spent large amounts of money on commercials unless he was sure they would elicit the cross-wired interest of a large percentage of viewers. Of interest is the level of objection to the TV and print ads, so great that Klein decided to remove the ads to prevent the possibility of legal action against him.

Advertisers and producers figure out how to get people to watch shows and buy products. Our deprivation of touch, sex, and intense coupling, accompanied by addictions to sexual energy in the form of sex and romance, set us up to pay close attention to stories and ads. As long as we do, and as long as the media profit, then we will continue to be assaulted by unhealthy sexuality. Those who are in the position of using our interests to sell products will not choose to stop. They have no motivation to stop. As we heal our sexual energy and find that these maneuvers no longer work, then the media will not use our cross-wired and addictive reactions to manipulate us.

§ BONDING FACIAL EXPRESSIONS ATTRACT US §

Magazines, such as *Cosmopolitan*, *Redbook*, and *GQ*, that sell millions of copies each month are also using sexuality to sell things. When I spread ads from these magazines across my living room floor, the facial and body expressions of the models reveal intensity. In real life, they would turn heads. The woman who laughs gaily while pulling off her jacket (advertising Panty Shields) has no sexual expression on her face, but she is looking at the viewer in a way that is reserved for lovers, children, or others who are very close to her. In the same way that erotic dancers in nightclubs look at their customers adoringly, their expressions laced with sexual energy to attract those who have been deprived of loving looks, intense looks in the media feel good to those who have not received enough of them while growing up. Since this is true for most people in our culture, we are set up to pay attention to ads.

The woman in the perfume ad who straddles a man's lap, facing him, sitting on the man's penis, is the recipient of a longing, sexual, desirous look from a man who is considered valuable by our culture's standards. The viewer can identify with the woman and receive this look herself. The male viewer can identify with the man receiving her delighted smile. Watching this scene may bring up envy and a wish to be one of the two people, thus eliciting a desire to purchase the perfume, with the hope of bringing this about. This wish must be unconscious, of course, because if the person were aware of the connection, it would be obvious that a perfume cannot create this scene.

Other readers or viewers will respond to models looking right at them in ways that others rarely, or never, do. The same fuel that brings lovers together, and that bonds infants and young children to adults, is used by advertisers to draw us in. Intense looks, deep feelings of connection expressed by face and body, adoration, and vitality and energy, are all expressed by parents loving their children, as well as lovers falling in love. (It is also the appeal of adoring dogs.)

"Beautiful" people moving away from us on the page can elicit feelings of abandonment and a desire to pursue. As children, dependent on adults for the continuation of life, our most basic fear is abandonment. Without others' care, we would not live. Some of the same attention we paid to our parents when they moved away from us is transferred onto the model, and the ad people get what they want—our attention. For those who were reigned in too tightly as children, such a picture may elicit relief. As the desired object moves away, the viewer doesn't feel suffocated or pressured. Instead, he or she gets to feel desire for another, a feeling rarely possible in a childhood in which parents submerged the child within their lives.

"Beautiful" people moving toward us can elicit relief, feeling loved, and feeling wanted, all of which are powerful experiences for those of us who grow up in a culture in which we do not receive enough loving attention. The feelings create powerful connections to the product for sale.

When children are adequately nurtured and allowed to decide when they have had enough, then they are not vulnerable to the manipulation of their feelings in adult life. But when children are raised by parents who were deprived of bonding, it is rarely possible for children to determine how much, when, and for how long parents will attend to them. Consequently, in adult life, each of us responds to a certain style of attention, a dynamic that dramatically affects our choice of mates, as well as our response to stimuli designed to entice us to buy something we don't need.

Intense, cross-wired expressions are also employed in magazines and television. We see hostile looks, direct, angry expressions, and aloof anger designed to tap into our past associations. Cultural views of sexuality and coupling relationships include power and control on both sides. A woman may be attracted to distancing, controlling men in order to exert control herself. If she can dominate this man by making him want her, she demonstrates that she is more powerful than the powerful man. Love or caring can become mixed up with hostility and anger if a person was raised by emotionally or physically abusive parents who also provided affection and support. Bonding can include the intensity brought on by fear and pain, and may feel stronger than a gently loving relationship. Such a person may respond more to the pictures of hostile, angry models (such as the cover of *Cosmopolitan*) than the affectionate ones.

The ownership of children by their parents and the typical expression of built-up anger toward children contribute to our attraction to hostile models. Our culture provides the backdrop for cross-wiring to sexually hostile people.

Ads can grab our attention by using our tendency to identify with the models. Romance novels provide this for women who cannot achieve the heroine's experiences. They get to feel irresistible to all men, while remaining innocent and pure. People who have within them the desire to dominate and control, or seduce, or castrate, to attract any man or woman they want, can find the expression of their desires. Advertisers give us a vicarious experience that isn't possible in real life.

§ ADVERTISING IS PORNOGRAPHIC §

Popular magazines are filled with scenes we are not allowed to see in real life. When I spread pictures from these magazines across my living room floor, I was startled to see what they really present. In glossy color, they show us scenes that are absolutely forbidden in public. Several totally nude women and some men were photographed in shadow, without revealing nipples or genitals. Other scenes of lovers kissing make them look passionately aroused and about to have sex. A perfume ad shows a woman sitting astride a man's penis. If they didn't have clothes between them, they would have difficulty avoiding intercourse. She is smiling, and he is lustfully moving his mouth toward hers. Six women in bathing suits show their bodies in classic sexual poses—backs arched, legs apart or one leg out, breasts pushed up—and we are expected to believe they are merely engaged in traditional modeling stances. I had become so accustomed to seeing models placed in these poses that I no longer perceived them as sexual. Somehow viewing them all together, spread out on the floor, gave me a new objectivity, so I could compare these scenes with real life.

Products for the skin are advertised by full-body shots of nude models, and even tennis shoes are shown on a woman pulling a jacket off her scantily clad, huge breasts. Almost all of the women and men in the top-selling women and men's magazines exude sexual energy. Even the gaily laughing Panty Shields model twists her body as she pulls off her jacket in a way that makes her look "sexy."

§ We Don't See the Sexual Stimuli §

Until I saw a grouping of these pictures, I was not aware that most of the scenes, if occurring in public, would bring about intense interest as well as discomfort, and the people engaged in them would be the objects of lust and condemnation. Yet millions of people, including children, see these pictures in magazines and on television.

In real life, when we happen onto sexual arousal, we refuse to see it. I watched a scene unfold in a fast-food restaurant in the early morning that brought up intense displeasure in the other customers. A young couple, waiting for their food, made love to each other—without touching sexually. They were both aroused and appeared to have left their bed only long enough to satisfy their hunger for food. A man came in, did a double take, and walked far around them, on his way to another clerk, turning his back as he ordered. I wondered if he were a recovering sex addict or if he typically avoided sexual stimulation. The scene that bothered him was a real-life portrayal of something that is very tame in the media. We have become accustomed to the constant barrage of sexual stimuli in print, yet the real thing, even with clothes and no genital contact, brought reactions from observers. *Americans have become able to look at sexual scenes when they are in a context that has been defined as normal, and at the same time, are uncomfortable when running across real sexual arousal.*

Walking down a street in New York City, I came upon a photographer and models preparing to film an advertisement. This ad was not as sexual as the ones I have described. It was rather ordinary, apparently for clothes. Yet when seen next to a fountain on a city street, the positions of the models were clearly designed to bring up sexual awareness. Although the magazine ads themselves have become so familiar that we easily forget they are conveying sexual energy, in this unusual context, I could see the truth.

When it comes to sexuality, we use our human ability to form compartments into which we can place different kinds of experiences. We put sexuality in the shame compartment to avoid feeling shame, and then when sexual stimuli appear unbidden, such as the couple at the fast-food restaurant, shame will be provoked. The defensive function of the shame compartment couldn't operate for the man who was an onlooker of the couple's public lovemaking. At other times, he could probably step into his shame compartment, even go to a club where women dance almost nude. Before he goes, he knows what to expect and prepares accordingly.

When confronted by such a scene, others are able to make a rapid shift and enter the shame compartment. Once inside, all kinds of things happen. The lusting, leering, sex-driven stereotype of a man might appear. We can observe this in a man who makes socially "inappropriate" remarks about sexual things, or who feels as if he can join the couple by feeling sexual with them. Sexual boundaries break down, and those around the man react either by joining him or finding him disgusting. Because this reaction brings up large doses of shame, most men remain out of the shame compartment unless they specifically choose to enter it. Alcohol and a party atmosphere allow people to enter together, but the next day, they may have intense shame when remembering what happened.

The media have created a category in which people can be in touch with sexual stimuli without feeling disgusting or being judged as such. Walking past the magazine stand of large grocery stores is like walking past a display of soft pornography. Nudity is even on covers, minus only bare genitals and breasts. Huge breasts are presented on many covers every month. *Cosmopolitan* cover women look as if they want to lure men with their sexuality, and at the same time, are prepared to violate them with anger. Women wearing bikinis or other scanty clothing stand next to cars in men's magazines. Magazines that have nothing to do with sex have sexual scenes. It is amazing how we are able to avoid seeing what is all around us.

Other advertisers use nudity to grab our attention. One manufacturer of skin-care products uses a series of photographs of skin. They range from a bare leg, stroked by a hand, to nude bodies, photographed in shadows to emphasize certain shapes and curves. The pictures are not overtly sexual; instead, they use our deprivation of skin contact (which is usually associated with sex) to draw our attention.

§ CONFUSING CHILDREN §

As we walk our children past these displays, offering no information to mirror their confusion, they grow up believing this isn't the sexuality they're not supposed to have. Here are overt portrayals, and no one is saying "Don't look!" However, if a child asks questions about the breasts and legs that are not seen among live people, he or she is not usually encouraged to explore further. He may be told this isn't good, or this is just the way it is, unrelated to regular life. Either way, the child learns that sexuality in the media must be put into a separate compartment. It is not identified as similar to shameful sex or to loving sex between partners.

Children of all ages become isolated when no one tells them the truth about their experience. They need to hear that these are sexual stimuli that might bring up sexual feelings, and there is no need to feel shame, because our culture conditions these responses. They need to know they are free to talk about their feelings of sexual arousal, of violation, of desire for sex with those they are attracted to, or of anger at sexual provocation they would not choose.

§ SUBTLE SEXUAL MESSAGES ARE HARDER TO SEE §

Although straightforward sexual pictures can be obvious to anyone who is willing to acknowledge them, we are bombarded by countless subtle messages that are difficult to label as sexual.

These pictures, or sounds, are perhaps even more effective, because we don't have to go into a separate compartment to take them in fully. The advertiser elicits our sexual reaction without our knowledge.

A magazine ad shows a woman in shadow holding a lipstick to her mouth. Her hand is also in shadow. The lipstick and her lips are lit, and a tube of light from her mouth to her jaw attracts our attention. Perhaps we could believe this picture was not intended to elicit sexual connotations if her jaw didn't have this strange beam of light hitting it right where a penis would penetrate if she were to have oral sex with a man. My acculturated inner voices still say it's just an interesting picture created by an artist, even though I know this artist deliberately intended us to feel as if we were observing a sexual scene. If the picture alone leaves us in doubt, the statement in red above the lipstick removes it. It reads, "When it feels good, you want it to last."

An even more startling, "subtly" sexual picture is a full-page perfume ad placed in several major women's magazines, in which a woman is holding a boy against her breast. She is dressed only in a gauzy wrap and is holding the child, who is between the ages of five and nine, in a consuming, controlling manner. He looks highly distressed whereas she, oblivious to his feelings, projects romantic bliss. Why are readers going to buy a perfume that is worn by a woman relating that way to a child? This picture suggests that enough women are sexually stimulated by controlling, sexually intimate contact with a male child to highlight the value of the perfume. Such women are allowed to associate a certain smell with their incestuous feelings, without ever consciously knowing they have them. The perfume is made by Calvin Klein, noted for blatant use of sex in advertising.

Advertisers know women will buy this perfume as a result of seeing (and feeling) this ad. They know what most mental health professionals still want to deny—that many women's sexuality is cross-wired to respond to dependent, controllable children.

§ "YES" TO SEX, "NO" TO PREGNANCY §

Vanity Fair magazine, in 1991, published pictures of actress Demi Moore, wearing no clothing, when she was in the last month of pregnancy. The cover picture of her naked, with one hand over her breasts and the other on her large belly, brought up intense indignation! Grocery stores removed the magazine from their shelves, and at the same time, the magazine was quickly sold out.

In the same month, the magazine *M* had two absolutely naked people on the cover, staring out from those same grocery store shelves. A man sat on a bench leaning forward, with a woman behind him, leaning on him, with her breast against his back. We could see all but her nipple, which was pressed against him. His genitals are hidden, but we can see all along his side and down his leg, so we can fill in the missing parts. This picture is clearly soft porn, definitely designed to arouse sexual response. Yet a bare, pregnant stomach was not permitted in "family" stores.

§ INHIBITING THE EFFECT OF ADVERTISING §

While advertisers are busy discovering vulnerable triggers to get our attention, we can employ four approaches to help remove or block their effect.

One is to stop partaking. By giving up television and not reading magazines that use such tactics, it is possible to remove the belief that this is just the way life is. After a year or so of avoiding the stimuli, it becomes easier to see how we are being manipulated and if the advertisers are succeeding.

A second is to spread magazine pictures on the living room floor, and take an objective look at how we are being set up to respond. By changing the context, it may be easier to perceive the hidden intent.

A third approach is to *look longer*. This might best be done with someone we can talk to at the same time, to bring the looking out of the shame compartment. The rules about glancing or looking only briefly add to the power of the piece. Staring at a naked body for five minutes, studying what it is that we might react to, can desensitize us to the advertiser's purpose. (For sex addicts, this may not be a place to begin.) Taping television shows allows us to replay or pause during the commercial or program segment. This approach may also work with pornography. By looking, having cross-wired arousal, and talking with another recovering person, in time, the cross-wiring can lose its ability to arouse.

A fourth tactic is to deliberately look at stimuli with the intent of examining and naming the ploy used against us. Perhaps, a group of people who want to stop the influence of advertisers might want to gather together, each person bringing along a sample, and spending a period of time sharing personal reactions, feelings, and observations.

Once our consciousness is raised, we have access to data we can use in sexual healing. Now, instead of responding with a sexual hum we didn't choose or cutting off feelings in order to avoid the sexual hum, it becomes possible to see how the media have put before us sexual stimuli to manipulate buying choices. It also becomes possible to see our sexual "hooks," those stimuli to which we are particularly reactive, so we can work toward releasing the cross-wiring that makes them work. In time, it will become possible for all of us to see sexual advertising and not be triggered into reacting against our will.

THE BILLION-DOLLAR
SEXUAL-SERVICES INDUSTRY

§

We, in our country, say that we want sexual intimacy. Most people agree that to bond with a partner, creating intense love and conceiving children, is the purpose of sex. Yet at the same time, billions of dollars each year are spent on pornography. Traditional sex therapists and others say that the use of pictures and videos can increase sexual arousal. Some therapists even suggest their use. (See Chapter 17 for more on traditional sex therapy). Others will say they can use pornography to become aroused, and then make love with their partner in an intimate way. A quick review of the reasoning behind such a belief reveals that pornography cannot be used by people who truly wish to have intimate sex. If a person has been aroused by observing others in sexual positions, and without clothing, then the sexual energy isn't beginning with the loving relationship. Instead, it is being deliberately provoked, because it doesn't emerge from within the relationship. The obstacles to natural, inside-out sex aren't obvious, because they are an integral part of our culture. We have no models of healthy sexual relationships to offer an understanding of what is wrong and what can be done about it. Instead, we have traditional sex therapists, who represent the "modern" approach to sexuality, offering solutions to sexual boredom and other symptoms.

Traditional sex therapists and feminists suggest that some pornography can be healthy as long as it doesn't degrade women or present sex with children. They do not see that all outside-in sexual stimulation is used only when the natural variety is otherwise unavailable. If a person has a choice between these two kinds of stimulation, the natural kind will always be chosen, because it is so much more pleasurable. There is no "healthy" pornography or erotica.

§ PORNOGRAPHY INTERFERES WITH INTIMACY §

Alecia's story illustrates a long-term search for a loving sexual relationship. She and Paul (discussed in Chapter 7) were married over thirty years ago, when a bride's virginity was valued. A "good girl," she believed Paul's lack of pressure for sex was respect for her, but when they married she learned the truth.

Paul equated sex with wickedness and was unable to be aroused unless he was firmly into the shame compartment, in order to feel wicked without shame. The first time they had sex, Alecia expected him to be the way her parents seemed, and to love her gently. Instead, he wanted her to rip off his clothes, while he did the same to her, and fall passionately into bed. He asked her to use slang expressions for sex to arouse him, and felt terrible when she refused.

Alecia was shocked, but at nineteen, she thought she must believe her husband, who was five years older and had a good deal of sexual experience. At the time, she didn't know that all of his experience was with prostitutes.

In the early years of their marriage, Alecia pleaded with Paul to make love with her, but the combination of her inability to "talk dirty" and join him in the shame compartment and his resulting feelings of shame, triggered by her "goodness," resulted in virtually no sex. Occasionally he could arouse her, sometimes to the point of orgasm, but once he attempted to put his penis into her vagina, he lost his erection. Paul could have sex with prostitutes or other "wicked" women, but sex with a "good" woman brought up his feelings of shame. It was difficult for him to enter his shame compartment, and he required intense "badness" so that he didn't have to feel the shame. Sexuality was intensely cross-wired to shame in his childhood, and so anything resembling overt, loving, gentle, "good" sex brought up his shame feelings. The usual secrecy that accompanies sex is sufficient for most people to enter the shame compartment. For Paul, it required far more.

Alecia could not have children, because Paul was unable to ejaculate in her vagina. She didn't know he masturbated to orgasm, and so didn't realize that artificial insemination was possible. Even if she had known, her outrage and hurt over his inability to do so with her would have contaminated the process of conception.

Although unable to be sexual with Alecia, Paul could masturbate with the use of pornography. The women in the pictures had to look like "bad" girls, and so *Playboy* centerfolds did not appeal to him. Those women looked just like Alecia but in sexual poses and with desire. They were the girl next door, the very image with which he could not feel sexual.

Paul primarily used pictures and books to take himself into the shame compartment. When he went out for sexual services, he preferred being sexual with an actual partner. Instead of having sex from afar in movies or peep shows, he engaged prostitutes.

During the first five years of marriage, Paul was also frustrated by the lack of sex. He blamed Alecia for not behaving in ways that stimulated him, believing that if his partner were lusty enough, he wouldn't have difficulty with sex. When this didn't happen, he took the next step. A neighbor and close friend of Alecia's made it clear that she was interested in having sex with him, and they began a long-term affair, which ended when Alecia found out about it. The ensuing years brought many more affairs, even though Paul felt strong love and bonding with Alecia. He had no interest in leaving her to marry someone else. The other women provided a way into the shame compartment.

By the 1970s, when sex therapy became popular, Alecia and Paul had spent twenty frustrated years trying to figure out sexuality. They had seen therapists who were unable to help, and then they saw several sex therapists over a period of fifteen years.

Their therapists took the approach of solving the problem of no sex. Because it was obvious that Paul was capable of having sex, the only solution they could see was to help Alecia become more like the women who aroused him (i.e., to become his cross-wired sex object). And so she did. She exercised and dieted, learned how to do her makeup and hair more flamboyantly and dress in ways he liked. She went from "plain" to "sexy." Nothing changed. She also set out to be more "interesting." She went to college, got two degrees, and went to work as a professional consultant. Nothing changed.

Paul desperately wished to please Alecia, because he feared their marriage would end if he couldn't make love to her the way she wanted. And so when she suggested that they go to yet another therapist, he willingly went. During this process, they received some benefit from the Masters and Johnson therapy clinic. Paul was able to follow the prescribed exercises that begin with nonsexual touching and gradually build up to sexual contact. Through this process, he learned how to please Alecia with his hands and mouth. Because he could see how pleasing this was to her, he felt pleasure and so wanted to do this more. The therapists forbade intercourse for a period of time, allowing the two of them to really learn about this kind of sexual loving, without pressure on Paul. But when the time came to move to intercourse, Paul consistently lost his erection. The times he was able to maintain it, he was unable to have an orgasm.

During these years, Alecia was convinced by therapists that her discomfort with pornography was not healthy, and that she should join Paul in the use of it, so that he could feel aroused sufficiently to be sexual with her. She went along with it for years, trying to quell her distaste and feelings of betrayal. Finally, she realized that she couldn't do it any longer, but she had no support for this decision. While her husband was away on a trip, she felt stronger and made the decision not to use pornography any longer. Coincidentally, her doctor told her about my book, *Reclaiming Healthy Sexual Energy*, and she made an appointment.

Alecia entered a period of intense grief as she began her healing from forty years of being told she was wrong. She raged over the lack of information about sexuality while she was growing up and for so much of her adult life. She felt deprived of having a healthy sex life and giving birth, as well as being allowed to use sexual energy to bond to her husband. She grieved deeply over the secrecy that endured throughout her life. Although she could complain about her husband, she hadn't revealed the reasons for her distress. Even after she joined the women's sexuality group, she spoke in generalities for a time, until she finally told the whole story in a way that allowed her listeners to grasp what she had been through. The tragedy was far more than her husband's inability to have sex with her. As with incest victims, she suffered from the total absence of a witness for her painful experience. Even therapists couldn't show her the truth in her perceptions, and she was prohibited from talking to parents, friends, and others by the cultural prohibition against talking about sex. Alecia had no way to grieve for the losses she lived with, because she had no one to mirror the existence of most of these losses. Attending the women's sexuality group and meeting with me allowed her to see that she indeed had been deprived and there was nothing wrong with her because her husband wasn't sexually interested. All past therapy and cultural myths supported the belief that there was something wrong with her. If she would only be more sexy, say "dirty" words, and learn how to be lusty, then there would be no problem.

Paul entered therapy too. He had no understanding of his need to move into the shame compartment in order to have sex. He grew up in a community where men were tough and prostitution was accepted and legal. "Real men" liked lusty women, and for the most part, sexuality was viewed as some-thing "dirty" and desirable. Sex jokes fit in with the perception of sex as "off color." At the same time, "good" women were seen as desirable for marriage. A gentle, loving, motherly kind of person was the one a man would want to take home to meet his parents and to mother his children. The environment Paul grew up in and the classic situation of the early 1950s, when he prepared to marry, set him up to fall in love with a woman with whom he couldn't feel sexual.

Additional influences from Paul's childhood supported the cultural ones. His grandmother was a gentle, loving person who adored him. She lived close by, providing a second home for him. Staying at her house offered a stark contrast to the alcoholic home in which he lived. His father was driven to make money and used anyone he could to do so. He forced his wife to have sex and demanded that she obey him in all ways. She was depressed, although she followed his orders. She showed little interest in Paul, instead finding him a bother with which she had to deal. Her anger found an outlet with Paul, because he was the only person who was in her power, the only person with whom she didn't feel inferior and controlled. She was mean to him, displacing her feelings from her powerful husband, where they might be danger-ous. He developed an intense anger toward her for not taking care of him. This anger became projected onto the women he was sexual with, while his relationship with Alecia was preserved from that by duplicating the love he shared with his grandmother.

It does not appear that Paul was sexually abused when he was a child, but his sexuality was damaged by exposure to parents whose sex was distorted and unhealthy. In some ways, Paul identified with his father, and in this way he saw sex as something to be obtained, however that came to be. At the same time, he hated his father's way of relating with women and felt shame for the ways he resembled him. As a result, he had to enter the shame compartment in order to be like his father—to use women for sexual gratification with little concern for them. His father, in contrast, seemed to live in the shame compartment at all times and so appeared to accept his sexual behavior without question. Because Paul couldn't do that, and because he chose a woman such as his grandmother to love, he wasn't able to have sex with his wife. His therapy involved learning about alternatives to his way of being sexual and examining his childhood influences, so he could relinquish his identification with his father's views of sexuality.

Until it was possible to learn about sex addiction and cross-wiring, Paul had no way to obtain help. Traditional sex therapy could not address his difficulties in a way that allowed him to change, in a manner that permitted a loving use of sexuality. He spent years trying to convince Alecia that she needed to change in ways that allowed him to get aroused and show her that he loved her! He was in an impossible bind. He couldn't show her love in the way she wanted, and he couldn't abandon his sexuality entirely. And so he made the only choice possible for one with his cross-wiring. He had affairs and used pornography.

§ THE NEED FOR OUTSIDE-IN STIMULATION §

Paul is not alone in his struggles. Countless men and women must be aroused by outside stimuli in order to feel sexual with their partners. Some succeed in obtaining sufficient arousal so that they can have sex with their mates, whereas others, like Paul, can rarely accomplish it. Michael could have intercourse and orgasm with his wife, but he always felt disappointed when they were finished. His fantasies were of a woman seeking him with love and adoration, and his wife no longer acted like this once their courtship period had passed. During his marriage, he had sex with two women who acted this way, but as soon as he had an orgasm, his guilt was so strong that he immediately left and never saw the women again. He found that videos with plots involving women who seduced men were stimulating, because he could identify with the men and feel as if he were the object of the woman's interest. He also read books that reflected this cross-wired sexual interest.

After eight months of therapy for sex addiction, Michael could no longer tolerate using pornography. He was too conscious of what he was doing. He could see the actors and actresses for the people they were and wondered why such beautiful women were allowing degrading sexual acts to be done to them. As he saw the unreality of the scenes, he could no longer be aroused by them. Michael was relieved by this, but at the same time, he feared he was losing his sexuality entirely, because he found sex with his wife disappointing. As long as his cross-wiring was in place, he was unable to enjoy sex that emerged from their intimacy. As with most people who give up all their old ways of being sexual before they access healthy sexuality, he and his wife went through a lengthy period without sex. Once they were free of the rule that they must have sex to be a man or a woman, or because they were married, they were free to drop the other expectations that limited their sexuality, and they began to uncover what is possible.

§ OTHER FORMS OF OUTSIDE-IN STIMULATION §

Brothels, street prostitutes, strip clubs, adult book stores, bath-houses, and massage parlors are among the services that allow people to experience their sexuality outside of an intimate, bonded relationship. Pornographic movies are easily available on cable television, and video stores offer large selections. Phone sex is a recent multimillion dollar, high-tech addition, which has now been followed by computer sex—an even more impersonal experience. The volume of such services in our culture is a symptom of how difficult it is for many people to bond inti-mately, and the extent of cross-wiring to sexual activities that are not readily available within the culture.

Imaginary Sex on the Phone

Phone sex has moved into a major role among the available sexual services. Phone companies make it easily available by doing the billing for companies offering the services. A person who wants to keep it secret can charge it to a long-distance phone card and have the bills sent to a private address. Sex on the phone allows a person to create fantasy that brings sexual arousal. The woman on the other end of the line can present herself as blond or brunette and with any combination of physical characteristics that may appeal to her customer, conveying her looks through her voice. She will describe sexual activities to excite him. The "obscene phone call" has become big business.

Sex on the phone with a stranger may have the advantages of safety from disease for the caller, physical safety for the phone prostitute, and independence from the crime world, because it is legal, but it is not healthy for either person. The one who calls a stranger for sex is seeking the most impersonal of sexual services, a choice that holds no interest for one who is capable of intimate sex.

Phone-sex operators say they are frequently asked to be the object of rape. They must play the role of a woman who is frightened, in pain, and sometimes enjoying being raped. They must act as if they are receiving a penis in their anuses or mouths without their consent. They are beaten or beat the man, and they are killed as they fake orgasm—all in their minds. It can't be possible for a conscious woman to relegate these imaginary abuses to some part of her that is unharmable. She will be affected, unless she is already capable of separating out abuses of her being from her usual experience of herself. The ability to do so is acquired by women who are already familiar with abuse, and all for $6 to $9 per hour, while the phone companies bring in millions of dollars every year and the telephone-sex services make millions every week.

Richard, a thirty-year-old married man who was highly successful in his work, was a sex addict who used telephone sex as well as prostitutes and paid almost nude women to dance at his nightclub table. His fantasy was so real that he believed prostitutes really loved him, although none would have sex without charge. Even though he was married, and his wife was willing to have sex, his desire for cross-wired human sexual contact felt like delirium at times. He searched for a woman who wanted him intensely and would be willing to risk everything to have him. Asking a woman on the phone to play this part felt real to his distorted, desperate mind—until his orgasm. He ran up thousands of dollars in phone bills and was caught by his wife when he wasn't able to intercept the bill. During my last contact with him, he wasn't willing to take steps necessary to reduce chances of acting out, and so was not able to begin recovery from sex addiction, even though he attended Sexaholics Anonymous meetings.

Although Richard believed the woman on the other end of the line really cared about him, she may have been conducting two calls at the same time. Phone prostitutes are trained to create fantasies for two men at once to increase their earnings. Only a person in a sexual trance could imagine something real was happening between himself and the operator. We might like to think that only a small percentage of people would regularly use such services, but we know this cannot be true because of the large amount of money spent each year.

Pornographic Videos Viewed at Home

In 1991, 410 million "adult tapes" were rented in the United States to be played at home on the VCR. The average is more than four per year for every American adult. These figures don't include movies available to any viewer on cable television or those purchased so they can be viewed again and again. Movies can also be taped from cable by people who want their own collection. This statistic only hints at the huge number of pornographic movies that are watched.

If shame were to drop from sexual activities, and people began to talk openly about what they watch and how it feels, we would have a more accurate sense of who watches what, as we do with theater movies. Instead, people only share when they have created a subculture of acceptability by moving into the shame compartment together. For example, men will invite other men over to watch a porno film, much as men might go together to a strip club. Some will not reveal their arousal, whereas others might masturbate together. But this form of revealing sexual activities doesn't remove shame, because it takes place in the shame compartment. The men agree that they will engage in their shameful activities for a time and not feel shame. If they were to seriously discuss it the next day at work with a group of male and female co-workers, the feelings of shame would emerge. As long as shame stays in place, each person is unable to find out what use of sexual energy would really feel good. Members of the men's sexuality therapy group experience intense shame once they are able to see what they are doing. It isn't until the shame passes, through extended discharge of it, that the alternatives begin to make sense. Those who insist that pornography use is fine, and those who condemn it and refuse to look, remain bound up in their cross-wiring. *Growing to accept one's cross-wiring is the first step to taking a serious look and making decisions from the inside out.*

In addition to the most common forms of sexual services that appeal to the typical adult who wants to be stimulated are the more atypical and illegal forms. These include child pornography, films, and pictures depicting violence, torture, and death. (The R-rated film *Basic Instinct* demonstrates the growing acceptability of acts previously found only in "hard-core" pornography by presenting a scene in which a man is stabbed to death while having an orgasm.) In addition, there are specialty films and magazines for less common cross-wiring, such as administration of enemas, sex with animals, cross-dressing, and particular fetishes. The cross-wiring that makes these activities sexually arousing (reviewed in Chapter 15) is of the same nature as cross-wiring that determines which hair color is attractive, or preference for oral sex or masturbation over intercourse. These socially unacceptable, and sometimes illegal, forms of sexual behavior are merely at the end of the continuum of unhealthy sexual practices.

Behind the Scenes with Table Dancers

When beginning his massage practice, a good friend of mine (I will call him Rick) worked in a nightclub that served alcohol and presented table dancers who offered to dance to one song for a certain price. These women were scantily clad, and they moved their bodies in ways to elicit sexual arousal in their male customers, to elicit more dances and tips. Although it is illegal for the women to have sex with customers, and in most states even to have physical contact, different clubs allow different levels of contact. These women can make large amounts of money, depending on the club they work in and the income level of the area.

Rick was hired by the owner of the club, a woman who wanted massages (nonsexual) at least once a week. It was convenient to have a massage therapist in the club, so she allowed him to set up his massage table in the dancers' dressing room, where the dancers had the opportunity to receive massages on their breaks. Rick got to be the proverbial "fly on the wall," gathering information that would not be available to me if I were to interview these women. He could hear the real stories of women who made their living this way.

It was obvious that dancing to arouse men (possibly to orgasm) and entertaining them by making them feel special and attractive isn't merely a variation on the usual use of sexual energy, as magazine articles and nonrecovering sex addicts would like us to think. Rick got to see that these women are not happy, don't enjoy their work, and are disgusted by the men they manipulate for as much money as they can get.

In this particular club, run by women in a small city, the dancers received a percentage for the drinks ordered by the men they entertained. They were given 50 percent of champagne sales, which brought them a minimum of $50 for a small bottle.

Rick spent hours each week in the dressing room, observing the behind-the-scenes action. He got to know over sixty dancers during his months there and observed that well over half were lesbians. They revealed this by talking about their partners or dating activities. Others, who were not obviously lesbians, flirted with each other and sexualized their conversations. These women may have grown up sexualizing and now did so with both sexes. Four of the sixty women had had sex-change operations from male to female. Rick said that all four used alcohol heavily and hated men. One in particular expressed intense disgust for the men she serviced.

Rick divided the women into two categories. About half of them used drugs and alcohol extensively and began using prior to going into the club to work. They needed to be in an altered state before they were able to engage in seductive activities with the patrons. The other half were obsessed with how they looked. These women were in their thirties and forties and did not use alcohol or drugs, because they focused on health and fitness. They seemed to be proving they were still attractive to men by getting men to pay them to be seductive.

Rick was acutely aware that most of these women were not naturally attractive by our culture's standards. He watched them use makeup, costumes, and hair to create an effect of beauty, along with silicone breast implants. As they walked into the club to go to work, few would have been given a second glance by prospective patrons.

The owner of the club wouldn't allow male partners of dancers in the club. When they saw their partner dancing for other men, they would became jealous and sometimes fight the men for whom she was dancing. In addition, their jealousy was often expressed by convincing their partner to quit, and the owner lost a dancer. In spite of media pressure to accept these situations as valid occupational choices, it seems that natural jealousy isn't limited to those who subscribe to monogamy.

The dancers talked about finding the perfect daddy, a man who wanted to spend time talking and drinking with them, who would give them large amounts of money and not require them to do much for it. The ideal was a married man who wanted a mistress, with no intercourse. The dancer would entertain him, make him feel special, and take his money. She would then return to the dressing room and report how much she had taken from him. The men were seen as marks, and the dancer felt skillful in taking them for as much as she could. Most of the women felt that dancing for men was a safe way to make money, in contrast to prostitution, at which they might not make much more money, were in danger of arrest and disease, and would not have protection from men who might be dangerous. The club offered a safe place to make money from men's interest in casual sex.

When a man paid large sums and was interested in only one woman, she said he was different. She didn't call him a pig or animal or other generic terms used for the customers.

When a woman was ready for a massage, she changed from the person she seemed to be while working. Clad only in a G-string and top that barely covered her nipples, she danced for men who masturbated on her. But when they took off these scant pieces of clothing, Rick described the women as feeling self-conscious and uncomfortable. Even though he was in the dressing room when they took off all their clothes to change from street wear to costumes and back and had seen them entirely nude, everything changed when he prepared to massage them. He used a sheet on his massage table and left the room when they undressed and dressed, as he did when giving a massage anywhere else. It appears that these dancers were able to transfer into their shame compartments when they danced and when they were preparing to dance, but when they put their bodies into the hands of a man who was going to touch them for nonsexual purposes, they moved back into their real selves. This self had boundaries, felt self-conscious, wasn't sexually aroused in order to overcome shame, and retained feelings of modesty that originated in childhood. Rick is a respectful person, who did not sexualize with these women, and whom they perceived as someone to trust. This relating threw off the hard, sexualized using that went on with the customers.

Rick related that when he came to work, he entered through the club door and went downstairs from there. Sometimes a dancer would not see who he was and approach him as if he were a customer. When this happened, he observed hard, plastic expressions and seductive body movements directed at him. But as soon as the woman recognized him, her face would change completely. The hard smile dissolved into a soft, friendly one, and she looked more like a real person. The posed expressions were designed to please the sex addict or the occasional man out for a sexual experience. But Rick wasn't one of the people they used for income, and so he didn't have to be lured. Instead, he was a friend.

§ THE DANCERS' STORIES §

I had the opportunity to interview two women who sold sexual services in the form of dancing in clubs in almost no clothing, bringing men sexual arousal and orgasms. Their therapist asked them if they would be willing to be interviewed. Both said they wanted to help with a book that might shed light on the life they had been leading. Each woman had been in therapy and so had been working on the shame that accompanied their professions, which allowed them to be able to talk openly. Catherine no longer works as a dancer. Trina continues in this work and occasionally supplements her income by charging for sex.

Catherine Gave Up Table Dancing

Catherine came to my office in a plain black dress, her hair pulled straight back, wearing no makeup, and with braces on her teeth. She didn't look anything like the stereotype of a woman who dances erotically for a man at his table for a fee. She leaned forward in her chair, looking at me intently while she talked. As her shame came up, it showed on her face, but she pushed through it, wanting to give me as much information as she could. I was touched by her desire to help.

Catherine had been a table dancer for three years, until she decided to stop three months ago. She started because it was easy money and required no experience. It seemed like a natural way for her to make money, because her father had paid her for sexual favors from the time she was five, including bringing him to orgasm in a variety of ways. She didn't have to think much about dancing in almost no clothing for a man and then rubbing her body on his penis to bring him to orgasm. She was, however, unable to touch her clients' penises for this purpose, because it brought up too much disgust at having done this for her father.

I asked Catherine why she stopped dancing. She said she was in recovery from drugs and alcohol, and knew that she couldn't continue the progress toward liking herself if she stayed in this job. I knew she was right. If she continued to service men sexually and live in a culture that condemns women for it, it would be difficult or impossible to move to a place where she could really accept herself.

Catherine understood, through therapy, how her cross-wiring was acted out in her work. For the first two years, she didn't get aroused when dancing, but once she stopped using drugs and alcohol to numb out her feelings, she found herself feeling sexual when she danced, and when she rubbed on penises, she had orgasms. Because this replayed her childhood abuses, she felt as if she were being abused—even though she chose to do these acts to make more money. She was living "in memory," feeling as if she were in childhood again instead of the present.

Catherine was able to describe the shame that comes with being a sexual dancer in this culture. She dated a number of men during the three years, soon telling them what she did for a living. The response was invariably the same. The men would either leave immediately or stay around long enough to get sex and then leave. They held our culture's view that a woman who is sexual with men for money isn't a real person and is not to be valued. (Such a reaction is also reasonable, because a man cannot form a monogamous bond with a woman who is exchanging sexual energy with others. If he tried, he would find himself naturally jealous.)

She didn't tell her most recent lover until they had dated for a month. Because he had gotten to know her, he was able to see the whole person she was and didn't abandon her. He was angry that she withheld that information from him, but she pointed out what had happened before when she revealed it quickly.

As I listened to her examples, I thought about how the men who paid her to dance sexually and bring them to orgasm are considered normal in our culture. Unless they spend all their money and go to the club every day, they are considered normal, red-blooded American males. Perhaps they are "naughty," but "boys will be boys." Most people, including most therapists, consider the concept of sexual addiction absurd. Men have been programmed in this culture to think that sex addiction would be a good addiction to have, and many respond "jokingly" with a comment to that effect. They also joke about wanting a woman like a dancer in their bed but, of course, they would never take her home to meet the family. Prostitution has been illegal for a long time, but until recently, only the prostitute was arrested, reflecting the difference in our culture's attitudes toward women who sell sexual services and the men who purchase them. (I'm not addressing homosexual services in this context. Our culture condemns all same-gender activity, even while supporting it. See Chapter 11 for further information on how homosexuality is treated in our culture.)

Catherine Is in Recovery for Sex Addiction

When she decided to stop using drugs and alcohol, Catherine discovered how addicted she was to sex too. As long as she could alter her mood with drugs, she was able to stop sexual feelings, unless she chose them, and to prevent herself from feeling much of the shame that came with servicing men sexually. But once she stopped "medicating" her feelings, they came back. Now she was able to feel sexual when she danced, using arousal as a drug to prevent herself from seeing how harmful her actions were to herself. But the orgasms she had from rubbing on the men's penises ended her arousal, leaving her with deep shame that came with the immediate loss of her drug. Unlike the gradual loss of a chemically induced, drugged state and the ability to regain it with further use of drugs, she became immediately "sober," unable to become aroused again for a time. She was then able to see what she was doing, feel the shame, and feel what it was like to continue servicing men.

Catherine found it difficult to stop dancing. She depended on the money but was also caught up in the shame–addiction cycle—the more shame she felt from sexual acting out, the more she wanted to avoid shame with further acting out. She joined a therapy group run by her therapist and through the support of other women struggling with sexual issues she was able to leave. Catherine also attends Sex and Love Addicts Anonymous (SLAA) to further explore her addiction to sexual fantasies and how the content resembles the way she was used sexually as a dancer and the sexual abuses of her childhood.

Catherine attended school during her dancing years and is now employed in a job she enjoys. She continues her schooling in computer graphics and told me that it felt very good when she paid her tuition from "job money" for the first time.

As we completed the interview, I asked Catherine if she were interested in reading any of my books. As I described them, I realized that *From Generation to Generation: Understanding Sexual Attraction to Children* would be a good choice. I had written it (in part) for those of us who are recovering from childhood sexual abuse in order to understand the people who did this. She agreed, and then added, "I'm afraid that I might abuse the children that I will have too, so I want to read your book." I nodded, telling her that all of us who were sexually violated carry the programming to do the same, and through our sexual recovery, we can make sure we don't act on it.

Catherine got up to leave, and we looked at each other with deep caring and understanding. We had touched one another, and we each had one more experience of talking to another survivor. Catherine has been off all drugs and alcohol for only a year, and she has made large strides in healing. With her courage in facing the pain of memories and her current life choices, she is on the path to understanding healthy sexuality in ways few people can now grasp.

Trina Is Still Table Dancing

Trina is thirty-five, and works out regularly in order to keep her body interesting to men. She stopped drinking and using most drugs a year ago, although she stopped using pot only three months ago. She has been attending twelve-step programs off and on for many years and presently goes regularly to meetings.

Trina is trying to deal with her addiction to sexual activity and to men who want her sexually. This one is harder for her than drugs. Although she has a sexual relationship with a man who lives with another woman, at the same time, she is beginning a new relationship with a man with whom she hasn't yet had sex. She laughs at the absurdity of abstaining from sex while she is still addicted to sex with someone else, but she is struggling to find out how to approach healing. She has been working with her therapist only a few months, and she is just beginning the hard work.

Trina got off the subject of dancing to tell me her concern with sexually abusing her own children. They live with their father most of the time now, but she remembers the past, when she realized that she had done some harmful things. One example was talking with her lover on the phone while her son, then eleven, lay on the bed next to her. She said she "had phone sex" with the man. She didn't realize this wasn't healthy for her son until the next day, when he rubbed his penis against her. She stopped him. I could hear the shame and despair in her voice, and I was glad that I knew she hadn't tried to harm him. I realized from my work with other women that she didn't understand sexual boundaries. In her own childhood, none had existed, and so she was unable to know what her children needed. I was glad she was able to tell me, so she could see herself in the eyes of a person who didn't minimize the seriousness of what she had done but also didn't shame her for it.

Trina had been fired many times from her dancing jobs. She was frequently in a bad mood. She felt the men took advantage of her, and she would become angry with them, snapping at everyone. She also asked customers for pot. Today, she is less angry about the situation. She has taken more control and feels better about herself. She has learned how to get men to pay more by bringing more of herself into the dance, looking men in the eye, and expecting them to pay for her services. As she has become more proficient at eliciting sexual reactions, her nightly earnings have gone from $200 to $800. The success has increased her self-esteem—even while the job itself decreases it.

I asked Trina why she thinks men come to her for table dances. She believes they are controlled by bosses and wives and girlfriends, and want to be in a situation where they can control someone else. By paying money, they get to say what they want. Other men want someone to talk to and will touch her in nonsexual ways. She sees them as lonely and starved for touch. She said this kind of man is "looking for something real in his life in bars."

Trina earned a four-year degree in psychology during her dancing years. She got a job working with retarded people several years ago but lost it because of having "no people skills." She was smoking pot and thought frequently about suicide. This seemed to be the bottom period of her existence, and she knew that she had to change her life or die. She began the several-year process of giving up drugs and alcohol and finally entered therapy. She believes she is on the road to recovery but doesn't know when she will give up dancing.

I wondered about Trina's feelings about aging, knowing that she had just crossed the midpoint of her thirties. She said that she gets scared inside, wondering how long she will be able to do this work that pays so well, but she doesn't receive negative feelings from her audience or customers. She saw a forty-seven-year-old woman dancing and figures that she can keep her body fit by working out for many more years. Trina won't have plastic surgery, because it isn't natural, and she doesn't like how it looks after a few years. She also believes that it isn't her body alone that attracts men but rather the "warm up and presentation."

§ SEXUAL SERVICES FOR GAY MEN §

"Adult bookstores" have long been available for impersonal sex for both homosexual and heterosexual men. These stores have small booths, which show pornographic videos that can be selected, much as channels on a television can be changed. Quarters buy time, and masturbation is typical. In addition, holes are made between booths, so men can put their penises through to be fondled or sucked to orgasm by another man. Heterosexual men also put their penises through the holes for an orgasm.

The most impersonal form of sexual activity is contact only between genitals and hands and mouths. It can be accomplished without awareness of the identity of the person on the other side of the wall. Men also have sex with each other in the stores or go elsewhere to do so. But the intent is different from the typical bars, where men go to pick each other up.

§ THE MEN WHO GO TO PORN BOOKSTORES §

I spoke with two men in their thirties who use the services of stores that permit them to put their penises through holes and be stimulated to orgasm. One is gay, the other bisexual. Both are recovering sex addicts and have been in therapy.

Greg continues to act out his sexual addiction occasionally. When existence seems pointless, he loses interest in life. In this state, he no longer cares if he engages in acts that are out of his integrity, or even threatening to his life. This empty, lonely, isolated state prevents him from knowing that he has a rich existence most of the time, and that he is "in memory" from childhood, when life held little hope. The thought of calling someone who would listen to his feelings of despair doesn't occur to him, because he can't remember that he has another life. He feels as if he will fade into oblivion if he doesn't do something to achieve a semblance of living. His cross-wiring tells him that the way to do this is to find a man with a thick penis who will let him suck on it. The draw to the activity, the sexual arousal, and the search, bring him energy and a feeling that life might have sufficient value. The fastest way to accomplish this is to go to a "bookstore" and into one of the booths with a hole in it.

When he has completed the act, Greg's shame makes him feel terrible, but the empty, hopeless feelings are abated. He scrubs his mouth and hands as he attempts to wash away the entire experience. The shame separates him from other people, creating intensified loneliness. Since he entered sexual recovery two years ago, he has found that the sooner he can tell someone what he has done, the sooner his shame will lift, and he can return to himself.

Sometimes Greg goes to the "bookstore" when he isn't feeling quite so desperate, and then he will talk to men in the hall, sometimes asking why they are there. On one trip, he was approached by a man to whom he wasn't cross-wired, and in whom he had no sexual interest. The man happened to be of a different race, which was not significant to Greg's cross-wiring, but the man wanted to know if that was the reason for his lack of interest. Greg explained that he had had sex with someone of his race in the past, and that his lack of interest was because he responded to men who looked like police officers or cowboys, or who had particularly shaped penises. He realized how the man attributed his own self-worth to Greg's interest or lack of it, even in this artificial situation. Sexual addiction, endemic to this culture, supports the idea that our worth is measured by how sexy we are to others. (See Chapters 9 and 14 for more on how our culture supports sex addiction.)

§ NEIL IS BISEXUAL §

Neil, the friend of an acquaintance mentioned earlier, agreed to tell me about how he had had relationships with women, but when he acted out sexually, he searched for men for impersonal sex. He did this in public places as well as "bookstores." Neil was sexually abused by his father, who had him suck on his penis from the time he was a baby until he was around four. He stopped when Neil became too old to keep it secret and was past an age that attracted him. Neil had been convinced that his father loved him when they were sexual, and so he felt greatly rejected when his father was no longer interested. In his adult sex life, he searched for penises to suck on to feel loved. Because this was an impossible task, when he became addictive, he chose the easiest route to his objective—a penis offered through the hole in a booth.

In recovery from his sexual addiction, he was able to work through this cross-wiring and relinquish it. He discovered that he could comfortably mate with either sex, and he married a woman. But his intense interest in penises, which, of course, required interaction with the same gender, came from his early childhood abuse.

§ WHEN THE CULTURE SHIFTS §

A decrease in the amount of money spent on sexual services will be one indicator of the shift away from the cultural shaming of sexuality. As more people tell their stories of sexual abuses, as more people know they are addicted to sexual energy, and as more people talk openly about sex to remove the shame, we will find that impersonal sex will lose its appeal. As this happens, the sale of pornography, prostitution, and other services will drop. Legislation will not be necessary to limit people's sexual behaviors. Instead, each of us will discover what is healthy for us.

ARE "SEXUAL PREFERENCES" UNHEALTHY?

§

We are all aware that some people like sexual activities that are culturally judged to be perverted or sick. Some are pedophiles, who prefer sex with children; some are rapists; and others prefer sex with partners who charge money. What hasn't been understood is that these people are at one end of a continuum of sexual distress, a continuum that includes almost all sexuality in our culture. All of us have our sexuality cross-wired in some fashion that prevents us from knowing healthy sexual energy.

As I have discussed in earlier chapters, we are born into a culture that distorts our sexuality right from the beginning of life. Our bodies are shamed when evidence of sexuality emerges. Many damaging rules are imposed on sexuality and are well understood by the time a young person reaches puberty, even though few of these were communicated with words.

Children are not allowed to develop their sexuality in natural ways. Instead, they are shamed, their physical and sexual boundaries are crossed, some are touched sexually, and all are prohibited from a genuine sexual unfolding. With this background, all of us have had negative experiences that became associated with sexuality. We can remove these negative associations, but to do so, we must talk about them and have the feelings that naturally accompany them (e.g., fear, humiliation, sadness, or betrayal). Because our culture prohibits most discussion of sexual things and also discourages the full expression of emotion, the feelings from our early negative experiences get wired up to sexual activity and to our choice of sexual partners.

We play out our past experiences until we can bring them to consciousness and release them, thereby creating the opportunity to reclaim healthy sexuality.

The media present examples of the connection between childhood experience and adult behavior. It is generally known that people who are sexual with children were probably sexually abused by an adult in their own childhood and are passing it on. It is also publicly understood that men who are abusive to their partners and children were abused in similar ways when they were children, and that women who tolerate abuse grew up with it. *We replicate those things that were unavoidable in childhood when we have no place to express the feelings that would have been appropriate.*

These connections occur most easily with sexuality because of the pervasive prohibition against seeing that it exists in children and the lack of talking about it. We get more easily stuck with the influence of both childhood experiences and cultural values in this area than any other.

§ CROSS-WIRING §

The term "cross-wiring," as I have defined it, reflects the incorrect associations between sexuality and anything else that is not inherently sexual. For example, a rapist who must angrily take sex in order to be aroused is clearly not in touch with healthy sexual energy. He or she had experiences earlier in life, which included cruel physical violation of boundaries, that left sex attached to violence.

A second example is the need for pain in order to achieve sufficient arousal for orgasm to take place. Known as sexual masochism, this form of cross-wiring can occur when a child lives with parents who are cruelly restrictive and humiliate the child for their own cross-wired pleasure. Such children may grow up to be controlling and humiliating in their sexual or nonsexual lives, duplicating what the parent did, and resuming the child's role in another area of life.

These and many other activities that are wired up to sexual arousal are defined by the mental health profession as deviations from "normal." The list includes sex with animals, urinating or defecating during sex, inflicting or receiving pain, the need to be punished or punish oneself, receiving enemas for arousal, focusing on objects or body parts (such as foot fetishes), the need to observe sexual scenes from a distance (voyeurism), the need to have one's genitals or sexuality observed (exhibitionism), and multiple hidden affairs when married (as evidenced by some politicians and spiritual leaders in the media). In addition, preference for masturbation over sex with a partner, the need for outside stimulation—such as pornography or fantasy—in a way that limits intimate sex, and sexually addictive activities, are among issues that people bring to therapy. Some people manage to incorporate their cross-wiring into their sex lives. For example, if a sexual masochist partners with a sexual sadist, they can play out their roles—or reverse them—by structuring their sex lives around S&M activities and establishing boundaries to create safety for each. Most people who make it to my office, however, feel cursed by their cross-wiring and are aware that it prohibits intimacy with a mate.

With the confusion in our culture about the subject of sex, it has been difficult for the mental health profession to decide what is normal and what is not. The definition of perversion has changed over the decades. In the past, homosexuality was considered perverted and a subject to address in therapy, even though the "cure" rate was low. After research on the subject and pressure from homosexual mental health professionals and organizations, it is no longer routinely labeled as such. But it has been confusing to know where to draw the line, and the line changes according to what is accepted in our culture. We have gone from believing that the only healthy sex is heterosexual intercourse between married people, with the man on top, to accepting any activities between consenting adults. Such assessments are based on the prevailing belief about right and wrong rather than on an underlying truth about sexuality.

Although sexual behaviors that are seen as unacceptable are examples of cross-wiring, in addition, most associations to sexuality are also cross-wired. Sex as love and reassurance or lusting for "sexy" strangers, are examples of socially acceptable forms of cross-wiring.

New Criteria for "Unhealthy" Sex

The concept of cross-wiring allows us to disregard the question of what is moral and acceptable and turn, instead, to a different set of criteria to decide if something is "wrong." These criteria might include the following:

1. Does my cross-wiring interfere with finding and maintaining a loving, intimate relationship?
2. Is my sexual focus more on how to achieve arousal and orgasm than on getting to see my partner more clearly and be seen?
3. Does my cross-wiring dictate my sexual choices (i.e., partners, activities, feelings, sexual frequency, etc.)?
4. Does my cross-wiring bring feelings of shame, either from within me or from the thought of others knowing?
5. Does my cross-wiring prevent me from using sex as a loving expression toward myself or another?
6. Does my cross-wiring inhibit the use of sexual energy to bond me into a monogamous, committed relationship?

§ SHAME IS AN OBSTACLE TO FINDING HEALTHY SEXUAL ENERGY §

Feelings of shame for any sexual activity that is between consenting adults are misplaced and an additional example of cross-wiring. It was not our doing that we were given associations that remain bound up to our sexuality. Events out of our control placed them there, and we are stuck with it until we have an avenue for change. We are not bad, awful people for wanting to have sex with animals or finding bondage arousing. Sexual fantasies of any kind are not indicators that something is *morally wrong. Fantasies are merely indicators of what got wired up during an earlier time of life and thus are valuable information.* (Guilt is appropriate when another person is being harmed, such as a child or someone who is coerced into sex. Toxic shame, however, is never useful to a person who wishes to change sexual connections.)

Once we are able to take a shame-free, curious look at our sexuality, then we can begin to look for how our connections were made. As I began my own curious exploration, I could see just how pervasive cross-wiring of sexual energy is.

The continuum approach began to make sense to me. The only problem with placing each cross-wired arousal pattern on a continuum is determining the criteria for placement from serious to less serious. The criterion of social acceptability may be useful, but it is limited, because the definition of "acceptable" varies greatly, even within our culture. I suggest that you place examples along your own continuum, making your own decisions about the seriousness of each pattern. Some of your cross-wirings may seem of no consequence, whereas others may greatly affect your life.

Below are categories of cross-wired behaviors and examples of each. Within these categories, the particular behaviors can be high or low on the scale of social acceptability. For example, a man who is aroused by overtly sexual, "dirty" language is not acceptable if he does this with strangers on the street, but he is tolerated and even encouraged when he does so with a partner who is sexually responsive to such behavior.

Categories of Sexually Cross-Wired Behavior

1. *Visual Stimuli*
   Partner's hair color
   Need for "sexy" clothing
   Partner of a certain body weight and shape and other physical qualities
   Body positioning and movement
   Nipple placement on breast

2. *Specific Sexual Activities Needed for Arousal*
Any sexual activity that is *necessary* for arousal, rather than just an option (may include oral sex, anal sex, certain body positions, etc.)
3. *Nonsexual Activities Needed for Arousal or Orgasm*
Spanking or being spanked
Being tickled
Bondage
Talking "dirty"
Genital pain (e.g., biting, pinching, scratching)
Urinating or defecating
Fetishism
4. *Erotic Stimuli in the Environment*
Watching a "sexy" person walk down the street
Watching someone undress
Hearing a zipper
Smelling perfume or cologne
Sex talk
Pictures or movies of sexual scenes
5. *Feelings That Produce Arousal*
Feeling aroused by a lover walking away from you
Wondering if the person will arouse you or not (e.g., during massage)
Needing to be seduced, or to seduce
Feeling special and important
Feeling sexy to your partner
Feeling admired, physically or otherwise
6. *Clothing*
Tight clothing that shows off the body to others and stimulates arousal
Men wearing women's clothing
Feeling well dressed
7. *Altering Oneself to Seem "Sexy"*
Body positioning
Strutting
Smiles

Sounds

Touching one's body suggestively

8. *Romance*

Needing to be charmed, swept off one's feet, made to feel special

Needing to feel like a real man, a stud, with above-average genitals and ability to perform

Needing to feel beautiful, sexy, and desirable

Taking care of, and being taken care of (financially, emotionally, physically, etc.)

Quickly believing that this is *the* relationship, and it is permanent

Reading romance novels frequently

9. *Discussing Sex as Wicked, Forbidden, Naughty, or Dirty*

Telling "dirty" jokes

Approaching potential partner with overtly sexual come-ons

Talking "dirty"

10. *Sexual Roles*

Being the "other woman" or "other man" in triangles

Being the "bad girl" (having sex with almost anyone)

Being the super stud (getting any girl)

Being a prude

Being the "good girl"

Being the gentleman, or good guy

Being the knight in shining armor

11. *Fear of Sex*

Avoidance of sexual activity

Lack of appropriate arousal

Staying out of relationships

Having impersonal sex to avoid fear brought on by awareness of partner

Preferring masturbation to sex

12. *Fear of Relationships*

13. *Preference for Sex without a Partner*

Fantasies of sex and sexual relationships preferred for arousal

Pornography replacing sex with a real person
Voyeurism (looking at strangers, telling sexual jokes, mentioning the night to come at a wedding, double entendres in conversation, flirting with relatives or friend's partners)
14. *Necessity of New Partners for Arousal*
15. *Inability to Say "No" to Sex*
Because you are in a relationship
Because you did it once before with that person
Because men can't turn it down
Because there seems to be no relationship without it
Because you're not allowed to say no
16. *Interpreting Sexual Activity as Meaningful*
Because you are loved
Because you are a loving person
Because you are valued
Because you are wanted
Because you are beautiful or handsome
Because life has meaning
17. *Interpreting Sexual Activity as Functional*
As a tranquilizer, sleeping pill, or other mood-altering effect
As something to do
As a means of creating closeness that doesn't occur in other ways
18. *Responding with Sexual Energy When the Choice Is Not to Be Sexual*
To television and magazine ads designed to trigger sexual energy
To flirtations of people who are not available, or when you are not available
To the walk, dress, facial expression, and so on, of those who exude sexual energy (charisma)

Cross-wiring is pervasive in our culture, as can be seen in many of the previous examples. The automatic sexual "hits" we get while watching television and even walking down the street are accepted as natural to our sexuality. They are not. Instead, they are examples of cross-wiring that almost everyone experiences. I watched a movie called *The Emerald Forest*, made in 1985, that showed how many of my automatic reactions are, in reality, just conditioned.

§ NATURAL BODIES §

The movie was set in South America, in a tribe in which the people were almost nude. My first reaction was to the breasts: I felt that I shouldn't look, and at the same time, I was curious to see. My "voices" said this was a sexual scene, and I might have sexual feelings. I felt tense because of the multitude of meanings associated with bare breasts.

But soon I was involved with the characters, and their breasts became just part of them. I was able to look curiously at the difference between the bodies of the young women and their mothers. Because they presented themselves naturally, in a way that isn't designed to elicit cross-wired sexual energy, I could see them as natural.

The scene shifted to the abduction of several of the young women, who were dressed in Western clothes and forced to be prostitutes. Now the cross-wired awareness returned. When they ran, I noticed their breasts bouncing—something I hadn't noticed when they ran uncovered. I also noticed relative breast size.

When the men of the tribe rescued the women, they all ran to the jungle. As the women ripped off the clothing, I found myself joyful to see their natural bodies and be freed from the cross-wired perception of them as sex objects.

§ CROSS-WIRED BY THE MEDIA §

Advertisers and television and movie producers have shaped our cross-wired associations by using psychological principles.

As I described in Chapter 12, they know that if they show us some but not all, and if they show us for only a short amount of time, so that we cannot fully experience what we see, our attention is riveted to what we are exposed to and will remain so for some time after the stimulus has been withdrawn. Sexual feelings are a drug for so many of us—lifting us temporarily out of dreary lives—that it is an obvious way to lure us. In addition, we are so deprived of our healthy sexuality that we search for any place it may be given expression without violating our inhibitions. Women's magazines, with sexy pictures of women, and men's magazines, with pictures of sexy men and women, provide low-grade sexual arousal that we can easily deny as sexual.

§ Mistrust of Children's Sexual Instincts §

Our childhoods, combined with the effects of our culture, shape our cross-wiring. Parents, and the rest of society, use a multitude of maneuvers to inhibit sexual expression from a young age, because it is believed that if you let children be as sexual as they want, they will somehow grow up to be oversexed or perverted. In fact, the reverse it true. Sexual shaming causes sexual addiction and unacceptable cross-wiring. However, children do not automatically forego their sexuality as a result, and they learn how to manage sexuality so that their parents think they have controlled it. Almost every boy was told directly or indirectly that he wasn't to masturbate. Almost every boy did so anyway. The stories I hear from my clients about their masturbation experiences are remarkably consistent. They were either told directly not to touch themselves, and were shamed when the adult thought they were going to, or they picked up the adult's discomfort with the topic, even if the adult's words said that masturbation was Okay. In either case, they knew they could perform this activity only in secret, acting as if they weren't sexual when in public.

Nowhere in the process of children's growth is there a place for the natural unfolding of sexual expression based on the inside-out experience of sexual energy. Except in a therapist's office, there has been no arena for the expression of feelings that are elicited by damage to sexuality—an event that is necessary to shed damage and reclaim health. Consequently, children store up the experiences in their brains and in each cell of the body. These memories are expressed in adult sexual activity, choice of sexual partners, arousal patterns, and the struggle to repress and express this vital part of being alive. No one totally abandons his or her sexual selfs, but the form sexual expression takes may appear unrelated to sexuality.

§ UNDERSTANDING OUR CROSS-WIRING CAN LEAD TO SEXUAL HEALTH §

Cross-wiring arises from childhood and cultural influences on sexuality. This vital connection is useful in recovering the healthy potential we had at birth. By examining the nature of cross-wiring and going back to early years, we are able to retrieve memories of events and/or kinds of relating that brought about the cross-wiring. For example, a man called me in his search for a therapist, because he found it necessary to bind his penis with a hanger, tie paper to the other end of the hanger and light it, so that the hanger burned his penis until he couldn't stand it any longer. Without an understanding of the influence of childhood, this behavior may seem beyond comprehension. But if we know (as he did before calling me) that he didn't make up the need for pain to bring on sexual arousal, and that such connections were made in earlier years, then we have a place to begin. We can also look at how his need for pain serves him now and influences his adult relationships. His cross-wiring from childhood relating will influence all his adult relating, not just sexual relating.

§ ROMANCE AND LUST AT CROSS-PURPOSES §

Terri was in a therapy group with Warren. One evening, they demonstrated how their cross-wiring interacted to create a relationship common in our culture. Both were addicted to sexual energy: Her cross-wiring was to romance, to being adored, the center of a man's attention for a man, whereas his was to the intensity of sexual scoring with a woman who thought he was wonderful. It started when Terri attempted to tell Warren that she liked him. This was a real feeling, based on his courage in revealing himself in painful ways. Warren received the information from his cross-wired addict, however, and lit up. He looked delighted, like a child who has just learned that he will get the expensive toy he has been asking for. As he was telling Terri that he was embarrassed and pleased, we could all see that he had taken her compliment as sexual interest, not the human connection she was expressing. Before I could point this out, Terri responded with her own cross-wired patterns. She told him that his response felt good to her, and she had immediately planned their entire relationship in her head. They would begin dating, soon have sex, bond into a couple, and be married in my office with the group members in attendance. And, of course, they would live happily ever after.

As Warren heard her putting into words the dynamics that many women in his life had unconsciously acted out, he could also express his own patterns. He told Terri that she scared him, and he wanted to run the other way. His interest included no plans for the future, only sex. He said he would like very much to *want* a relationship, and that was the goal of his recovery, but the fact was that he was cross-wired to want to score. Getting a woman sexually interested in him and willing to have sex made him feel as if he were a worthwhile person. He felt strong, as if he could manage anything. This "fix" was so powerful for him that he was unaware that Terri was not sexually interested—in fact, her patterns dictated romance and marriage, not sex—and that she had offered him a real compliment, not a cross-wired one. He was also not influenced by knowing that he was prohibited from having any relationship—particularly a sexual one—with a group member he didn't know before joining the group. Warren is an intelligent man, competent, and easily manages other areas of his life. But in this one area, he appeared blind to other group members, and he felt blind as well.

Terri's romance addiction took over as she watched Warren show interest in her with his expressive face. His energy flowed strongly in her direction. She told him and the group about how appealing his reaction was to her, and how her "voices" were telling her how they would create a relationship. Warren assured her that he was interested only in sex, but this real information could not turn off her cross-wiring. Both were able to observe their cross-wiring, because they were in the presence of group members and me, but their description of the nature of their cross-wired desires resembled drug addicts needing a fix to prevent the excruciating experience of withdrawal.

As Warren heard Terri's picture of the perfect marriage, he could see that all the women he had been with had wanted the same. He described how they acted, and how he had felt too guilty to leave them. What followed was a painful period in which he longed to run, and his partner felt abandoned, thus clinging to him even more. As he told Terri he could see this with her, she filled in the gaps. She would do everything she could to be attractive to him, as she had with other men. She became conscious of her clothing and makeup, and fought the tendency to suck in her stomach to look thinner. Several of us commented on the increase in her flirtatious smiles and head turnings.

She said she would think of him constantly, waiting for him to call, even when he hadn't said he would. He said he would feel guilty if he didn't call and angry if he obeyed the unwritten rule that he must. She said she would pout and withhold information because she was hurt, and he said he would try to have sex to bring her out of withdrawal. She said she would feel used and objectified by his desire for sex when she was obviously not interested. He said he would feel rejected and unloved, the feeling he was trying to avoid when she showed her initial interest. They both said that it was time to go into therapy to save the relationship, and they turned to me.

With a startling wave of insight, I saw how couples seek therapy to save something based entirely on cross-wired interest and doomed unless it is possible to introduce massive amounts of honesty into the system. We agreed that the forty-minute, abbreviated relationship should be put to rest, and both parties got to see how impossible it is to create something real and life sustaining out of illusion.

As the list of cross-wiring examples shows, many areas of our sexuality and our lives are affected by the experiences of our childhoods and the cultural dictates passed on to each of us. When we can respect the existence of this process and learn about the role of our culture in distorting our sexual nature, the route to cultural change will be open to us. The growing awareness of the existence of sexual addiction and the presence of incest in a large percentage of American families is opening doors for changes in our culture. But until we each know how we have been affected, and how to remove the effects, the process of change will move slowly.

15

"SEX DRIVE"

§

A Product of Our Culture

Men and women both experience a strong desire to have sex, often after going for a period of time without it. Sometimes masturbation will satisfy it, and at other times, sex with a partner seems necessary. This desire can be very intense.

Even though this experience is real, the intensity is not caused by an innate sex drive. When we reach puberty we get a spurt of hormones that ensures sexual arousal and orgasm so that we become able to have children and perpetuate the species. Most people find themselves focused on potential sex partners— also historically necessary for survival, because two parents ensure the provision for offspring. This intense interest in sex and partners is part of being human, but a misuse of it results in our belief that we have sex drives that must be satisfied or "serviced," usually by another person.

The point is made by those who believe in a "sex drive" that our hormones influence our interest in sex and the ability to become aroused and reach orgasm, as if this were support for the existence of a need that must be regularly satisfied. We can look at it in reverse. When we have a strong need for sex (resulting from its repression), then additional hormones are created to bring about the intense experience. As well, when a person does not want to be sexual, the body decreases the production of hormones to decrease sexual feelings. Hormone levels are not a given, causing predictable responses. Instead, they are the physiological tools with which our gender was created, and with which we mediate our physical responses. This is demonstrated by menopausal women. Women who are sexually active maintain higher levels of sex hormones than those who are not. Perhaps a sexually healthy culture would have a lower average level of sex hormones than ours. Even that might vary, depending on the status of individuals—higher for those just falling in love or searching for a partner, lower for those in long-term relationships, and lowest for those who are sick or otherwise not ready to express sexuality.

The experience of a sex drive comes from a number of sources. First, our culture supports sexuality that resembles that of postpubescent young people—romance, infatuation, and reaction to body parts. When men are less interested in sex as they age, it is viewed as a loss instead of possible maturity. A second source is the cross-wiring from childhood and cultural influence that programs us to experience intense sexual feeling in response to certain stimuli. A third is lack of access to natural, gently passionate, inside-out sexuality.

§ Our Experience of a Sex Drive §

Our *experience* of a sex drive is real, but it is an artifact of growing up in a society that tries to inhibit sexual feelings and activities in all but a few, narrowly defined piaces. Sexuality is a vital part of being human—a necessary part. Without it, we would cease to exist as a race. Without it, individual humans dramatically lessen their existence. If we are comfortable with sexual feelings, they can accompany us through most of the day, rising at times into the form of overt arousal and subsiding at others into sexual potential. Our sexual energy is a powerful source of feeling alive. We can feel plump, sensuous, and fully in our bodies, in contrast to other valuable times when our intellect dominates. *Sexuality is one of our options for how to feel at any given moment.*

Having sex with a partner or masturbating to orgasm are only two ways to express sexual energy. Yet, in our culture, it is believed that all men and some women, particularly when they are young, must have this kind of sexual expression on a regular basis. We don't validate the presence of sexual feelings that have no urge for expression, or the power of flirting with a partner or potential partner, as being truly sexual.

Soon after we were born, the outside world stopped mirroring the natural, life-giving nature of sexuality. Instead, we were nonverbally instructed to get rid of it. Shaming looks and forcibly removing hands from genitals were only two of the ways we were told not to do that. Some of us were used as emotional lovers and required to share sexual energy covertly with a parent. Others were dressed in ways that denied sexuality, as parents tried to repress it entirely until the magical day of marriage. Still others were used as sexual partners, while sexuality was denied in other contexts. All of us were expected to withhold evidence of sexuality in public, creating an illusion of nonsexuality, and then somehow introduce sexuality only at the proper time and place. Even now, when sexual activity and "sexiness" bombards us from television, magazines, and all around us, we are somehow expected to absorb it all without reacting sexually.

Each of us makes unconscious choices about our sexual energy. Some people entirely repress its existence, then are not able to be sexual when it is appropriate. The other extreme is the behavior of the sex addict, who feels sexually driven most of the time and whose life is dominated by it. Wherever we lie on the continuum, none of us are supposed to talk openly about it. If we feel aroused in the presence of others, such as during a discussion of sexuality or while watching a movie with sexual scenes, we are not to share it. Each of us feels alone with our sexuality, except when we have a sexual partner with whom we can share. The fact that we are only allowed to feel sexual in the context of a relationship makes relationships even more necessary in order to experience ourselves as sexual beings.

§ THE VICIOUS CYCLE OF SEXUAL REPRESSION §

A vicious cycle has evolved over time. It goes like this.

1. We all feel sexual. It is in our nature. We are born with the capability of sexual arousal, and the tendency to experience it increases after puberty.
2. Some other people are not comfortable with evidence of this, because it triggers their own sexual feelings.
3. Evidence of sexual energy was shamed by those who were not comfortable in order to inhibit evidence of it.
4. The shaming resulted in our hiding evidence of sexual feelings.
5. Hiding sexual feelings resulted in having no mirrors (or only shaming ones).
6. No mirror for normal, healthy feelings made us feel as if we were the only ones who had these feelings, even though indirect evidence is available that others do too.
7. Each of us becomes accustomed to our sexual energy being isolated from shaming influences, and so we no longer want our sexual energy stimulated accidentally. Our internalized shame emerges when it is.
8. Each of us helps create artificial boundaries around sexual stimulation, so that we don't accidentally find it triggered. We do this by showing our shame with laughter or other evidence of embarrassment when a joke or innuendo is made. We also are willing to experience ourselves as nonsexual people, particularly in the presence of children or adults who are not in our age range. We isolate sex in a shame compartment and can only express it freely when the rules permit, after we switch into the shame compartment.
9. The effects of public shaming and internalized shaming are like a pressure cooker. Sexual energy must be expressed, because it is part of our aliveness, but it is held in by artificial constraints. *The intensity necessary to*

*override the constraints gives the appearance of an intense sex
drive that must be satisfied.*

10. When it is expressed, it feels shameful, and if it is
    observed by others, will be shamed, furthering the need
    to isolate sexuality from others and the sense of being
    alone with it.

This vicious cycle has been going on for centuries in many
cultures, and it has become self-perpetuating. To reverse this
process, we must take the shame off of sexuality, which requires
bringing it out in the open, where it can be seen for what it is.
The truth is that sexuality is a normal, natural, life-giving part of
being human, and it is meant to be welcomed into our lives. As
we are able fully to have our sexual energy, we will express it
only in ways that serve us.

§ SEX ADDICTION OR CROSS-WIRING CAN FEEL LIKE A SEX DRIVE §

Sex addicts, both male and female, feel as if sexual behavior is
absolutely necessary to sustain life. The form of the addiction
varies from person to person and may include compulsive
masturbation, addiction to sex with one's partner, affairs, pornography, buying prostitutes or seeking other sexual services,
such as massage parlors and topless bars. It also includes getting
picked up, romanticizing any potential partner, and flirting with
many people.

These addicts will begin to feel very uncomfortable if they
cannot have their addictive drug, in the same way that a heroin
addict begins to panic if he or she cannot obtain the drug prior to
the beginning of withdrawal. I frequently hear stories from
partners of those who seem to "need" sex at a given frequency.
Partners can sense the change in their mate when it has been too
long since having sex. This experienced need has been described
in the popular press, as well as by traditional sex therapists, as a

sex drive. However, searching a little further, it can be seen that this isn't the case. If one needs an orgasm, masturbation can produce one quickly. Although this may not be as satisfying as sex with a partner and doesn't serve the coupling need, it will take care of the feeling of "horniness," if this were strictly physiological. When people need sex with their partner at a certain frequency, whether the partner wants it or not, cross-wiring is involved. In a nonaddictive, healthy sexual relationship, a couple may have sex every day for weeks and then go for weeks or even months with none. The bonding needs, along with other needs in their lives, play a role in the desired frequency. The need for bonding will instruct them, *together*, when sexual activity is needed to bring them intensely back to each other. If one person wants sex more than the other, then other variables are intruding. Among these are one partner's inhibitions due to past sexual damage; association of sex with love, care, reassurance; and feeling needed and valued. Desire for more sex than your partner may also be an expression of anger and control and may be unconsciously intended to drive him or her away. It is not the result of a "sex drive."

R. J., a lawyer for a major corporation, was convinced that he had a sex drive that had to be satisfied at least every two days. When the time came, he found himself looking at attractive women and creating a fantasy about sex with one of them. As soon as it became possible, he would quickly masturbate, relieving the desire for another day or two. After two decades of this, he saw it as a need he was born with and required to satisfy. The few times he tried to disregard his urge were met with failure, further reinforcing his belief.

R. J. felt shame following his ejaculation and wished he did not have a "sex drive." He had been provided with the shaming our culture attaches to sexuality, with an added emphasis on morality. He felt cursed by his need, because he saw it as sinful. In addition, his view of sexuality as being beneath a person of moral character placed him in a position of not wanting to have sex with his wife. He had been able to have sexual relationships with women that lasted up to one year, because the bonding urge allowed him to override shame. But once the relationship settled into permanence, he could not continue to be sexual. Each of his relationships ended after a year, for reasons that did not seem related to sex.

R. J. married in his thirties, because he wanted to break this pattern, and he found a woman he enjoyed being with, even when their sex life faltered. This relationship brought him into therapy, because he was no longer willing to blame the relationship and end it. As we looked at his views of sex, we began to see that intense shame prevented him from continuing a gentle, loving sexual relationship.

R. J. was surprised to hear me say that we don't have a sex drive that needs to be satisfied on a regular basis. He was curious to learn about this, because it differed from his experience, and also because it held out hope that he might be able to let go of the long-standing behavior he didn't like.

As we talked about his masturbation, it came to light that R. J. couldn't stop. I introduced the concept of the addictive nature of his use of sexual energy. Because this made sense to him, we began to map out ways for him to collect more information about it, so that we could see how to intervene. We began by agreeing that R. J. would allow two days to focus on his sexuality, even to the exclusion of work. If necessary, he would take time off from work to allow himself to focus on his sexual compulsion. After years of masturbating every two to three days, we could predict that by the second day, the need to masturbate would soon arrive.

R. J. found that, for the first time, he went four days before the compulsion became strong. Apparently, looking at his behavior allowed him to begin seeing what he was doing, and it reduced the compulsion. But by the fourth day, it was intense.

We had discussed the possible functions of his routine fantasy and masturbation, alerting him to what to look for as he refused to use the release in the old ways. As he set aside the possibility of creating a fantasy love affair for an afternoon, terminated by orgasm, he began to see that his life felt empty. In spite of a loving relationship that had lasted over two years and his position as an attorney, he didn't feel that he was living. As we explored, R. J. told the story of his younger years, when he wanted to do well in law school, so he could have an impact on injustices he saw around him. He felt alive and dedicated to his studies, seeing a future with meaning. But after leaving school and finding a safe job, he had somehow abandoned his hopes.

R. J. saw no way out of this bland, empty life, and so he created a substitute. Every other day (he probably would have done it every day if he had not felt shame and remorse afterward), he created a mini-illusion of a human connection. Sexual feelings would emerge, preparing him to go for a walk until he saw the kind of woman that fit his fantasy. He would look at her only briefly, not wanting to violate her by staring. As he returned to work, or home, he would begin the fantasy about a woman who adored him. The afternoon at work became something to get through, so he could go home to his fantasy woman. The intense fantasy filled his vacuum, and he had a reprieve from emptiness.

As we examined the fantasy experience, we learned that his use of sexual energy was addictive. It was a mood-altering drug that made him feel differently than when he was with real people and having real sex. We could now see that our task was twofold. First, we worked on limiting R. J.'s use of sexual energy as a drug, so that the feelings he found distressing became more available to work on. Second, we began examining the life R. J. had chosen and the influences from his childhood that brought him to choose it, so he could begin seeing what he really wanted to do with his life. As he became more able to choose his life, based on his talents and interests, the need for a made-up life subsided. In addition, we also examined his difficulty in sharing his sexuality with his wife and discovered an intense sexual shame. He felt he was violating her with sex, even though she expressed a strong interest. As he was able to examine his shame-based beliefs, he could begin welcoming a healthier sexuality.

After a year of therapy, R. J. was able to forego addictive masturbation, and he spent the next year with no sexual activity.

He came to see that he did not have a drive for sex that had to be satisfied. During that year, he had only an occasional desire for sexual activity. As he was able to resolve some of his feelings, he began to have sex with his wife.

§ We Have a "Coupling Drive" §

We humans certainly have a strong interest in our sexuality, and and we still would even in an ideal culture. Bonding to another, having families, and creating community are essential components to a fully led life. We might even say that men and women have a "coupling drive," an intense interest in finding a mate and joining together. When we reach puberty, we find ourselves with strong sexual feelings and an intense interest in potential partners. Sexual arousal is the fuel for the coupling drive.

Coupling has also been distorted by our culture in ways that are transmitted by our parents and those around us. These distortions are different, however. Coupling hasn't been driven underground, and is seen as a normal part of community. Controls have been placed on it by most cultures, such as the age at which it is appropriate and the way partners are selected. Our culture states clearly that we are to be with people of the opposite sex, near our own age, and we are to have children. We are also supposed to limit ourselves to our own race, and we are encouraged to mate with those within our subcultural community, based on socioeconomic status. We are to mate with those like us.

We are permitted to show some affection in public and indicate that we are bonded with sexual energy, but we are not allowed to reveal either with our bodies or our words that we are sexual with each other. We are given nonverbal messages by those around us that doing so is not acceptable.

Infatuation and "falling in love" are looked on with delight, tolerance, or criticism, depending on the attitudes of family and friends. Many parents delude themselves by seeing their children's bonding activities as "puppy love" or something less than the feelings that lead to marriage. This isn't true—the feelings are the same, perhaps even more intense, because they are new to teenagers. Using such labels allows parents and other adults to separate it from the "shameful" nature of sexuality and look down on it as trivial. These mechanisms also allow adults to avoid knowing that their children are fully sexual beings, whether or not they are having sex. Even for those who choose not to engage in sexual activity, the feelings of sexual arousal are very intense, experienced either in the genitals or diffusely throughout the body or, normally, both.

If we were allowed to use sexual energy in the ways it is intended, it would be a powerful fuel for bonding into a relationship. But we are not allowed to use it overtly. Instead, we must pretend that we aren't really having sex, or talk about it only in stereotyped ways. Men are allowed to say they "got some," and women can talk about how romantic he was. Except in unusual circles, neither are allowed to bring sex out of the shame compartment, to talk openly about their decision to introduce it into their relationship, and talk about what it is like or ask open questions about it.

Coupling with the "right" person is accepted and sanctioned. How to integrate this part of sexual life with sexual activity is confusing to everyone. If one is right, and the other shameful, then how does the individual integrate the two? Some people reduce sexual frequency after the marriage has been well established. Others use myriad possibilities for avoiding shame or moving into a shame place that does not feel inconsistent with the act. Others separate their sex lives from their love lives.

16

TRADITIONAL SEX THERAPY

§

Perpetuating Unhealthy Sexuality

Masters and Johnson applied for their first research grant in the mid-1950s, before the sexual revolution opened up the field. The early study of sex had to push against public objection and only since the 1960s has it become easier to study without fear of public opposition. These two pioneers were the first to revolutionize the study of sex, preceded only by Kinsey's studies in the 1940s. Their courage has influenced sexuality for all of us.

Helen Singer Kaplan, M.D., Ph.D., head of the human sexuality program at the New York Hospital–Cornell Medical Center, arrived on the scene a decade or so later with her book *The New Sex Therapy*.[1] She offered additional approaches for sex therapists. During the 1970s, as the numbers of sex therapists grew, authors appeared with books on sexual subjects to help people increase their awareness of sex and enjoy it more. These professionals and writers have served several important functions.

§THE CONTRIBUTIONS OF SEX THERAPY§

First among the benefits of large numbers of people reading books on sex is that the subject has become more acceptable. Sex is receiving more accurate coverage than locker-room talk and quilting bees ever provided. The books of sex therapist Lonnie Barbach,[2] beginning in the mid-1970s, offered information to women about sexual activities. Readers could find out what was really going on with women sexually, something we hadn't been able to know, because women were not allowed to sit comfortably together and discuss the details of their sex lives.

Second, the popularity of sex therapy is reducing sexual shame for the first time in history. In spite of the changes that took place in the 1960s and 1970s, most people still feel shame about sexual activities and thoughts that are different from what we have been told is the norm. The norm is being revised from preliminary sexual stimulation followed by intercourse between opposite sex partners to include a large variety of activities. The result is a growing change in our culture as the truth about the actual variety of sexual activities becomes apparent. However, the shame-reducing effect of this communication is offset by lack of accurate information about where sexual fantasies come from, their meaning, and the possibility of changing one's personal history, so the fantasies are no longer appealing. Traditional sex therapists claim that in order to reduce shame, individuals must accept their sexual fantasies and all activities that do not harm others as normal and healthy. It is possible to give up shame and, at the same time, know that we can have more than fantasies and sexual activities that do not provide the most loving use of sexual energy.

A third function that sex therapy serves is providing the public with sexual information that has only become available in the past two decades. After Masters and Johnson reported their research on human sexuality, the door opened to all kinds of research in many medical schools and universities. The results have answered questions that couldn't be answered in the past. We know how the body works during sexual arousal and activity, and how to help those who have been affected by shaming and sexual silence in ways that inhibit use of sexuality.

A fourth function is the widespread knowledge that therapists can help with sexual problems. Prior to Masters and Johnson's research and resulting treatments of sexual dysfunction, the general public had little hope of "curing" lack of erections and orgasms, and premature ejaculation. Now, when people experience such symptoms, they know it is possible to find help.

§ DEFICIENCIES OF TRADITIONAL SEX THERAPY §

Traditional sex therapy, by presenting the *typical* sexual expression as *normal*, hasn't gone far enough. It is not enough to say you aren't sick if you have fantasies of sexual bondage, sex with animals, or rape. It must also be said that these fantasies and behaviors are symptoms of our culture, that these symptoms can be changed, and that there is a healthier sexuality available to all of us.

Ruth Westheimer, Ed.D., known as "Dr. Ruth," had several years of popularity on radio and television during the mid-1980s and wrote a best-selling book. She was the most visible sex therapist and self-declared expert in America, and so, in the eyes of the public, she represented the field. It might have been easier to dismiss her advice as eccentric and unfounded if she hadn't had academic credentials, including training at Cornell Medical Center, and a foreword to her book written by her teacher, Helen Singer Kaplan, a highly respected researcher, clinician, and writer, mentioned earlier as a major contributor to early sex therapy. Although Dr. Ruth's popularity is fading, most people still recognize her name, and she remains a contributing editor for *Redbook* and *New Woman* magazines.

Dr. Ruth and other traditional sex therapists have advised people to use pornographic pictures, movies, and books to arouse sexual energy. At the same time, they give lip service to the concept of sexual "intimacy." The two are mutually exclusive.

§ INTIMACY §

Writers about sex usually assume that intimacy is valuable while we are being sexual with our lover. *And yet, traditional sex therapists are trained to offer suggestions that not only don't encourage intimacy, but also actually decrease it.*

Intimacy is not defined by the act of taking off clothes and rubbing bodies together to bring up sexual feelings. These activities can be done with no intimacy at all. Intimacy is an experience of truly seeing another and being seen. It comes from out willingness to be open and honest about our present experience and receptive to the experience of the other. When we can do this, we get to have the most basic experience of relationship to another—one we originally needed as newborn infants, and one that creates our sense of community and reason to live. Sexual energy provides a powerful supplement to the desire to open ourselves. The primitive act of bringing naked bodies together allows us to feel as we did when we were little bundles of infant feeling.

If intimacy is one of the most important reasons to be sexual, then discovering obstacles to it and removing them are obvious directions to take. Traditional sex therapy, however, too often offers suggestions that remove us from intimacy.

One of these suggestions is the prescription for the use of fantasy to enhance sexual arousal. Because traditional sex therapists focus on helping people perform sexually, they don't see that fantasizing about other people or other activities takes people *away* from the present and makes intimacy impossible. Dr. Ruth talks about a man who couldn't achieve an erection when his wife grew to be 60 years old, because she no longer looked like the kind of woman required for arousal. Instead of learning about his ageism and helping him discover how to be delighted with his wife, no matter what her body looked like, Dr. Ruth helped him to create fantasies of his wife when she was younger so he could have an erection! *What kind of intimate loving is going on when a man needs to pretend he is with someone else, in another time?* He was told not to tell her this, because it would hurt her feelings. A second lie has been added onto the first.

Sexual fantasizing is a sickness in our culture. We do it too much, not too little. Sex addicts spend hours in fantasy as they anticipate their next score or replay the last. Some men masturbate to pornography or fantasies until their penises hurt or are severely damaged. Women and men spend large amounts of time imagining romantic interludes, taking themselves out of an uncomfortable present by bringing on pleasant thoughts. One function of extramarital affairs is providing someone to fantasize about when work or family life seems boring. Eighty percent of married men and 50 percent of married women act out such fantasies. We already know these life-depriving pastimes. Then traditional sex therapists suggest that we use fantasy— avoidance of real life—to be able to have sex, whether we want to or not.

An assumption is made that we must be sexual, either for our partner's sake or to live up to some outside-in idea of what it means to be human. If sex is accompanied by the use of fantasy or any other activity that takes us away from ourselves and away from our partners, then it is not life enhancing.

I believe it is healthier to be celibate in a loving relationship than to have sexual feelings elicited by an outside-in stimulus. Let us no longer go along with our culture's belief that any sex is better than no sex. Even if it means we won't be sexual for periods of time, let's not settle for anything less than intimate sex.

§ FANTASY DOESN'T ENHANCE SEXUAL LOVING §

Here are some examples of how therapists have mistakenly recommended fantasy to enhance sexual performance.

Kaplan, in *The New Sex Therapy*,[3] describes a man who was impotent when sexual with his wife but able to have erections with a masturbatory fantasy in which he was Superman, rescuing women who were being harassed by brutal men. He was told to use this fantasy while having intercourse, which he did, and he became able to maintain his erection. His wife was told what he is doing, and she liked the idea. The therapists worked with both of them to reduce guilt and anxiety about using a fantasy in this way—forbidden by our culture's stated view of sexuality.

If the goal of sex therapy is to help a couple have intercourse, then this approach can be effective; however, if they
want an intimate use of their sexual energy, then these suggestions work against them. Reducing feelings of guilt and shame
for having sexual fantasies is a major service in our shame-
ridden culture; however, *advocating* fantasy only encourages
people to continue to be separate from each other.

Barbach, in *For Each Other: Showing Sexual Intimacy*,[4] gives
women permission to have sexual fantasies. After telling us that
many women cannot have orgasm without fantasy, she offers an
example of a woman who used fantasy to climax when she
masturbated but couldn't let herself do that when she was with
her partner. "After finally accepting the idea that it was perfectly
normal to fantasize, she decided to try fantasizing during partner sex and, to her surprise, had no difficulty attaining orgasm."

She goes on to point out that women try to squelch their
fantasies, because they are illicit or because they fear they might
act on them. She does a nice job of pointing out the difference
between fantasy and reality and by speaking so openly about
sexual fantasy, she gives people permission to reduce guilt and
shame. But she doesn't explain that it is possible to have even
richer sex by examining the content of the fantasies, healing the
wounds that brought them about, and getting to have real sex
with a real person.

Barbach does acknowledge that wounds of childhood may
be the cause of the fantasies. She gives examples: A child for
whom spanking is coupled with sexual feelings might have
spanking fantasies many years later, or a child who peeks
through a door and sees a couple having sex may later form
voyeuristic fantasies. "Feeling turned on by fantasies of being
forced to have sex could stem from our adolescent years when, in
order to maintain our reputation, we had to fight our boyfriends
at each step of the highly sexually charged exploration. This may
have trained us that it was all right to feel turned on as long as
we weren't responsible, if we were being forced or coerced."

The following sentence demonstrates that Barbach is unaware of arousal emerging out of intimacy: "an erotic mind-set,

free of worry and excessive self-consciousness, is as necessary as the proper physical stimulation for sex to be exciting and orgasmic." Barbach is only one of many therapists who have written that we must work to create sexual arousal, so we can use our sexual energy. Our culture has prevented these people from finding out what inside-out sex is like, so they can perceive the error of their teaching.

§ PORNOGRAPHY DOES NOT BRING INTIMACY §

Dr. Ruth responds to a letter from a woman named Della in her book *Dr. Ruth's Guide to Good Sex*.[5] Della's husband wants her to see pornographic movies with him and accuses her of being unaffectionate and not caring about his needs when she refuses. Della makes the point that she doesn't want to watch such movies before having sex with her husband.

Dr. Ruth gives her permission not to watch the movies but encourages her to consider doing so. She tells Della that there is nothing wrong with the husband's going to pornographic movies. She says, "They are harmless and serve a good purpose—they enrich people's sex fantasies and improve their sex lives." Westheimer apparently is not aware that primary purchasers of pornography are sex addicts obtaining their drug, and secondary purchasers are people who have difficulty gaining access to sexual arousal from the inside out. In any case, these movies lead away from intimacy.

Della says, "I said I'd hate to [go to a porno movie] and to my surprise he was very upset and accused me of being unaffectionate and unresponsive to his needs. I found out he had been going to porno 'flicks' alone since we've been married. My impression had been that it was something he did a couple of times out of curiosity . . . when he was a bachelor." Della is describing behavior that is typical for sex addicts who want their partner involved in their addiction. The pressure, guilt, and secrecy are classic and fit with the many stories I have heard from sex addicts who want to control their partners. Dr. Ruth is approving behaviors common to addicts of pornography.

Even though Della states in her letter that she doesn't want to "make love" after seeing a sexually explicit film—a limit that is necessary in order to use sexual energy from the inside out—Dr. Ruth suggests that she invite her husband to go to a movie and then have sex. "Ask him why doesn't he go to a sex movie sometime and then meet you after at a hotel. Or come straight home and you will be waiting for him, waiting to have a good two-person orgy with him. In a sheer negligee or sexy underwear."

This advice is fraught with difficulties. First, Della doesn't want to invite other people into her sex life, and this is what she would be doing if she had sex with a man who had been aroused first by movies of other people being sexual.

Second, to plan such a thing prohibits the two of them from finding out what they are feeling and wanting at the time. A more important focus for Della might be her feelings of betrayal that her husband had to be aroused by others before being sexual with her. If she arrives at a hotel dressed in sexy clothes, what will she do with her anger? If she suppresses it and has sex anyway, she will reabuse her sexuality.

Della's husband will also be required to play a part. He may not want to go to a pornographic movie and then meet his wife for sex. He may feel pressured to go along with it to make her feel that he still loves her, in spite of his behavior.

Dr. Ruth seems not to understand that regular use of pornography is symptomatic: it is not a healthy use of sexual energy. It can feel like a need to the following people: those who are cross-wired to stimulation that is not available in their sexual activities; those who prefer to limit their sex life to pictures; those who cannot achieve sexual arousal in an intimate, inside-out way; and to sex addicts who search for new and greater stimulation to fuel their arousal drug.

Dr. Ruth would be helpful if she told Della that she is respecting herself when she refuses to have sex after watching pornography. She might advise her to read more on sex addiction and see if her husband has a problem, and if the answer is yes, then to take a look at her sexual codependence. It is harmful to encourage her to believe that her husband's behavior is fine and to do the very things sexual codependents must learn to stop doing.

§ THE MYTH THAT NO SEX MEANS SOMETHING IS WRONG §

Surveying the rack of women's magazines any month of the year will reveal that people are not having as much sex as they want or think they should. The editors of the magazines know that offering articles about how to have passionate sex (along with diets, clothes, and relationships) will sell magazines. I purchased many of these magazines to study what is appealing to readers and soon learned that one issue of each would have been sufficient. Month after month, magazines tell people how to make sex more fun, more passionate, or how to have more of it. The articles must not work any better than diets, because the following month, women are buying yet another magazine in the search for answers.

Perhaps there *is* something wrong if people are not having sex. Sexual energy is a vital part of being human, and if we don't allow it to emerge fully in our lives, we are missing out. *But the advice given in these articles is how to drag sexual energy out of us rather than how to allow it to emerge.* Readers are told to use fantasies that will arouse them and make up new ones that will be ever more effective. Traditional sex therapists who write the articles, and journalists who quote experts, make up ever more stimulating things for women to do to arouse themselves and their partners. As with all addictions, each new drug level wears out in time, requiring more or different drugs. As a certain sexual activity fades into boredom, as have the prior ones, women are advised to drop their shame and up the level of stimulation. New fantasies, new clothes, new sexual activities—anything to keep it going. In time, these techniques have to give out. Then what?

Readers are given the message that this is all there is to sex. In the beginning, it is exciting, but it becomes boring after a few years with the same person. Then, to make sure the man continues to want her, she is given things to do, so he will continue to want sex, and he is taught how to be more romantic. This perverted marriage contract does nothing for people's desire to use sex to re-create a loving bond. Instead, it deprives people of finding out what sexual loving really is. Our culture's distorted perception of sex is again supported, and the sexual health of the individual and couple is violated.

Why Do People Not Have Sex?

Although there are many reasons why people don't have sex, traditional sex therapists focus on a limited number of them. In addition to sexual "dysfunctions" and resulting difficulties in becoming aroused, maintaining erections, and having orgasms when wanted, there are other factors to examine, even before looking at the symptoms.

Sexual abuse in childhood. Sexual abuse is so prevalent in our culture that the first question I ask myself when evaluating a client's sexual issues is "How was this person's sexuality damaged?" The answers lie in several areas. One is overt, physical, sexual abuse as a young person. We now know that at least one in five people were sexual with adults when children. Other research, and my own and others' experience from therapy, indicates that the figures are really much higher. Patrick Carnes, psychologist and originator of the concept of sexual addiction, found that his samples of sex addicts with several years of recovery reported higher levels of childhood sexual abuse than those with little recovery.[6] This difference is a reflection of the higher level of recovered memories among those who had been in treatment longer.

Nonphysical abuse of sexuality. Many more people were sexually abused in ways that didn't involve physical contact. Lustful attention from adults, triangulation into an unhappy parental relationship as one parent's love object, exposure to sexual stimuli and jokes, and being called sexual names are some of the many abuses.

Shaming of bodies and sexuality is almost universal in our culture. Parents attempt to control their children's sexuality, as their parents tried to control theirs, believing that children who are allowed free sexual expression will end up in trouble. *They are not aware that children who are permitted to discover their sexuality in their own time and in their own way will not abuse it in adulthood.* The very shaming and control damages sexuality and results in its misuse in adulthood.

Even if parents have clear sexual boundaries, school personnel, friends' parents, and other adults will provide shaming and other abuses. The most basic shaming of sexuality comes from requiring silence. Children cannot escape from our culture's damaging views.

In teen years and adulthood, sexual relationships are contexts for further abuses to both sexes. Instead of being able to explore sexuality lovingly, girls and boys are bound by stereotypes: Boys must want it; girls must withhold it and judge boys for wanting it. The girls feel pressured and violated, and the boys feel judged and further shamed for being sexual.

Therapists might ask, "What were the particular abuses this person experienced prior to arriving in my office?" This could yield more information than asking if he or she was abused or not. When people tell me their sex life has been fine, I ask questions that will reveal just what damage has been done. We have been so well trained not to be aware of sexuality that it is hard to speak clearly about events that have been damaging.

With this kind of respect for our culture's effects, a therapist would not simply set out to help clients have sex more often. Instead, the therapist and client can uncover the whole picture and go from there.

Prohibitions against talking about sex. In addition to historical influences, the present circumstances are important as well.
When couples can't talk about sex, they have no way to understand what is not working. Learning to talk about sexuality is
always the first step. Therapy groups, support groups, and good
friends are places to practice and practice, until sexual conversation is as ordinary as talking about work.

The present relationship. In relationships, anger, proof of
love, control, relationship smothering, fear of fusion, sex addiction, and so on, interfere with a loving use of sex. When couples
search for a healthier way to be sexual, these issues are the
center of therapy.

A choice not to be sexual. Traditional sex therapy does not
honor the fact that there are times when no sex is the right thing
for people—even for extended periods. Depression, life crises, or
major losses can reduce interest in sex. This is natural, and it
needs to be accepted by the person and his or her partner.

Some people choose to be celibate in order to learn about
their sexuality. Sex addicts usually find that they naturally
give up sexual activity of the old variety before they are ready
to enter into new sexual relating. Others know that what they
have been doing is not serving them well, and they elect to go
without it to gain the objectivity necessary to observe their
sexuality.

Still others find their attention naturally drawn to a different
area, such as a creative project or the health of a child, and sex
just doesn't fit in. When partners are in tune with each other,
when one waxes or wanes in sexual desire, the other may too.
Contrary to having a "need" for sexual activity, we have a
wonderful power available to create bonding with our mate and
to rebond when we have been apart physically or emotionally.
Sex serves our need, it isn't the need itself. The needs that sex serves
are not on a daily, weekly, or monthly schedule. They exist at
some times and not at others.

§ IGNORING THE PAST §

In their work with sexual complaints, traditional sex therapists focus on the present, searching for solutions to current problems. Although a great deal of change can come from creating new situations, it is also necessary to take a look at the past. To remove the effects of sexual shaming that inevitably went on in their childhoods, people must break the silence.

For example, a sizable number of men, homosexuals and heterosexuals alike, are sexually aroused by wearing women's clothing. Our culture shames such behavior, calling it perverted. As a result men with such cross-wiring either hide what they are doing or join together with other men who are doing the same.

In Seattle, a group of such people meet regularly, so they can wear clothing that is otherwise unacceptable. Such gatherings reduce their shame and may be an important first step toward being able to take an objective look.

A leading sex therapist in Seattle recommends these gatherings as an end in itself, with the goal of acceptance. There are some people for whom such a recommendation is suitable: people who are not able to enter a process of reclaiming their inherent use of sexuality. For them, accepting themselves as they are is vitally important. By providing an environment in which they can be with others who understand how they feel, won't shame them, and give them a sense of community, the therapist is performing an important service.

But the therapist stops there. As with so many traditional sex-therapy approaches, he or she doesn't go on to look at how this person developed the penchant to wear clothing of the opposite sex, felt sexual arousal when doing so, and engaged in sexual activity or masturbation. If a person can explore the history that brought about the behavior, he has the opportunity to let it go. Until he can let it go, he must choose between intimate sex with a lover and cross-wired sexual arousal elicited by what he wears. As long as he is focused on his clothing to feel sexual, he cannot be aware of the other person. The interest in sex and the arousal of sexual energy doesn't come from the two of them—or from inside himself. It is instead manufactured by a stimulus from the past.

A man I saw in therapy wore his mother's underwear and masturbated when he was a teenager. He didn't develop a long-term interest, and he gave up the activity when he left home. As we explored his relationship with his mother, we found that he had been severely neglected and then abandoned when he was nine. Her life changed radically after she divorced, and when her two older sons left home, she deposited the youngest, my client, in a boarding school. When he was with her on school vacations, he was left alone for long periods. It was during this time that he put her clothing on, feeling comforted, as if by her presence, and used sexual arousal to intensify the positive feelings. This was the beginning of a life of sexual fantasy about the perfect woman who would rescue him and take care of him as his mother hadn't. His therapy took him into many avenues of history in which his mother had abandoned him. Further abandonment came from her denial that she was doing so, making him think that his life would be enjoyable if only there weren't something wrong with him.

By studying the causes of his cross-wiring, he was able to find its roots and use this information to discharge past hurtful experiences. If I had stopped at "deshaming" his use of women's clothing—which was an important part of his therapy, both with me and in the men's therapy group—he would have been denied an important piece of his story.

§ UNHEALTHY ADVICE §

Dr. Ruth's position as the most public sex therapist concerns me, because some of the advice she gives is contrary to that offered by most other therapists and more damaging. For example, she advises a woman not to talk to her husband about his decreasing levels of affection; instead she advises her to rub her breasts against his back while he is washing his hands and pat him on the behind to "remind him that he likes to pat you, too." Dr. Ruth's belief in our culture's admonition not to talk shows up in her last sentence to this woman: "If you try doing this regularly, in a nice affectionately sexy way, you may never have to say anything about it in words."

Why *not* say it in words? Talking about it is the only sure way to find out what is going on. I don't think he "begins to forget to show enthusiasm," as Dr. Ruth suggests. Something else is happening. He may be following the natural rhythm of a relationship, which begins with intense bonding and then moves on to a quieter period. He may still love her but no longer needs to touch her constantly. Or he may be angry with her and unable to express it. Or his own sexual patterns may be surfacing, now that the relationship is stable, and he is uncomfortable with sex. If the latter is the case, then he will feel violated by his wife's rubbing her breasts against his back when he is not feeling sexual. They *must talk* to keep their relationship developing in positive ways.

A second recommendation that is damaging is the use of alcohol. Dr. Ruth recommends it for relaxation and as a mild aphrodisiac. Alcohol, as with any drug or fantasy, will take people away from the present and cast sex into the realm of illusion. As with most of her recommendations, it might provide a quick fix.

No mention is made of the effects of childhood sexual abuse on the sex lives of adults, or the possibility that sexual abuse may be occurring in the present. For example, a woman writes in saying her teenage daughter asked her and her husband not to hug and kiss her in front of her friends anymore. Her husband was hurt by this and after observing her with her boyfriend, commented, "She doesn't want her father to kiss her, but I see other people can." I would wonder about the nature of the father's interest in the daughter and encourage the mother to provide the daughter with a place where she could talk about her feelings about him. Since we know that at least one-third of women have been touched inappropriately, and many more have been the object of nonphysical, sexualized relating, it is very possible that the father's interest in the daughter and his jealousy of the boyfriend are indicative of an unhealthy interest on his part. At the very least, he isn't respecting her right to create boundaries with him. She kisses in a sexual relationship, not a parental one.

§ SEX BY NUMBERS §

Traditional sex therapists created and use the term "foreplay." This word reflects the belief that intercourse leading to orgasm is sex, and anything else is preparation for the main event. This concept is incompatible with the inside-out unfolding of sexuality. It identifies the woman as "needing more time to become aroused" and the reason that "it" must be postponed. *Natural sex has no predictable order, no goal, and no predetermined end.* The term "foreplay" is inappropriate, because there is no such thing. Our culture has defined the order of sex, and traditional sex therapists have gone along with it. We must eradicate the word from our vocabulary.

§ WHEN ONE PERSON DOESN'T WANT SEX §

A common complaint brought to sex therapists involves one person wanting the other person to want more sex. This is commonly labeled a difference in sex drive or in sexual appetite, or it is diagnosed as "inhibited sexual desire."

One of the dangers of traditional sex therapy is that it addresses sexual issues as problems to be solved, implying that once they are solved, a couple will be able to have enjoyable sex. If you can fit your problem into categories such as impotence, premature ejaculation, inorgasmic, or inhibited sexual desire, then there is a program to fix it. The solution is a set of exercises that will allow a satisfying and intimate use of sex. People with inhibited sexual desire or impotence are told not to have intercourse and are instructed to touch each other's bodies in nonsexual ways, graduating to sexual touch. Men who ejaculate before they want to use "start–stop" techniques to increase awareness of impending orgasm. Although such activities may be useful, they do not address the more basic areas of sexual relating between a couple and for each individual.

For example, my client, Robert, came to me alone after seeing several other therapists for impotence, meetings in which he was accompanied by his wife. As we talked about marriage, he told me that his wife was having an affair: He had recordings of conversations with her lover and could prove to her that he knew. He learned—through the tapes—that she lied to him not only about the affair, but also about countless other things, and that she lied to others too. These issues were not addressed in previous therapy, because the problem had been defined as his impotence and her desire for intercourse. They were assigned the classic sex-therapy exercises for impotence, which, not surprisingly, they didn't do.

I asked Robert to imagine that he could get and keep an erection anytime he wanted. Then I asked him if he wanted to have sex with his wife. His astonished answer was "No." For the first time he could see that he wasn't getting erections, in part, because he just didn't want to be sexual with her. According to cultural myths, he should always want to have sex with a willing woman. Not getting an erection is considered failing to be a man, and so he had never been able to question if he even wanted to be sexual with his wife. From this point on, Robert was able to think about what he wanted, instead of focusing on what she wanted. He was soon able to see that he needed to respect his penis and not force it to do something that wasn't right for him. As he explored his sexual relationship with his wife, he realized he had never enjoyed sex with her. As soon as she became sexual, her personality changed. She adopted seductive noises, body movements, and "dirty" talk that he found unappealing. It was as if she became someone else. Sex was not loving.

Robert had other issues with erections that had to do with perceived failure in life, and difficulty pursuing what he wanted. These issues could be addressed once he removed his focus from his wife's stated "needs." When he could see that he wasn't entirely to blame for their difficulties and responsible for fixing them by learning to have erections, his self-esteem rose. He could begin the process of finding out what was really going on—for him, not for her. At this point, his therapy really started.

Meg, a woman in her late twenties, wanted to be able to enjoy sex with her husband but did not find traditional sex therapy useful. She told me that when her husband wanted her to tell him what to do, she couldn't, because she didn't know. Meg had been seeing a counseling couple with her husband before coming to me. This couple had encouraged them to see movies of explicit sex and had given Meg permission to do things that her churchgoing parents had indirectly forbidden. She sought me out when it became obvious this approach wasn't working.

As we talked about her relationship with her family, in the present and the past, it became clear that our first focus would be the way she had been trained to do what she was told and fit neatly into a mold. Over several months, Meg came alive. She discovered that her brothers had identical issues with sex. As she openly talked—breaking a major family rule—she gathered information not only from her brothers, but also from her grandparents and aunts. As her comfort with speaking grew, she was able to sit down with her parents to confront the countless negative things that were going on and bring them out in the open.

The result was an opening of her sexuality as well. When we met, I thought she was sexually numb and unable to enjoy sex. But once she could see herself, she could tell me that, in fact, she really enjoyed both giving and receiving oral sex, as well as breast stimulation and kissing. She had trained her body not to reveal this pleasure, and she was able to override her perception of it, so she could feel that she was like the image her parents wanted. In truth, she wasn't, and by talking to relatives and with me, she was able to find out what was really going on with her. We were then able to take a look at her discomfort with intercourse, whereas in the beginning, she hadn't been able to provide any information about the nature of her pain.

A large number of couples seeking help with sex do so when one person is addicted to sex with the other, and the other is feeling pressured and used—as with Robert and his wife. If a therapist were to address this issue as it is presented, then a number of damaging things would happen to the partner who wanted less sex. First, the addict would receive confirmation that wanting more sex/drug is appropriate. Second, the addict's partner would be given the message that the addict's "need" for sex is valid. *Differences are often called a difference in appetite, when, in fact, one is using sex as a drug, and the other is failing to be the supplier.* The partner is not supported in refusing to engage in sex that is not loving, which entails the emotional absence of one or both of them.

Therapists must look at the entire dynamic that is presented rather than taking complaints at face value. I have heard countless sighs of relief in my classes and therapy sessions as I say that there is no requirement to have sex just because one is married, and that to have sex when you don't want to is reabusing yourself. I add that to be able to really say "yes," we must be able to say "no."

The difficulty with saying "no" comes from our childhoods. Our bodies were owned by our parents: They decided what was to go on with us. None of us had completely perceptive parents. We were all abused, for example, in the way our genitals were washed, and with unawareness that our genitals could be stimulated by touch and rubbing even through clothes. We were controlled by teachers, baby-sitters, and all other adults. This gets replayed when our partner wants sex and we don't, and when we believe we must have sex if we are married. Now we are the parent who won't respect our body and boundaries.

The work of Patrick Carnes on sexual addiction is filtering into sex-therapy organizations. Changes in understanding this vital cause of difficulties in relationships are occurring. But the focus on the present, to the exclusion of addressing cultural and personal abuses from the past, will prevent therapists from helping people truly heal from damages to their sexual energy.

§ THE FALLACY OF "HAVING BETTER SEX" §

The proliferation of sex books and magazine articles indicates that sex isn't going well for readers. We, as a culture, are trying to find answers to puzzling questions about sexuality, but as yet, few have been offered that truly help.

When sex is treated like an act with ordered activities and goals, then no amount of advice will provide lasting change or real improvement in pleasure. *We cannot follow a prescription and find out the meaning of this powerful energy in our lives; instead, we can learn how to get back into our bodies and let sexual energy unfold.*

Cosmopolitan magazine, read by millions of women between the ages of twenty and thirty-five, has always offered advice about having better sex—a subject valued by its editor, Helen Gurley Brown. An issue had an article called "Secrets of Sensational Sex." The journalist, who quoted sex "experts," had strong feelings about "lusty" sex and made assumptions that all men are like the male cultural stereotype. She said, "Men go wild when you whisper *dirty words* while *making love*," (these phrases don't belong in the same sentence) and "Leaving on a garter belt and stockings during lovemaking is *guaranteed* to jack up his temperature." These activities may increase his cross-wired arousal by helping him move into shame-based sexuality, but they will distract from intimacy.

The author went on to tell her readers to "learn to indulge in erotic daydreams" and read erotic literature when having difficulty becoming aroused. She said, "You can't be a sensational lover without at least some willingness to lick, suck and nibble . . . hot sex is largely an oral experience." She went on to give more advice about how to use cross-wired arousal patterns: "For some lovers a touch of the taboo is needed . . . Such 'naughtiness' includes bondage, anal sex, spanking, and lovemaking in public places." Velvet-lined handcuffs were recommended for bondage. When recommending X-rated videos, she said, "Understand that he isn't comparing your body to the ones on the screen—only indulging in another form of fantasy." On the contrary, he most likely is comparing her body (these videos select actors' bodies that are most likely to elicit cross-wired arousal). Videos and fantasy are used, because love with the partner isn't sufficient to create arousal. The mixed message is that you don't turn him on enough, so use these other devices—but at the same time, know that he finds you desirable and that he is "making love" with you.

§ Orgasms Do Not Determine Good Sex §

Sex therapy has been useful to women who do not have orgasms by making it clear that orgasms are a natural part of sex and creating sexual exchanges that include them is appropriate. Historical silence about sexual matters, except for a few "marriage manuals" written by men, made the discovery of orgasms an individual event for women. Now we know what they are, how they work physiologically, and what to do to have them.

The disadvantage of these discoveries is that our culture has created a new value that women must have orgasms. Although the subject is popular in women's magazines, read by millions of women each month, no articles address the possibility of women and men having sex without orgasm if their bodies so choose. People are not encouraged to find out what sex will be like; they are encouraged to set goals and meet them.

Dr. Ruth believes that if people are having orgasms, then everything else is fine. A man speaking on her radio show (transcribed in her book) said that when he started to have difficulties getting erections about a year ago, he began to buy pornographic magazines and look at them before and during intercourse with his wife. Then she began buying the magazines and using them the same way. This graduated to the use of movies, which she watched "while we're going through our routine." At this point Dr. Ruth interrupted to ask, "Do you have orgasms?"

"Oh, yeah."

"And she has good orgasms?"

"Yeah."

"Nothing to worry about, then. You've found a way that's right for the two of you. And you both enjoy it. So everything is fine. Bye bye."

Not only did she interrupt before she found out what his problem was, she declared that having satisfying orgasms is the measure of good sex. This man may have wanted to talk about his feelings of abandonment by his wife as she watched the movie while using his penis for sex. His partner, rather than being in the room with the man she loved, was joining the actors in the movie set while having a warm body and genitals to use in her own bed. And she also was abandoned, when he brought the first magazines.

The fact that he had difficulty obtaining an erection with his wife, his feelings about that, her feelings about that, and the possible causes were not addressed. Instead, sex was seen as an activity that is evaluated by successful orgasms, even when intimacy is totally impossible. These people haven't rebonded, and they won't feel close to each other when they are finished. The shame that accompanies their sex will hold them apart. It was a cold act. They are victims of our sexually silent culture, trapped in sex lives that are filled with shame, that aren't satisfying, and that require intense stimulation to maintain. I would like to hear their histories that led them to this unfortunate place and look at the effects our culture has had in not allowing them to change. The husband reaches out to make a phone call and receives no help at all; instead, he is cast once more into the night, with no way to change his situation.

§ WHEN SEX IS BORING §

Sexual experts, and journalists quoting experts, present sex as something we all want but are hindered from doing by boredom and routine dullness. As I write this, I wonder how sex can be boring! It is a subject that fascinates all of us, frightens most of us, and is the focus of much of our lives.

For a person to characterize sexual activity as boring, something else of major importance is going on. One or both partners are afraid of sexual intimacy, are out of touch with their bodies' messages. The buildup of deceptions creates distances, or something in the nature of the relationship is keeping them emotionally apart.

When a couple is intimate, sex can look the same but feel entirely different from one time to the next. It is possible to have intercourse in the same position many times and yet experience different kinds of relating with one's body and with one's partner. Energy flow within the body and between bodies varies, based on what we bring to the sexual encounter, not the variety of sexual positions. When we can access sexual energy from the inside-out, we cannot be bored, and the particular activities we engage in will unfold of themselves, with no predetermined order. We may have only intercourse for weeks, and then a period of exploring each other's bodies with our mouths, or touching only with hands. Other times can include all of these activities.

A successful case of boredom relief is presented by Dr. Ruth. The husband and wife had stopped having sex because of boredom. The wife was instructed to begin the boredom-relieving process by seducing her husband when he would normally have gone to bed. His turn came two days later. As they practiced doing things differently, they graduated from sex on the desktop and in the kids' rooms to what Dr. Ruth calls "illicit sessions" in hotels, and " 'shack up' weekends at motels." Then came the black garter belt and stockings, which Dr. Ruth calls "her tart's getup." She goes on: "Once they started, nothing could stop them. They tried all those positions in the sex manuals, and they tried really naughty things. Oral and, *you know.*" But when he suggested adding "a third party to their partying," she objected. Instead, she went to a sex shop and bought a blow-up doll to include in their sexual activities.

Dr. Ruth's suggestions are drawing on their cross-wiring to overcome fears. Sexual arousal comes from illicit activities, from acting like and observing a "tart," and graduates, for him, into setting aside all sexual boundaries. They are taught to use our culture's damaging, shaming attitudes toward sex to overcome the effects of other damaging, shaming attitudes. It is not suggested to her readers that perhaps we can relinquish such cross-wiring and discover what our real sexuality might be like. I don't believe that Ruth Westheimer is capable of doing so, because she herself has not worked on her own sexual shame and has not experienced the alternatives.

Dr. Ruth sets herself up as the one who decides what is acceptable kinkiness and what is not. She is merely changing the rules by which we can and cannot be sexual and doing nothing to help people learn from the inside out what is right for them. She does not know that if these people take a look at their feelings about sex and *undo the cross-wiring,* they will find a different kind of sex that can never be boring and may allow them to love each other in ways that "illicit" sex cannot. When clients interview me on the phone before making an appointment, many ask if I am going to recommend that they watch videos and wear sexy clothing—advice they have heard from traditional sex therapists. The effects they receive from such activities are a temporary, intense interest in sex and a feeling that something is wrong. They want to find out why they feel hooked on pornography, so they can stop. They don't want a therapist to tell them what they are doing is "normal," and to keep doing it—perhaps doing it even more. Or the partner of the one who wants "kinky" sex feels that something is very wrong, and these feelings are not validated. Instead, they are denied.

§ HOT MONOGAMY §

Helen Singer Kaplan coined the term "hot monogamy." (A book by this title was later written by Patricia Love). The term is in response to the growing interest in monogamy as a reaction to the freely experienced sex of the 1960s and 1970s, and the

proliferation of sexually transmitted diseases. Kaplan, a contributing editor of *Redbook* magazine, is frequently interviewed by
writers addressing the subject of sexuality.

The idea that sex should be "hot" is startling to me, as
startling as the idea that long-term sex with the same partner
can become boring. *Kaplan and other traditional sex therapists don't
know there is an alternative to hot or boring sex, and so they reflect
back to us the damaging sexual culture that created these ideas in the
first place.*

Redbook magazine put out an issue in February of 1992 that
portrayed Dr. Kaplan's views. The cover attracted readers by
putting "Hot Monogamy" in large letters. Under this came three
seductive, bulleted headings:

- Making Lust Last
- Saying Yes to Fantasies
- Secrets of Sexy Marriages

The subject of monogamy is popular in books and magazines now, so writers are trying to figure out how to promote
both the excitement of new sexual relationships and the safety
and stability of long-term monogamy. But without an understanding of genuine, inside-out monogamy, they come up with
only the typical cross-wired methods of eliciting arousal intense
enough to override sexual inhibitions. *In other words, publications
are encouraging people to use maneuvers long known to sex addicts
seeking more of their drug.*

Redbook addresses sexual fantasies under the heading "It's
All in Your Head." Sexuality specialist Domeena Renshaw, M.D.,
is quoted as saying, "Erotic fantasies are a strong mental aphrodisiac that triggers sexual arousal." Another expert says that
"fantasies also work to maintain arousal." Both functions are
useful if one wants to force arousal, but they work against the
natural use of sexual intimacy.

The article takes a look at fantasies that involved rape,
torture, homosexuality, and group sex. A revealing theory put
forth by Helen C. Meyers, M.D., clinical professor of psychiatry
at Columbia University, is that "women use fantasies of getting

hurt, humiliated, and abused to give themselves permission for their pleasure." I would ask "What is the cultural prescription that would lead women to abuse their sexual energy in order to express it?" If this is a common phenomenon, it is a strong statement about what our culture has done to female sexuality.

The *Redbook* writer Ronie Landroff makes the point that guilt and shame about sexual fantasies are misplaced. She cites studies that conclude that 94 percent of women fantasize during sex—far from a rare activity. If a woman is cross-wired to the use of sexual fantasy to have arousal and does not allow herself to use it, because she feels it is perverted, then she also prevents herself from accessing information that can be used to recover her healthy sexual energy. The fantasies can be welcomed as a source of information if the shame can be diminished. The damage that is being done by articles such as this one is the implication that this is all we can have—nonintimate, fantasy-induced sex with a lifelong partner.

Redbook says, "Some women feel guilty when they fantasize about other men, especially if they do it when they're making love to their husbands. They're afraid it's a form of infidelity, betrayal, or an insult to their partner's sexual ability. But sex therapists emphasize that . . . fantasies are normal and useful."

The use of fantasy *is* a form of betrayal of one's partner. When Dr. Renshaw's patients object to fantasizing about someone other than their partner, she recommends that they ' "think about their partner in their courtship days, whether it's three years ago or thirty years ago, when he was thinner, had all his hair, was more attentive." ' Speaking of insulting your mate! This advice encourages readers to accept their negative feelings about their partner and force themselves to have sex by living in the past! Loving sex is not possible when we are imagining anything beyond the present, even if it is the same person at a different time. Instead, an illusion of intimacy has just taken place. Each person has been violated once again.

After stressing how the experts encourage the use of fantasy as healthy and useful, the article moves on to say, "Be careful about sharing your sex fantasies with your partner," Georgia

Whitkin, Ph.D., Assistant Professor of Psychiatry, Mount Sinai Medical School, is quoted as saying. "In my experience, when a woman tells her lover about fantasies with other men, he often ends up being insulted. He won't like to think about sharing you with a movie star, a previous boyfriend, the woman who lives next door, or seven other men." This kind of dishonesty is one root of jealousy and deterioration of marriage. It is very harmful advice. How can it be helpful to advise a woman to enhance her marriage by doing things she must lie about? This is a violation, even within our culture's beliefs about male–female relating. It is particularly harmful for those who go to an expert searching for ways to truly enhance monogamously bonded relationships based on a healthy use of sexual energy.

The final section of the article, called "Keeping Lust Alive," describes cross-wired passion as normal. "There is nothing more powerful than passion, nothing more debilitating than desire and certainly nothing more all-consuming than the sexual frenzy that is part and parcel of a new love affair." This describes my experience, back when I was fully into my sexual fantasy and relationship addiction. The debilitating desire prevented me from having real conversations with my friends and enjoying my work. The "sexual frenzy" prevented me from making rational choices about my time, getting enough sleep, and meeting the genuine needs of others. It was truly a sickness. In contrast, the period of bonding with my husband Rex, although very intense, did not erase the rest of my existence. Instead of replacing it, love expanded life.

This article is only one of many published each year on sexuality. Over my four years of reading, they have become increasingly explicit. The encouragement of women to do the things men have been known to do is only increasing the amount of cross-wired sex taking place under the guise of aiding monogamy and loving marriages.

This issue of *Redbook* contained an ironic twist. Whereas women are told to lust and fantasize and seduce in ways not permitted in the media a decade ago, a separate article describes a woman giving another woman a short kiss on the mouth on prime-time television. The television show was met with strong negative reactions as well as greatly increased ratings. Cultural views of marital sex are changing dramatically, but homosexual sex remains in the gray zone of forbidden curiosity.

§ STOPPING SHORT OF SEXUAL HEALTH §

Westheimer, in her book, describes a couple who shared fantasies with each other and then acted them out. "One of his favorites was 'playing rape,' in which she pretended that he was a stranger, and he made love to her while she 'resisted.' " (Again, the words "made love" don't seem to belong in this scene.) Sometimes he "tied her hands behind her back and 'forced' her to have sex with him."

If a woman found herself aroused by the idea of a man raping her, I might suggest she ask her partner to play out the role in slow motion, allowing her to gain access to all the feelings. (He also will have feelings to observe.) By slowing down the process, the goal becomes learning about the feelings rather than increasing arousal, even though arousal may also increase. If she can, with little shame, allow the feelings to emerge, then other feelings and memories can emerge as well. Perhaps she will find that she was forced to be sexual as a child, or that the control of her child's body became linked with sexual arousal. We all tell our stories through play and other behaviors (the essence of play therapy for children), and if we can find the code, we can learn to interpret the meaning of our cross-wired feelings. Once the meaning is discovered, avenues to relinquishing behaviors that prevent loving become possible. My book *Reclaiming Healthy Sexual Energy* explains how to do this.

The damage comes from the open recommendation to use such cross-wiring to enhance sex. Although it can, of course, increase sexual arousal and draw people's interest, the reasons it does so are the focus of therapy that can help people find their healthy sexual energy. I encourage people to search for the causes of the cross-wiring that made such activity arousing.

I agree with sex therapists that feeling shame for such thoughts and activities is not useful. Talking about it brings it out into the open and demonstrates that these things are common. This is an important service, because one source of shame is people's beliefs that they are the only one, or one of a few perverted people, when most of us are cross-wired to be aroused by control and force.

Anna was a client who was cross-wired to arousal through anal stimulation. Although anal stimulation can supplement sexual arousal for most people, Anna's was also of a cross-wired variety. Soon after deciding to have sex, she would think about anal stimulation, using such thoughts to arouse her. At this point, her focus was away from her partner—she was no longer with him, but was now in the near future. As they engaged in other sexual activities, she felt an increased yearning for anal stimulation, waiting for it to come, but putting off asking for it. As the intensity of the desire for it built, she would reach a place near orgasm. As long as she didn't yet want to have an orgasm, she would postpone the anal stimulation. No other kind of stimulation would bring orgasm. When she reached the point where the intense sexual urge felt out of control, she would ask her partner either to touch her anus or to have anal intercourse with her. The orgasm quickly followed.

Traditional sex therapists told Anna this was healthy and useful, and to keep doing it. The one valuable function this served is that by telling her story, and receiving no judgment, Anna could reduce feelings of shame that accompanied her behavior. She felt uncomfortable asking her sexual partners for anal stimulation and was relieved when they liked to do what she suggested. When she was with a man who wasn't comfortable with it, she ended the relationship—her shame was too great.

Anna's understanding of her predilection for anal stimulation grew when she entered therapy to learn about memories of incest that were beginning to surface. The body work of Rolfing elicited body memories, and she had a diffuse sense that something was not right with her sexuality. As she worked in therapy, she was able to retrieve memories from guided imagery, understand her body memories, and gather information from family members that supported her growing belief that her father had been sexual with her when she was under two years old. He fell "in love" with his little daughter in a sexual way and used her little body to enhance his cross-wired feelings of sexual love. He rubbed her body against his penis, intending to have orgasms from this contact. However, as his arousal grew and his perception of her diminished, he would allow his penis to penetrate her anus. On at least one of these occasions, he penetrated so far that her flesh was torn and bleeding. Most of the time only the head of his penis entered, still causing pain. Anna's body learned that sexual arousal would allow her sphincter to open and admit the intrusion. Sexual arousal diminishes the experience of pain and can transform it into further arousal. As a result of the repeated penetration, she became able to bring on sexual arousal in the same way her father had—with anal stimulation accompanied by some pain.

As Anna continued to retrieve this information, and to have the feelings about the sexual intrusion that she couldn't have when she was a baby, she found herself becoming more conscious of the use of anal stimulation when she was having sex. She explained what she was learning to her husband Peter, and he joined her in learning more.

As they brought their sexual activity out in the open, he became aware that he had negative feelings about his role, but had been inhibited from knowing about them because of the requirement to be a good lover. He believed that he had to bring his partner pleasure, and so had been gratified to find out what to do to bring Anna rapidly to orgasm. He had not had the luxury of examining his own feelings. Now he could see that when he felt very close to Anna and wanted to use sex to expand their loving, she "left" him by moving into an experience that left her unaware of him. He didn't like it. Eventually, he refused to be sexual with her when this was happening—once he could see it.

Anna appreciated Peter's new awareness, because she benefited from learning that she had "left." With this feedback, she was able to differentiate between cross-wired arousal and arousal that came from within her, and from their relationship. The cross-wired arousal dropped over a period of months as she attended to the feeling itself (comparing it to the inside-out loving that kept her connected with Peter) and the memories from childhood, and discharged the stored-up feelings from those memories. She also faced new levels of shame as she became increasingly conscious of what had happened to her. She discharged these feelings as well.

The benefit of Anna's ongoing sexual cleanup was that she found out what it is like to remain in the present, fully with her partner. This experience, the very one we all say we want so much, was indeed preferable to the intense, driven sexual experience she had considered "good sex."

Her sex therapist had stopped at reducing shame and did not see that her sexual behaviors were also telling a story from childhood. The couple who made a game out of rape scenes are telling their stories too. When they find out that games only arouse them for a few weeks or months, and they are left with feelings of discomfort with "raping" the one they love, perhaps they will look further to find out why they are aroused by rape. At that time, I hope they find a therapist who goes further than giving permission to use cross-wired sexual images. Although most of us are cross-wired to such scenes, it is possible to examine our history and the influence of our culture to let it go. The benefit is enormous—we get to really love our mate with intimate sex.

§ HARMFUL SEX MANUALS §

Principles of traditional sex therapy are offered to married people to enhance their sexual relating in a book called *The*

Marriage Bed.[7] The authors, sex therapists Womack and Stauss, fall right into the traps of our culture's attitudes. Instead of enlightening people about a different way of having sex, they reinforce the very things that prevent people from using sex in the ways it is intended.

First, they begin by saying that the intense pleasure derived from new sexual relationships is because they are new and consequently more stimulating. They do not understand that the intense process under way is one that is basic to a mating animal: Sexual energy bonds us together into a couple. When we find a person with whom we wish to mate, the natural behavior is to spend large amounts of time together, look deeply into each other eyes, find the other the most wonderful creature in the entire world, and use sexual arousal to enhance this process. This usually results in a lot of sex.

When the relationship is safely bonded, and both people feel like a couple, then this process abates, and sex has different functions. A less intense process is the rebonding that sex achieves, or the spiritual awakening that sexuality may permit, or the exploration of one's inner workings that sex can elicit so well.

Womack and Stauss go on to say that some of the things occurring during that early courtship period can be done again (dressing attractively, making our bodies appealing, and doing special things for our partner). They spend three pages talking about how we must accept our bodies and, at the same time, advise us to get our bodies in shape and buy new clothes that make us attractive. This advice can only support the belief that we aren't enough as we are, and that if our partner is to desire us, we must present ourselves as well as we can (i.e., we are to create an illusion of who we are). If we make ourselves feel good by being attractive by society's standards, we are not intimately relating with our mate. Intimate sex comes out of *relating*, not the programmed reactions that marketing experts play on. And what happens when one's partner ages? Do we need him or her to have plastic surgery to remove wrinkles, loosening skin, and extra fat to be attractive?

Womack and Stauss state, "It is especially important to accept yourself as you are and the way you look right now. Most of us have things about our appearance that we wish could be different. Some of them we can change and some of them we can't. The ones we can't change, we have to learn to accept the way they are." These statements imply that there is a good way to look. If you don't, then you just have to accept it. Instead, I want to suggest that our task is to eliminate negative perceptions of ourselves by sifting through the causes of such cross-wiring, so that we can truly love ourselves just as we are. It is possible to love a body that is thirty pounds "overweight," sixty-five years old, with wrinkles.

The reader is told to prepare for sexual exercises mentally by reading an arousing novel or magazine, and physically by "making yourself appealing to both yourself and your lover . . . Splash on your favorite cologne. Put on a sensual outfit. In short, let yourself look and feel sexy." The last preparation they recommend is to "try to do some little things . . . that let your partner know he or she is special—a card, flowers, candy, a pint of ice cream or an unexpected phone call would be nice."

They are recommending that the reader distort him- or herself to create romance. Make yourself smell different, look different, and "try" to "make" your partner feel special. These maneuvers are the opposite of intimacy. Intimacy is being who you are, revealing yourself, and receiving the openness of your mate. If people must change themselves to feel sexual, they will not be able to have intimate sex; instead, they will engage in a cross-wired and temporary interest in sexual activity.

The authors of this book, similar to Dr. Ruth, set themselves up as experts who can tell readers what is good to do, what to do next, how to do it, and how they should feel. Such attitudes replay childhood relationships of most people and will not enhance intimacy. Instead, each person can uncover her or his own experience and history, and allow their unique sexual selves to unfold. Books such as this are damaging to sexuality.

§ LESS HARMFUL SEX MANUALS §

The book *Super Marital Sex*, by Paul Pearsal,[8] also comes from the discipline of sex therapy. Pearsal, however, expresses convictions that disagree with accepted sex-therapy beliefs and enhance real intimacy. For example, he stresses the need for honesty in all aspects of relationships. He states,

> My colleagues suggest that it is unwise to disclose extramarital affairs. They say this is only a "guilt dumping" on the partner, a way of clearing one's own conscience at the expense of that partner. They say the affair is irrelevant; just go on working on the marriage.

This is an excellent summary of advice from traditional sex therapists that denies the fact that we know everything anyway, and when the truth is withheld, we are only prevented from understanding what we know. Pearsal continues, "I say that such an approach is totally without support in the literature. It is opinion, and it helps a marriage survive, but not thrive . . . The question is how to deal with major problems in marriage, not how to cover them up and go on."

I appreciate Pearsal's straightforward discussion of sexual matters. He does not encourage the reader to use quick, cross-wired solutions, but instead to try new ways of relating to one's partner.

At the same time, his book is difficult to use, because he substitutes new rules for the old ones. He establishes himself as the expert who has the answers, instructing his readers in what to do to have "super marital sex." Although some of his exercises can be very helpful in uncovering attitudes developed from living in our culture, and from childhood, he does not take his understanding far enough. Pearsal remains in the arena of finding out how to have better sex, rather than showing people how to find out what their natural, healthy sexual energy is.

Barbara DeAngelis's best selling book *How to Make Love All the Time*,[9] is also among the more helpful sources. DeAngelis believes that sex is only one component of love, and so the subject of the book is love. She says, "Making love works best when you are already making love before you get into bed." In addition, she does not agree with other traditional sex therapists that stimulating sexual arousal with pornography or fantasy is compatible with sexual intimacy. She also knows that "love thrives on truth."

Like Pearsal, however, DeAngelis looks at much of sexuality as simple cause and effect. For example, she says, "If you want to avoid early ejaculation, learn to avoid these situations, habits or ways of behaving" (she provides a list). Anytime a writer says, "learn to," the reader is left with an impossible task and is once again set up for failure. Even more important, this approach to "better sex" is based on repairing what isn't working instead of scrapping the old ways of sex in order to discover the new.

§ THE NEW SEX §

An ever-growing number of us are finding out what sexuality really is. The truth has long been overshadowed by cultural definitions of sexuality, by inequality between the sexes, and by personal damage done to each one of us as we've attempted to grow into sexual beings. In order to discover what has been hidden, we've had to violate our culture's rules about the use of sexuality.

Those of us who are rediscovering intimate sex are recovering sex addicts, incest survivors, and people who couldn't stand to be touched sexually without large amounts of alcohol or other drugs. We were the porno lovers, the ones who wanted sexual orgies, the ones who went to strip clubs for "hand jobs" and bought prostitutes—the ones for whom an ongoing, committed sexual relationship seemed impossible. We were the sexual misfits who couldn't tolerate the way we were and had to change. So we scrapped the whole program and began again— only this time discovering sexuality from the inside out. Because sex was so troublesome, we had to discover alternatives. We couldn't afford to follow the myths of our culture—we weren't able to "fit in."

What we are learning won't be found in sex manuals or other instruction on how to have better sex, or in therapy for sexual dysfunction. It is absent in strip clubs and in most bedrooms. Almost all experts who teach about sex haven't experienced intrinsic sexuality and so cannot teach it. We won't learn about sex from those who are "well adjusted"—they haven't had to abandon their cultural ways in order to achieve a life of meaning, and so they haven't had the chance to experience what sex can be.

17

ALLOWING "ABUSERS" TO RECOVER

§

Adults who are sexual with children are seen as the lowest form of life. Our culture judges them harshly. Yet their behaviors are symptoms of the very culture that condemns them. Sex with children is only one way that people become cross-wired during formative years—it is only one symptom of our sexually sick culture. As long as we ostracize pedophiles and others who are attracted to children, we are prevented from seeing the whole picture of sexual sickness and recovery.

Those who are sexually aroused by children cannot tell others, because no one will have compassion or understanding. If they have been sexual with a child and tell, they will immediately be prosecuted. If they cannot tell, they are effectively cut off from the possibility of healing. And yet their recovery is essential for the prevention of further sexual abuse.

I have written an entire book on this subject called *From Generation to Generation: Understanding Sexual Attraction to Children.* I told the stories of many people, both men and women, who were sexual with children or had sexual attraction to children that they didn't act on. All but one were in recovery and had made significant progress in relinquishing their cross-wiring to children. In this chapter, I will take a brief look at the issues and tell the stories of two recovering men.

§ CROSS-WIRING TO CHILDREN IS SHAMEFUL §

We live in a society that causes people to feel intensely shameful about sexual attraction to children and, at the same time, promotes these feelings by not allowing people to heal themselves from the causes. By enforcing silence and hiding, we have prepared more and more people with each generation to have this cross-wiring and to act on it.

Things have been changing quickly in the past decade, as sexual abuse is being talked about and studied. The survivors are now believed and can come forward with their stories. But the other half still cannot. We look at the problem as if it were two separate groups of people—the victimizers and the victims. The victimizers were also victims. People who have grown up with sexually healthy families will never be sexual with children. Such people will know what is good for children and act accordingly.

The stepping forward of victims of sexual abuse is creating a brand new environment for sexual recovery. People are now allowed to see what happened to them, tell the stories, and hear the stories of others. It is a powerful time in sexual history, and the consequences will be far-reaching. But we are preventing these survivors from addressing one vital part of their lives: the tendency to repeat what was done to them, either in action or thought. They must be able to know they have cross-wiring with children, to feel the feelings when stimulated, and to talk about it with others who are doing the same kind of recovery. We must know that they are not limited to the small percentage who are reported or to those who have done the most damaging behaviors with children. We must know that most of us have had sexual thoughts or sensations that involve children. We must know that shame does not help; it only inhibits change. We must know that silence promotes shame, and talking is required. We must also realize that shaming people for what they are thinking, feeling, or doing perpetuates the very problem to which we have such a strong emotional reaction.

Each of us must take a look at why we have strong feelings against those who have been sexual with children. This may involve finding out that we share some feelings with them. If we don't take a look at our own feelings, we are helping to perpetuate sexual abuse of children. No amount of money or passionate speeches will help if people do not look within themselves. We are victims of a cultural process that has prevented healing and thus increased sexual abuse of children. To reverse this process and decrease child sexual abuse, our culture has to change. This can be accomplished by bringing the truth out in the open, so we can remove the shame from it. As shame decreases, each of us will automatically know what children need.

Following are the stories of two men who found recovery immensely difficult, because they had to deal with their own intense shame over their actions as well as shaming and condemnation from our culture. Both were successful.

§ RANDEL'S PAIN §

Randel was sexually abused by an uncle when he was a young boy, beginning when he was around three. The uncle was so out of touch with himself that he could not control his cross-wiring to be cruel—probably as the generation before him had been. He burned Randel as he told him that he mustn't tell about the sexual activity, and, if he cried, burned him until he stopped. Randel reclaimed these memories long after he had gone into therapy for his own sexual activities with his young son. (Randel's story is told in detail in *From Generation to Generation: Understanding Sexual Attraction to Children.*)

When Randel discovered an intense need to be sexual with his child, he was loaded with shame. He fought the compulsion, wanting to ask someone to help him. But, of course, there was no one to help, particularly in the late 1970s. He couldn't tell friends, who would condemn him, or his wife, and he knew

314 BODY AND SOUL

nothing of twelve-step programs or therapy. He lived with an affliction that grew with each year of his son's life, finally becoming so intense that he acted on it when the boy was five. Once out of the sexual-trance state, which allows sex addicts to leave their sense of themselves entirely while being sexual, he was filled with intense shame and remorse.

Randel began to drink heavily just after he first touched Billy sexually. At first his drinking seemed to be explainable by long work hours and difficulties with his wife. But within a year, he was drunk every night and weekend. His job was threatened, and eventually he was fired for not performing up to the standards of the company. His shame was increased by the alcoholism and losing his job.

AA meetings were one recourse, and Randel tried them. For periods of time, he would stop drinking and attend meetings, but he was not able to discuss the underlying cause of the need to numb his feelings. Many times, he left meetings and went immediately to the closest bar. Although many alcoholics feel as desperate and shame-laden as Randel, most are able to tell their stories in meetings and relieve themselves of the deadly shame associated with alcoholism. These people can form a community with others like them and receive support as they go through the agony of recovery, finally facing the feelings that had been eliminated or controlled by the effects of alcohol. When Randel stopped drinking, he was not able to use the meetings to air his pain, because he feared he would immediately face condemnation and a jail sentence.

Randel's alcoholism quickly cost him his marriage, home, and income, and he became a street person, obtaining only enough money to remain drunk. He felt as if life were not worth living. There was no point in working to become sober, because the pain he would have to face would be intolerable. It seemed better to kill the pain. Randel spent many years as a severe alcoholic who had no other life than drinking and finding a place to sleep.

Finally Randel couldn't tolerate the life he was leading, and he turned himself in. He had resumed AA meetings, no longer able to live with his secret. In fear, he went through the judicial system, believing he would be imprisoned for years. Instead, he was given an eight-year sentence that was suspended as long as he entered a two-year sex-offender treatment program. Vastly relieved, he immediately began the court-ordered program.

Randel entered a treatment program run by therapists who believe that controlling sexual behaviors is the only reasonable goal for sex offenders. He was given a thorough evaluation, including a plythesmograph, in which a strain gauge was placed on his penis to measure the various levels of erection while he was stimulated by audiotapes of sex scenes. Once it was discovered what scenes with children aroused him, he was subjected to a conditioning program that would make him dislike being sexual with children and encourage him to become aroused when thinking about being sexual with a woman (see *From Generation to Generation: Understanding Sexual Attraction to Children* for more information on behavioral programs for sex offenders).

Randel was given tapes to play while he had the strain gauge on his penis. When he would begin to have an erection, a low-level electric shock was administered. He was also given ammonia capsules to carry with him to smell when he found himself aroused by the sight of children. The ammonia acts as an immediate aversive stimulus, that then becomes associated with the forbidden object.

At the same time, he was instructed to create fantasies and look at pictures while he masturbated. He was assisted in the creation of fantasies that included a loving exchange.

After one year of the program, Randel's shame and desire for sex with young boys continued, although he was well versed in how to stop the feelings when they came up. He felt some relief to know that he would not act out, but he was still cursed by the desire.

Randel could now become a core member of his AA home group and feel some sense of community. But even here, his shame was not alleviated. Even the alcoholics like himself, who had lived on the street and seemed destined for an early death, were not as a group able to hear his story with compassion. Even here he was shamed by those who did not see the parallel between their desire to drink and his desire for sex with children.

However, Randel was now determined to survive. His treatment program wasn't working well enough, and his AA program, although vital for his recovery from alcoholism, wasn't sufficient for his sexual addiction. Randel prepared to move to a smaller town, away from the scenes he associated with his sickness. Prior to moving, he had to find a new treatment program to meet the requirements of his sentence. He found one.

Randel entered treatment with a professional who understood the connections between childhood traumas and adult sexual choices. At last, Randel found someone who could help him begin the long process of examining his childhood experiences, permit him to have the feelings that he couldn't have then, and relinquish the sexual connections with children. He became highly involved in the process and, two years later, no longer felt sexually compulsive. He married again and, in his last communication with me, spoke of how he and his second wife are learning about healthy sexuality. He was able to sexually bond with her, and he joyfully talked about how they missed each other when he worked out of town for six weeks. Randel's recovery allowed him to discover the real nature of sexual energy, and at age forty-five, he fell in love for the first time— with his wife.

I spoke with his therapist, Steven Zimberoff, Ph. D., to find out about the difference between his program and the more typical sex-offender therapists who receive referrals from the court. Steven told me about his program and, as he spoke, included references to the childhood experiences of his clients, in addition to the focus on helping the person understand and control his present cross-wired desires. I asked him how it was that his clients focused on the historical causes of their behaviors. He laughed and said that it was because he regularly brought it up. In group therapy he occasionally asks, "What about when you were sexually abused in your childhoods?"

Many do not have memories of this, but those who do have a chance to retrieve their experience and relinquish the effects. When therapists focus only on the present connections between behavior and its antecedents and consequences, clients will rarely bring up past experiences.

As I questioned Steven to find out what he did that helped Randel and resulted in his deep gratitude, Steven spoke of his respect for the men he works with. He said he doesn't call them "sex offenders," and he clearly differentiates between their actions—which he sees as terribly wrong—and the person who committed them. He joins with the person to find out how to help him or her reduce shame and find out the causes of their behavior, at the same time, taking full responsibility for what they have done. It is a magical combination that allows a person who has damaged others to recover.

Steven's work with Randel is reflected in his letter to the Department of Corrections regarding the completion of required treatment. He wrote,

> Mr. S's progress has been excellent. He developed from a typically suspicious, rather withdrawn, defensive group member to an open, involved leader of the Program. He has learned a great deal about himself, his motivations for offending, and most important, how to control his sexual attractions to youngsters.

This statement reflects the power of exposure to an environment in which a person is not shamed and instead is truly helped to recover. Randel continued to see Steven beyond his graduation from the program, so that he could retrieve memories from the past and continue his recovery.

Randel has a life again. His wife is also a recovering alcoholic, and they understand the need for being entirely honest about everything so they don't slip into silence and secrets—the behaviors that feed addiction. Randel's son (whose mother died when he was ten) lives with Randel and his wife. Now seventeen, he is no longer the age that appealed to Randel's cross-wiring. Randel has a job and supports his son.

There is no happy ending, however. He cannot tell new friends about his past, because they will judge him. While working in another town, one of his bosses learned about him from a newspaper article. She didn't mention the information directly to Randel, but instead she shamed him for his job performance and eventually had another boss fire him. He was told that she wasn't comfortable having him around. The shame will be with him for years to come.

Randel does not have a community in which he can openly acknowledge his cross-wiring and ask for help to avoid triggering it. When he sees a child of the right age and stature, particularly if the child is in a state of undress, he alone must make sure he doesn't look, and that he leaves the scene. When working in the home of a woman with children, a young boy ran up to him with no clothes on. Randel had to leave the job and not return. He couldn't say to the mother, "I may respond sexually to your child, so it is necessary to clothe him when he is around me." It is perhaps safe to say that virtually all mothers would be upset by this information and want him out of the house immediately.

When it becomes possible for parents to know that many around us are cross-wired to children and speak openly about this, then we will have an environment in which this cross-wiring will no longer be harmful. As responsible adults are able to see when others are responding sexually, which they will be able to do once the cultural requirement of not seeing is removed, then they can comment on the behavior of others. Without shame, one person can say to another, "I see sexual energy coming from you when you talk to this child. You look like you are flirting with her." The one who is flirting can take a look at his or her behavior and see what might be changed.

This also provides the child with a mirror for the events. This mirror lets the child know that, indeed, something sexual is going on, that it doesn't need to be hidden, and that he or she can know it is true. Although directing sexual energy toward a child is not healthy for that child's developing sexuality, the damage is small compared to that experienced when the child is required to keep a secret.

When children intuit that they must accept sexual attention, when they see that no one else sees what is going on (consciously), and when they interpret the cause as belonging to them, then the damage is severe, even if the child is never touched sexually. But children are able to survive severe abuses when they have a mirror for what is happening, are not required to keep a secret, and know that it is not their fault. Our culture has much to do before we will be able to talk openly about these issues instead of believing that only a handful of "bad" people do "these things" to children. Those who can tolerate their shame in order to speak out, as Randel was unable to do for many years, will pioneer the second wave of sexual healing. The first wave is the massive learning about sexual activity between children and adults on the part of those who remember what happened to them as children. Now it is the turn of those who are on the other side—those who are sexually attracted to children.

§ ALLEVIATION OF SHAME §

A friend in college told me a story about a teacher who had a stroke while in her mid-forties, and much of her body was paralyzed. The teacher told her class on the first day about the congenital problems that set her up for the stroke, even though she was in excellent health. She was also susceptible to seizures and wanted the class to know what to expect if she had one in class. If she did have one, she encouraged them to watch so they would not be afraid of them in the future. My friend was aware that she made her students comfortable by talking openly about her condition and sparing them from the difficult task of acting as if things were normal when they obviously were not. She could reduce her own shame as well as theirs by being straightforward and open.

I was touched by her story and could see the parallels and differences with the ASCs. This teacher brought out sympathy, and it was easy to be affected by her courage. She returned to the classroom obviously impaired and asked to be accepted. She was. The pedophile, by contrast, has to have the courage to face his or her illness but will not receive the heartfelt response to a plea for compassion and understanding.

People who have sex with others of the same gender can together affirm their worth, in the same way that people of color and women have done, and create a synergy that brings about cultural change.

People who have been sexual with children cannot affirm their respectability. Their situation is more like the struggle of alcoholics to be recognized as suffering from a disease that deserves treatment, except that pedophilia is more seriously condemned. How can they hold their heads up and say they deserve to be given treatment? We must respect the severity of compulsion and the lack of awareness brought about by the defense mechanism of denial and know that any person who can see beyond his or her shame will want to change. Then each of us must work on our own prejudices so that we can see them and their needs. We must do this not only for the pedophiles themselves, but also for all the children who won't be touched sexually, because the needs of those who want to stop doing so are being met.

Randel's story demonstrates the benefit of prosecution for sexual offenses. He had to stop avoiding his shameful behavior and take responsibility for change. In addition, help was now available to him. For most people who are sexual with children, arrest begins the process of challenging their denial, which is necessary for most to even know they have harmed children. Although condemning the pedophile is not helpful to the person or the victim or our culture, judgment of the behavior is vital if we as a culture are to heal from sexual abuses.

§ STEVEN WAS ATTRACTED TO HIS PUBESCENT DAUGHTER §

Steven was a minister who discovered that when his daughter became a young woman, he had intense sexual feelings toward her. He found his attention riveted on her presence. Pictures of the family (including another daughter and his wife) revealed his romantic facial expressions toward her, as a lover might have with a new partner.

Steven went into therapy after becoming severely depressed when he was unable to control his feelings. Through therapy and collecting information about his family and ancestors, he discovered a long line of sexually addicted ministers who were sometimes thrown out of their churches when their sexual activities came to light. There was no treatment available for his ancestors, and so Steven was faced with the legacy of trying to integrate spiritual leadership with the curse of sexual and romantic desire for forbidden women.

Steven took his work as minister very seriously. He was dedicated to understanding spiritual needs and learning how to assist his congregation (and himself) in making changes in their lives that could help them learn about spiritual unfolding. However, his own cross-wired sexual attractions, and the shame and secrecy that accompanied them, prevented him from being able to lead well. Until he began his sexual recovery (he had been a sex addict long before his daughter became the object of his interest), he had no way to tell his story, reduce the shame, and seek help.

Steven knew that he could not tell his superiors in the church structure about his pain. As in the past, they had no understanding of the nature of his affliction or how to help him with it. Some religious institutions will give their pastors "another chance" when they have been sexual with members of the congregation. Few would give second chances to one who was sexually attracted to children.

When secrecy is necessary for a minister to continue his work, then it prevents spiritual health or healing. To be spiritually available, we humans must remove the obstacles from our bodies and lives that prevent us from gathering all the data available from within us to be able to have access to the breadth of understanding of life. Making ourselves available to as much "truth" as we can allows this unfolding to take place, whereas keeping secrets from our leaders and followers prevents this process. Steven had no support in our culture and his work environment to tell truths, have feelings, discover causes, and gain greater access to himself and to life. We must make this available to him and to others in spiritual leadership and healing professions. We cannot help others if we must isolate our core selves to prevent public condemnation and rejection, as well as our own shame.

Steven has taken major steps in telling first his wife, and then his children, about his sexual obsessions with his oldest daughter. He was terrified when the idea was first presented to him, but from his addiction recovery program with Sex Addicts Anonymous, he was aware that addiction has more difficulty living in the face of truth. When all those around him know he is having these feelings, and they mirror back to him the truth of the damage caused by his obsessions, he will not be able to feed his obsession so well. Addictions are fueled by lies, secrets, and silences.

A meeting was set up with Steven's family, his therapist, and a family therapist to meet the requirements of Child Protective Services, and also by recommendation of Steven's therapist, who knew that he must bring his family into the treatment. As long as he did not do so, the unhealthy part of him could continue to believe that his thoughts were not damaging to his daughter. Having his family involved forced him to see that he was not living a separate, isolated existence that had no impact on others.

The first meeting included Steven's wife. The children were brought in after two of these sessions. Steven had told his wife the whole story two days prior to the session. She already knew of his sex addiction that involved masturbation to voyeuristic fantasy, and she was supportive of his recovery work. But when she learned about his feelings for his daughter, she became distraught. She entered therapy of her own soon after the first meeting and expressed her rage and hurt over the situation.

Steven's shame intensified when he understood his wife's reactions. He didn't want to feel like the responsible party for such pain and anger and, at the same time, he was aware that this was the case.

If Steven were able to tell the important people in his life that he has sexual feelings toward his daughter, and not be shamed for it, he would be able to recover more quickly. He could seriously accept the responsibility that he is damaging her sexuality—even though he has never touched her sexually—and that he is having an impact on the family. By receiving support for his desire to change, he would be able to tolerate the remaining shameful feelings more easily and so uncover the causes.

In an ideal world, Steven could share what is going on in his life with his congregation, using his healing as an example for those who are struggling with the same issues. He could prepare sermons about how addiction interferes with spiritual unfolding and offer guidance to those who cannot find their spirituality, and he could offer information to the rest of the people about how best to support those who are inhibited by shame.

Instead, he works in an environment that does not encourage the honesty necessary to recover. His church would censor him, and he would probably lose his job if his superiors knew what was happening. The church reflects our culture's belief that shaming people for wrong actions is the way to change them. In truth, the opposite is true. Shame has to be removed before a person can access the courage to take a look at things they have done that have harmed other people, especially children.

§ WOMEN ARE SEXUAL WITH CHILDREN TOO §

Our culture has an especially difficult time believing that women are sexual with children. Mothers are supposed to be loving and pure, and if a mother were sexual with her child, she would be seen as highly perverted. As a result, professionals have a more difficult time realizing that women are violating children. When women and men are caught molesting children, the man is more likely to be seen as the one who caused it, and the woman is less frequently prosecuted. Women who are arrested for sexually abusing children are sent to jail far more often than arrested men. I think this is because only extreme abuses by women result in arrest.

EPILOGUE
§
Healing Our Culture

Our culture is shifting. Recovery from sexual abuse has taken on cultural proportions and will continue to make clear what has been going on for centuries. As we become increasingly conscious of healthy sexuality, the unhealthy forms will stand out as the distortions they are.

Our culture will change through the process that is under way. As each one of us takes on our sexual recovery, the effects of our change will ripple out to people around us, making the process easier for those in the next ripple. As we are able to parent more openly about sexuality, our children will have less damage to undo and be even better parents themselves. "Generation to generation" will become a positive dynamic.

In my own frustration at wanting the cultural shift to hurry up, I remind myself of the truth. My role in the cultural shift is to work on my own change, removing my sexual shame. As each of us takes on this task, cultures will follow. The sexual crisis can be resolved in favor of healthier, shame-free sexuality.

NOTES
§

Preface

1. Eliana Gil and Toni Kavanaugh, *Sexualized Children* (Rockville, Launch Press, MD: 1993).
2. Anne Stirling Hastings, *Reclaiming Healthy Sexual Energy* (Deerfield Beach, FL: Health Communications, 1991).
3. Anne Stirling Hastings, *Discovering Sexuality That Will Satisfy You Both* (Tiburon, CA: The Printed Voice, 1993)
4. Anne Stirling Hastings, *Healthy Sex*, audiotape (Tiburon, CA: The Printed Voice, 1994).
5. Anne Stirling Hastings, *From Generation to Generation: Understanding Sexual Attraction to Children* (Tiburon, CA: The Printed Voice, 1994).

Chapter 1: Culture in Conflict

1. Mohrbacher and Stock, *The Breast-Feeding Answer Book* (Franklin Park, Il: La Leche League International, 1991).
2. Patrick Carnes, *Don't Call It Love* (New York: Bantam, 1991).
3. William Masters and Virginia Johnson, *Human Sexual Response* (Boston: Little, Brown, 1966).
4. William Masters and Virginia Johnson, *Human Sexual Inadequacy* (Boston: Little, Brown, 1970).

Chapter 2: Cultures Resist Change

1. Hanny Lightfoot-Klein, "Human Rights: Crimes against 30 Million Women," *New Statesman*, August, 1979, 266–268.
2. Alice Walker, *Possessing the Secret of Joy* (New York: Pocket Books, 1992).
3. Hanny Lightfoot-Klein, *Prisoners of Ritual* (New York: Harrington Park Press, 1989),
4. Ibid., p. 14.
5. Ibid., p. 41.

6. Ibid., p. 116.
7. Al Santoli, "Fighting Child Prostitution," *Freedom Review* 25 (1994): 5–9.
8. Brett Kahr, "Historical Perspectives," *Journal of Psychohistory* (1991).
9. Robert T. Michael, John H. Gagnon, Edward O. Laumann, and Gina Kolata, *Sex in America*, (Boston: Little, Brown, 1994).
10. Elisabeth Bumiller, *May You Be the Mother of a Hundred Sons* (New York: Fawcett Columbine, 1990).
11. Betty Friedan, *The Feminine Mystique* (New York: Dell, 1963).
12. Bumiller, *May You Be the Mother of a Hundred Sons*.
13. Anna C. Salter, *Treating Child Sex Offenders and Their Victims: A Practical Guide* (Newbury Park, CA: Sage, 1988).
14. Robert T. Michael, John H. Gagnon, Edward O. Laumann, and Gina Kolata, *Sex in America*, (Boston: Little, Brown, 1994).
15. Peter Rutter, *Sex in the Forbidden Zone* (New York: Fawcett, 1991).

Chapter 4: Healthy Sexuality

1. Gary R. Brooks, *The Centerfold Syndrome: How Men Can Overcome Objectification and Achieve Intimacy with Women* (San Francisco: Jossey-Bass, 1995).

Chapter 6: The Beginning of Bodily Shame: Pregnancy, Birth, and Breast Feeding

1. Sheila Kitzinger, *Women's Experience of Sex: The Facts and Feelings of Female Sexuality at Every Stage of Life* (New York: Penguin, 1983),
2. Penny Simkin and Phyllis Klaus, *When Survivors Give Birth*; to be published in 1997.
3. Kitzinger, *Women's Experience of Sex*.

Chapter 9: Our Sexually Addictive Culture

1. Patrick Carnes, *Out of the Shadows: Understanding Sexual Addiction* (Minneapolis: Comp Care, 1983).

Chapter 10: The Mating Dance Gone Awry: Sexual Harassment and Objectification

1. Susan Webb, *The Webb Report: A Newsletter on Sexual Harassment*, August, 1991.

Chapter 16: Traditional Sex Therapy: Perpetuating Unhealthy Sexuality

1. Helen Singer Kaplan, *The New Sex Therapy* (New York: Brunner/Mazel, 1974).
2. Lonnie G. Barbach, *For Each Other: Sharing Sexual Intimacy* (New York: Doubleday, 1984).
3. Kaplan, *The New Sex Therapy.*
4. Barbach, *For Each Other: Sharing Sexual Intimacy.*
5. Ruth Westheimer, *Dr. Ruth's Guide to Good Sex* (New York: Warner Books, 1986).
6. Carnes, *Don't Call It Love.*
7. William Womack and Fred Strauss, *The Marriage Bed: Renewing Love, Friendship, Trust, and Romance* (Seattle: Madrona, 1986).
8. Paul Pearsal, *Super Marital Sex,* Ivy, 1988).
9. Barbara De Angelis, *How to Make Love All the Time* (New York: Dell, 1991).

INDEX

§